THE FASHION BUSINESS

This book provides a clear understanding of the different business strategies and models across all markets of the fashion industry.

Providing a holistic and practical approach to strategic fashion management and marketing, the book covers brand image, supply chain, communication, price point and social media. Based on examples from international organisations – including Off-White, Nike and Zara, as well as leading luxury brands – the author identifies 13 core market sectors and explores the strategies applied in each: from creativity to their supply chain and sustainability, from segmentation strategy to brand policies and from pricing to distribution. Each chapter includes features to aid student learning, including interviews with a wide range of experts from across the industry as well as student activities and reflection points.

Theoretically grounded yet practical in its approach, this is important reading for advanced undergraduate and postgraduate students of Strategic Fashion Management, Fashion Marketing and Communications, Fashion Merchandising and Luxury Fashion.

Dario Golizia is a visiting lecturer at IULM University and a senior lecturer in Fashion Marketing Strategies at Istituto Marangoni, both in Milan, Italy.

"This is a much-needed contemporary academic book related to fashion business that has excellently managed to critically examine and precisely dissect the challenging retail environment ... At first I read the whole book in one sitting, but I knew immediately that I would return repeatedly to refer back to key sections for future research. This is a book I would wholeheartedly recommend to current fashion industry experts across the globe, and of course to the future fashion business leaders: our students."

— **Sally Heale**, *Senior Lecturer, University of Westminster, UK*

"This is a comprehensive and much-needed new text on the theory and practice of strategic fashion management that is highly suited to students wishing to investigate this subject in significant depth. The author identifies thirteen core fashion market sectors, exploring the strategies applied in each. What stands out is the critical approach, in-depth comparative analysis and the additional input from a superb selection of contributing authors."

— **Harriet Posner**, *Director Undergraduate Programmes, Condé Nast College of Fashion & Design, UK*

THE FASHION BUSINESS

Theory and Practice in Strategic
Fashion Management

Dario Golizia

Routledge
Taylor & Francis Group

LONDON AND NEW YORK

First published 2022
by Routledge
2 Park Square, Milton Park, Abingdon, Oxon OX14 4RN

and by Routledge
605 Third Avenue, New York, NY 10158

Routledge is an imprint of the Taylor & Francis Group, an informa business

British Library Cataloguing-in-Publication Data
A catalogue record for this book is available from the British Library

Library of Congress Cataloging-in-Publication Data
Names: Golizia, Dario, 1966– author.
Title: The fashion business: theory and practice in
strategic fashion management / Dario Golizia.
Description: Milton Park, Abingdon, Oxon; New York, NY: Routledge, 2021. |
Includes bibliographical references and index.
Identifiers: LCCN 2021002071 (print) | LCCN 2021002072 (ebook)
Subjects: LCSH: Fashion merchandising. | Clothing trade—Management. |
Clothing trade—Marketing.
Classification: LCC HD9940.A2 G65 2021 (print) |
LCC HD9940.A2 (ebook) | DDC 746.9/20684—dc23
LC record available at https://lccn.loc.gov/2021002071
LC ebook record available at https://lccn.loc.gov/2021002072

ISBN: 978-0-367-49053-9 (hbk)
ISBN: 978-0-367-49055-3 (pbk)
ISBN: 978-1-003-04424-6 (ebk)

Typeset in Bembo
by codeMantra

CONTENTS

PREFACE

Which are the most successful fashion companies? What business models have they implemented? How are they facing the challenges of the near future? Is there only one successful business model in the fashion industry? Or are there several?

The book aims to give concrete answers to the above questions through the experience of the author, and by means of interviews with industry professionals, as well as of an analytical research of about 50 international companies.

Currently, there are many fashion business books, none of which focuses on business models. Moreover, they do not identify the different strategic groups[1] competing in the fashion industry, and each uses a different business model. Consequently, these texts do not highlight the differences among the creative, productive, segmentation, marketing, communication, distribution and omnichannel strategies, which are specific for each cluster and their companies.

But are the strategies applied by LVMH really similar to those adopted by Hermès or Giorgio Armani? Furthermore, is the strategy chosen by the Armani Privé haute couture line similar to that applied by the same company for the Armani Exchange line? The answer is "absolutely not".

When analysing the fashion industry, generalising makes no sense. We cannot largely describe a strategy – at every level – unless we first identify the different clusters and their companies belonging to the fashion industry. There are many (too many) differences within the Fashion System: it is a hypercompetitive sector with hundreds of companies, but only few of them achieve excellent results.

The features that distinguish the book are the following:

- it gives a new perspective to segment the fashion industry, adopting a new and different approach;
- it identifies 13 typologies of strategic groups, each one applying a different business model, which are the following:

  1. large unspecialised fashion companies (Chapter 2);
  2. historic fashion brands (Chapter 3);

3. contemporary fashion brands (Chapter 4);
4. industrial fashion brands (Chapter 5);
5. fast fashion brands (Chapter 6);
6. emerging brands specialising in ready-to-wear (Chapter 7);
7. brands specialising in formal menswear (Chapter 8);
8. brands specialising in casualwear (Chapter 9);
9. brands specialising in underwear (Chapter 10);
10. brands specialising in activewear (Chapter 11);
11. brands specializing in streetwear (Chapter 12);
12. brands specialising in bags (Chapter 13);
13. brands specialising in footwear (Chapter 14);

- it identifies the main players of each strategic group;
- it describes every strategic group, in a dedicated specific chapter, through an overall exhaustive vision: from creativity to their supply chain and sustainability; from segmentation strategy to brand policies; from pricing to distribution, with a strong focus on omnichannel;
- finally, each chapter begins with a reading describing one of the several professional figures of fashion companies, to then conclude with an interview with a protagonist of the cluster and student activities.

Note

1 The author uses the terms strategic group and cluster as synonyms, as defined in Chapter 2.

ACKNOWLEDGEMENTS

I have reached the conclusion of this very long work. I would like to thank all the people who offered a concrete or moral contribution to its writing.

In particular, I am grateful to my now-former students for their precious contribution in the research: Rubina Biancardi, Camilla Cenci, Raffaella Gemiti, Ileana Brendaglia, Alessia Breviari, Monica Bucalo, Marco Casciello, Francesca Danesi, Luca Grillo, Manon Leclerc, Luca Lutri, Hana Matsuura, Luna Nardi, Anna Péterfi, Alice Sebastiani, Sophie-Therese Solderer and Mia Vukasovic.

I would like to thank the professionals who supported me in the writing of some paragraphs: Lavinia Biancalani, Benedetta Breschi, Celeste Corso, Andrea Doroldi, Sennait Ghebreab, Daniela Guariento, Michele Leoni, Diana Marian Murek, Antonio Patruno Randolfi, Andrea Pittana and Sabrina Pomodoro.

A special thank you goes to my life partner who stood by me and also was by my side in this long work.

Chapter 1 is translated by Catherine Bolton, Cassese Amber Faith and Michelle Schoenung and revised and completed by Valentina Guzzo. Chapter 3 is translated by Aubrey Hill and revised and completed by Valentina Guzzo. Chapters 2, 4–15 are translated by Valentina Guzzo.

1

FASHION BUSINESS AND STRATEGIC MARKETING[1]

Reading: managing a fashion company

What's behind a dress, a T-shirt, a skirt? There's much more than a designer, a model and a fashion show. There are a company, its strategy and its management. Moreover, a fashion company is characterised by a very complex organisational structure encompassing many professional, creative and managerial roles. From the Chief Executive Officer (CEO) who decides the strategy of the company, to the Head of Designer who is in charge of the creative process. From the Product Manager, who takes care of production, to the Fashion Buyer who is responsible for purchases. From the PR Manager in charge of brand communication, to the Visual Merchandiser who takes care of the shop fitting. Moreover, a fashion company is supported by the work of many people who operate behind the scenes, but having an equally important role. From the Fashion Stylist, who takes care of the style and of the image, to Influencers who contribute to conveying them. Only a synergic and strategic management of all these managerial figures/competences allows the company to achieve excellent economic and social results. The above-mentioned roles, and many more, are briefly described in the following chapters.

1.1 Definition of industry and the strategic business area

The point of departure is "industry", which Porter defines as "as the group of firms producing products that are close substitutes for each other" (Porter, 1980, p. 5). Of course the boundaries of an industry, especially in fashion, are not always clear and well-defined. However, defining the industry is not the same as outlining "where the firm wants to compete (defining 'its business')" (Porter, 1980, p. 32). Thus, the "decoupling industry definition and that of the businesses the firm wants to be in will go far in eliminating needless confusion in drawing industry boundaries" (Porter, 1980, p. 39). Most industries can be subdivided into distinct and strategic business areas (SBAs), each one made up of its own characteristics. An SBA represents a specific area of the market, which becomes the aim of the products sold by the business. Thus, an SBA has the following characteristics:

- it is strategically relevant and it can be managed independently;
- it has similar products and similar prices;
- it satisfies similar needs;
- it has similar distribution and production strategies;
- it presents similar factors for success (Valdani, 1995).

1.2 Definition of strategy, strategic model and strategic group

In almost every industry, there are companies that attain different economic results. The reason why some make higher profits than others is in one magic word: strategy. Companies implement strategies to convince potential buyers to buy their product and not that of their competitors (Porter, 1985). So what is strategy? Strategy implies deciding how to satisfy the needs of potential consumers, how to respond to the competition and the choice of the industries, markets and segments to compete in (Pellicelli, 2005).

Since we've explained what we mean by strategy, we'll explain the meaning of strategic model and strategic group, the two key concepts of this book. The former is defined as the "simplified description of how a company does business and makes money without having to go into detail of all its strategies and processes" (Corbellini and Saviolo, 2009, p. 121). We are now able to understand the meaning of strategic group, which Porter defines as "the group of firms in an industry following the same or similar strategy along the strategic dimensions" (1980, p. 129). Having defined the industry, SBA, strategy, strategic model and strategic group, we will see how these concepts apply to the fashion business in the following section.

1.3 The sectors in the fashion industry, according to the literature

What is fashion business? Does it correspond to or is it different from luxury fashion? How is it possible to segment (luxury) fashion? Let's consider six books dedicated to the topic and see how their authors dealt with first two questions and then the third:

1. *Inside the Fashion Business* by Jeanette Jarnow and Kitty G. Dickerson (1997);
2. *Luxe… Stratégies Marketing* by Danielle Allérès (2003);
3. *Luxury Fashion Branding* by Uche Okonkwo (2007);
4. *Managing Fashion and Luxury Companies* by Erica Corbellini and Stefania Saviolo (2009);
5. *The Luxury Strategy* by Jean Noel Kapferer and Vincent Bastien (2009);
6. *Marketing dei beni di lusso* by Fabrizio Mosca (2010).

We can divide the authors' approaches into four lines of research. The first group embraces those who defined only the fashion business; the second group unites those who have distinguished the concepts of the fashion business and luxury fashion; the third group consists of those who have included only luxury fashion and the last group applies the two concepts indifferently.

Jarnow and Dickerson are part of the first line. They define only the fashion business, saying that it is "generally understood to refer to all companies and individual concerned with the design, production and distribution of textile and apparel goods" (1997, p. 2).

Those who distinguish fashion and luxury include Corbellini and Saviolo (2009) as well as Kapferer and Bastien (2009, 2012 reprint).

The first authors maintain that until the beginning of the 1980s, the word "fashion" was only associated with clothing; later on, it "has increasingly spread to additional segments – fur and hosiery, perfume and cosmetics, eyewear, accessories (watches, jewels, pens, mobile telephones), furniture and household goods, and even destinations and domestic pets" (Corbellini and Saviolo, 2009, p. 6). In addition, these same authors clearly distinguished the concepts of fashion and luxury, specifying that "luxury is connected to one or more segments, defined by price" (Corbellini and Saviolo, 2009, p. 19) and that neither fashion nor luxury defines one single industry or product category; nevertheless, they affirm that though the two terms have different meanings, they are often used as synonyms. Kapferer and Bastien also affirm that the relationship between luxury and fashion is "ambiguous and confusing" and "the overlap between luxury and fashion is in practice extremely slight" (Kapferer and Bastien 2009, 2012 reprint, p. 29). However, they add that they "represent two worlds … very different … and they overlap only marginally (limited to haute couture)" (Kapferer and Bastien 2009, 2012 reprint, p. 31).

Mosca and Allérès define only luxury fashion. Mosca (2010), who wrote a book that focuses on the markets of symbolically high-value goods, asserts that there are eight traditional industries for goods with a high symbolic value, and they are commonly defined industries of the fashion system: clothing, footwear, cosmetics, jewellery, eyewear, watches, leather goods and fragrances; he argues that luxury crosses through each industry, adding emerging industries to the eight previously identified: art and cultural heritage, sailing, cruises, automobiles, hotels and restaurants, food and wine, tableware and cultural services. Allérès (2003) defines a luxury item as an object having characteristics of perfection on every level, from its existence to the consumer; regarding what industries are part of luxury, she maintains that the luxury universe comprises a vast number of business industries. Most importantly, the author identifies three types of luxury: absolute, intermediate and accessible, and she dedicates a specific marketing strategy to each one.

Okonkwo seems to use the two terms interchangeably, first writing that "fashion is a strong force that has always played a significant role in the evolution of mankind's society" (2007, p. 1). A few lines later, she says that "luxury fashion played a prominent role in the social and economic order of previous centuries and continues to influence our modern societies, economies and governments" (2007, p. 1).

Let's continue to examine whether the authors consider how to segment the fashion business. From the above-mentioned texts, only Jarnow and Dickerson and Saviolo and Corbellini have looked at this.

Jarnow and Dickerson, using the "*Standard Industrial Classification (SIC)*" (1997, p. 6), subdivide the fashion industry into four segments. Corbellini and Saviolo maintain that "the fashion system is made up of many industries… . Luxury is a segment defined by price within the fashion system but also in other industries… . These industries in turn can be further subdivided into different competitive segments" (2009, p. 102); then they go on to segment just the clothing industry, emphasising that the other industries have a similar structure, through three macro criteria: "product end uses, groups of clients, and price" (2009, p. 102).

1.4 The sectors in the fashion industry, according to the author

We agree with the positions of the above-mentioned authors to some extent. We share the authors' opinion when they say the fashion business is (no longer) made up of just clothing, but many industries. We are aligned with Saviolo and Corbellini and Kapferer and Bastien about the need to distinguish between fashion and luxury fashion in the fashion system. However, we differ from the other authors who focus on just luxury and do not proceed to illustrate any specific characteristic of the fashion business as well as with those who use the phrases *fashion business* and *fashion luxury* as synonyms. Overall, we maintain that, with the partial exception of Saviolo and Corbellini, the boundaries they outline are not sufficiently defined to specifically explain the (luxury) fashion business, and, in my opinion, it presents a degree of complexity that makes clarity indispensable. Therefore, in this book, we are proposing an alternative vision that is articulated as follows:

- the macro fashion business;
- single-industry fashion;
- the sub-industry;
- the price range.

The macro fashion business is made up of a set of different industries that identify with the product category: clothing, leather goods, footwear, watches, jewellery, eyewear, perfumes and cosmetics. Our position is that it is impossible to offer an exhaustive and definitive list of industries included. The process of diversification adopted by many companies, which has led them to compete in numerous industries, extending the boundaries of the fashion industry, is evolving and in continual expansion.

Single-industry fashion is identified by a single category of products: clothing or footwear rather than leather goods, etc. As we explained above, every industry represents a distinct SBA since the product category is different and, consequently, so are the average variables we use to identify the strategic business area (prices, customer needs, etc.). Undoubtedly, there are fashion companies that compete in only one industry, for example, Ray-Ban, which specialises in eyewear; others in a few industries, such as Tod's, which competes in footwear and clothing; yet others compete in multiple industries of the macro fashion business, such as the American company Ralph Lauren.

Some industries can be further subdivided into sub-industries, in relation to their product sub-category. In considering the clothing industry, we see that it is made up of many sub-industries: haute couture, casualwear, activewear, underwear, etc. They are all totally different from each other, in that all the conditions that characterise a strategic business area, as evidenced in Section 1.1, are specific to each one. For example, if we consider the activewear and formalwear sub-industries, the players are different, given that the companies typical to activewear include Nike and Adidas while Kiton and Brioni are typical to formalwear. Their respective products reflect this difference: clothing and accessories for informal occasions and sports for the former and suits for formal occasions in the latter. Consequently, the strategy implemented by Nike is totally different than what Brioni uses for formalwear. The strategies would also be different for companies that compete in both activewear and formalwear. For example, Giorgio Armani S.p.A. implemented two different strategies for the brands EA7 and Giorgio Armani, which work in activewear and formalwear, respectively.

The price range is a further average variable that could be used to segment one industry (or sub-industry) and, consequently, identify the strategic business area. Both are made up of multiple and different price ranges, from very high to low, and each could represent totally or partially different conditions from other price segments. Let's take the example of leather

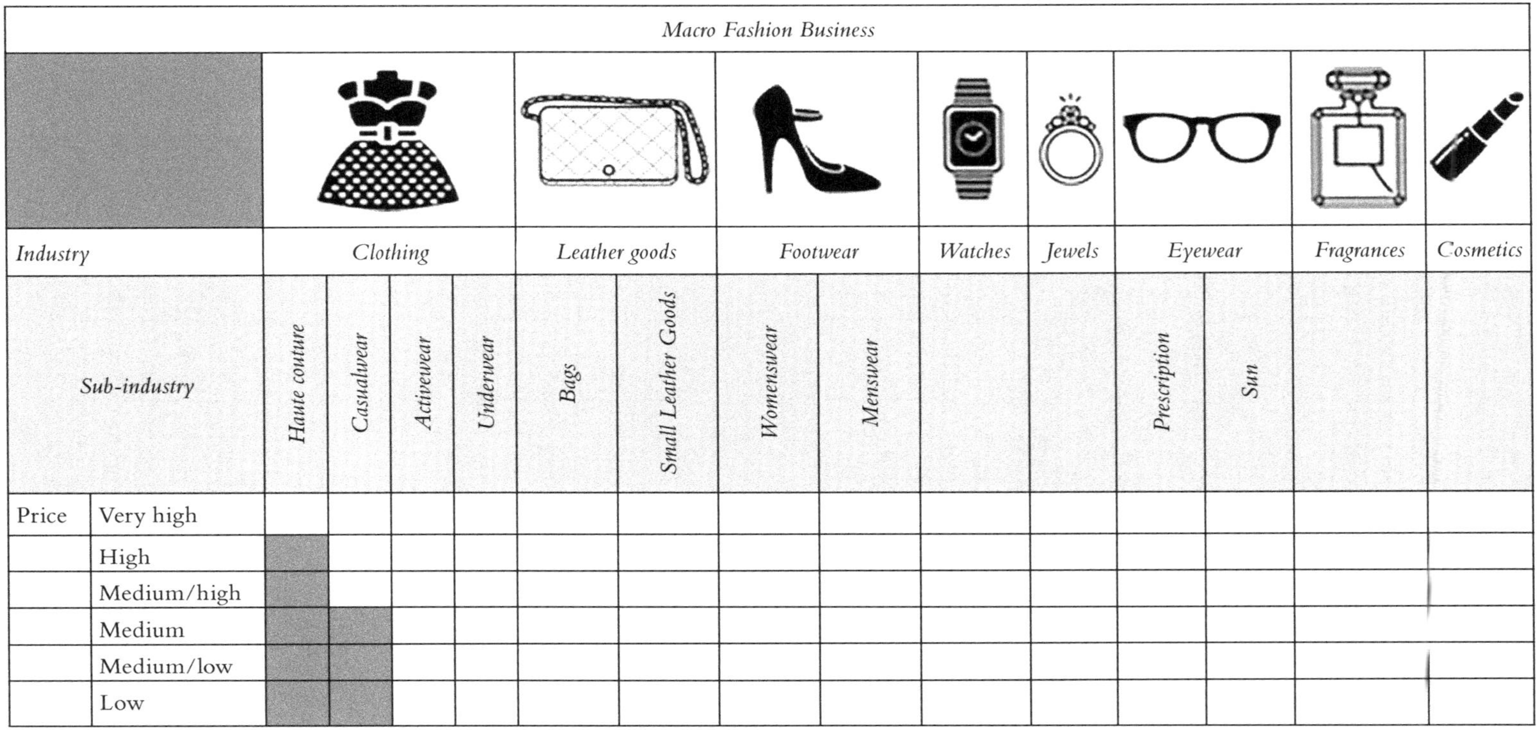

Macro Fashion Business

Industry	Clothing				Leather goods		Footwear		Watches	Jewels	Eyewear		Fragrances	Cosmetics
Sub-industry	Haute couture	Casualwear	Activewear	Underwear	Bags	Small Leather Goods	Womenswear	Menswear			Prescription	Sun		
Price														
Very high														
High	▨													
Medium/high	▨													
Medium		▨												
Medium/low		▨												
Low														

FIGURE 1.1 Macro fashion business

Source: author's elaboration.

goods (handbags): in the very high-price range, companies, such as Hermès and Dior, offer very high-quality artisanal products, relating a long and exclusive history, offered at only a few mono-brand stores, which are mostly owned by the company itself. In the mild-price range, we find companies, such as Furla and Coach, which offer industrially made products, marketed for an accessible price and sold in many different distribution formats. It is clear that the strategy Hermès implemented to find success in the high-price range of the leather goods industry would be different than the one Furla would use to achieve excellent results in accessible luxury.

1.5 Strategic models and strategic groups in the fashion business, according to the literature

We're going to examine if and how the same authors mentioned above have theorised strategic models and identified strategic groups. As to strategic models, we can see how some have theorised business models, dedicating ample space in their books and providing a major contribution to academic writings; on the other hand, others have dedicated little space to the topic or did not even address it. Let's look at them together.

The first include the studies of Kapferer and Bastien (2009, 2012 reprint) and especially Corbellini and Saviolo (2009). Kapferer and Bastien "distinguish four major types of luxury business models, according to whether the product or the service is dominant" (2009, 2012 reprint, p. 297):

- "luxury products with a profitable core trade";
- "luxury products with a too restricted core range" (Kapferer and Bastien 2009, 2012 reprint: pp. 298–305);
- luxury services;
- luxury high-tech.

Even Corbellini and Saviolo (2009) provided an essential contribution to the literature based on the fashion business. First, they define the luxury fashion model as the following set of elements: the "value propositions" (2019, p. 122), the groups of clients targeted, the distribution and marketing channels and production-chain management. They then identify the following four business models[2]:

1. *fashion griffe*;
2. *luxury brands*;
3. *premium brands*;
4. *fast fashion retailers* (2019, p. 122).

Okonkwo's book is among those that dedicated minimal space to the strategic model. She dedicated Chapter 9, "The Luxury Fashion Business Strategy Model", to the topic. The author begins by asserting that managers give little attention to the idea; however, she emphasises the great need for fashion companies to implement strategic models and writes that "business models are brand-specific because every luxury brand has features that make it unique and different from others" (Okonkwo, 2007, p. 269).

Finally, Jarnow and Dickerson (1997), Alléres (2003) and Mosca (2010) do not address the theme of a strategic model in their books. We'll end this discussion by observing whether the authors above have identified a strategic group that operates in the fashion business and the strategic models they used. At first glance, we must point out that no one has explicitly identified the strategic groups competing in the fashion business. However, those who do submit their vision of a strategic model implicitly identify the relevant strategic groups.

1.6 Strategic business models and strategic groups in the fashion industry, according to the author

We (partially) agree with the opinions of Kapferer and Bastien and Corbellini and Saviolo who present some specific business models for the fashion industry. However, we take issue with the small number (only four) of models offered by each of them. We believe that such a small number cannot reflect the complex and heterogeneous situation in the (luxury) fashion business. However, we disagree with Okonkwo's position that, on the contrary, it is impossible to come up with a characteristic business model for the fashion industry considering that each company adopts its own strategic model. With these approaches, these illustrious authors have not identified the many strategic groups that compete in the fashion business, each of which adopts a similar business model. As a result, they haven't differentiated various strategies used by each of the main companies in the fashion business.

1.7 Macro strategic groups in the fashion industry, according to the author

In this book, we propose a model that allows us to identify, first, four macro clusters by applying two variables. Second, by means of other variables, it allows us to break up the last two macro clusters; thus, we identify 13 other clusters that are analysed in the following chapters.

The two characteristics that make it possible to identify the four macro clusters are as follows:

- product (un)specialisation;
- the applied growth strategy.

The former highlights whether the company is specialised in a product category or unspecialised with an extended product portfolio. The latter considers whether the company adopted mainly a *buy* growth strategy, that is, the acquisition of existing companies, or if the growth has taken place chiefly thanks to a *make* strategy, that is, through the launch of new categories of merchandise by the same company. Combining these two variables, I identify the first four macro clusters:

1. big specialised groups;
2. big unspecialised groups;
3. unspecialised companies;
4. specialised companies.

TABLE 1.1 Four macro clusters

Four Macro Clusters

	Big Specialised Groups	*Big Unspecialised Groups*	*Unspecialised Companies*	*Specialised Companies*
Product-specialised	Yes	No	No	Yes
Growth strategy	Mainly buy	Mainly buy	Mainly make	Mainly make
No. of players	Few	Few	Some	Many
Example	Luxottica	Lvmh	Armani	Adidas

Source: author's elaboration.

The first two strategic macro clusters share the same growth strategy, which is (mainly) buy-based. They differ because the first is product-specialised, whereas the latter boasts a comprehensive merchandise offer. There are a very few examples of fashion companies having these characteristics; as stated by David Pambianco in his interview available at the end of the chapter, there is a natural economic barrier that prevents businesses from adopting such a strategic model – specifically, their annual turnover must reach at least a threshold of €10 billion.

The third and fourth macro clusters share a (mainly) make growth strategy; yet they are different in terms of specialisation: companies from the third cluster are not specialised (anymore), while those from the fourth cluster are still specialised; these last two macro clusters can be broken down into different subsets, each of which is characterised by specific features. This further subdivision allows us to properly segment the fashion industry and to have a representation that is more in line with different kinds of companies that make up this industry.

We now proceed with a short description of each macro cluster to then analyse them in greater detail in the following chapters.

1.8 Big specialised groups

A premise is necessary: many professionals of the fashion industry are used to applying the word "group" to define those organisations that have adopted a mainly buy-based strategy. We have accepted this definition. Besides the typology of product characterising the specialisation of these clusters, this macro cluster is not present in other sub-categories. We can mention Luxottica,[3] operating in the eyewear industry, and Richmont, active in those of jewels and watches. This cluster is not studied in this text because we focus on companies whose business models are concentrated on apparel and/or footwear and/or bags.

1.9 Big unspecialised groups

This macro cluster is made up of organisations that have expanded their original product offering, mainly by adopting a "buy" model and therefore acquiring existing companies or brands. They compete in many different businesses, with many brands, and their sales volume is very high. Louis Vuitton Moët Hennessy (LVMH) and Kering offer the most significant example. This cluster is analysed in Chapter 2.

1.10 Unspecialised companies

The third macro cluster, unspecialised companies, features two characteristics. The first, and most important, is that these companies have expanded upon their original product offering by adopting a "make" strategy. The second, which is a result of the first, is that they are perceived by the market as being lifestyle companies. At the beginning, almost all of these companies showed a high level of specialisation in a specific product/price/target market. Then, thanks to the fame and brand identity they garnered in their original specialisation, they expanded their selection to include other products. Thus, some that started by offering their own ready-to-wear lines (Armani and Versace) followed up by gradually diversifying into other industries, such as leather goods, eyewear, fragrances, etc. Others that started out in leather goods (Prada, Hermès) later expanded their product offerings to include clothing, eyewear, fragrances, etc. Three major factors involved in the way in which these companies have repositioned themselves from *specialised companies* to *unspecialised companies*. First, they (obviously) expanded into other categories of product; second, they offered up a new identity for the brand, shifting the focus in communications from the tangible characteristics of the product to those of the brand that elicit emotions; third, they changed their distribution policies from a wholesale strategy to more of a focus on direct retail; this allowed them to express their new brand identity, their "lifestyle". This repositioning process is recent compared to the centuries of history that many of these companies have. It has also been gradual as well because it required many years – decades actually. Let's take Prada as an example. The Milan-based company started its business in 1913, selling leather goods from its own shop, which opened the same year it was founded. For about 70 years, the business was limited to the leather goods sold through just one shop. The diversification into women's ready-to-wear and the opening of the second shop "only" took place in the early 80s, while during the 90s, there was expansion of the product range into men's clothing. Most importantly, this is when there was a change in direction in terms of communication in order to represent the new lifestyle image, with the debut of the Fondazione Prada and the sponsorship of the Luna Rossa sailing team at the America's Cup. The beginning of the 2000s saw the launch of eyewear, the first flagship store – Epicentro – and decisive expansion into international markets. While *unspecialised companies* may still be strongly specialised in their initial product category, which still provides the majority of their sales volume, they are perceived by the market as lifestyle companies. These include companies that Fabris and Minestroni would define as "culture brands" (2004, p. 156), in which the name of the designer (Giorgio Armani) corresponds with the name of the company (Giorgio Armani S.p.A.), which represents very different products: from clothing to fragrances, from accessories to sweets, from hotels to eyewear, but all the while maintaining that stylistic and image continuity necessary to creating a strong, overall identity – a lifestyle. Such companies offer a true way of life to their consumers.

This third macro cluster can be further split into four groups by applying the following variables, summarised in the chart below (Table 1.2).

- *the historic origins of the company*: is it a company for which its origins are very important, such as the historic brands (Chanel)? Or a company for which it is important but not as much as for the previous category, such as the contemporary brands (Giorgio Armani)? Or is it a company for which its origins are of little or no importance, such as the case of the industrial brands (Liu Jo) or fast fashion brands (Zara)?

TABLE 1.2 Unspecialised companies

Unspecialised Companies				
	Historic Brands	Contemporary Brands	Industrial Brands	Fast Fashion Brands
Diversification	Yes	Yes	Yes	Yes
Growth strategy	Make	Make	Make	Make
Historic origin	Very important	Important	Medium important	Not important
Made in	Very important	Very important	Medium important	Not important
Founder	Couturier	Designer	Entrepreneur	Entrepreneur
Positioning price ranges	Very high	Very high/–medium	Medium/high	Low
Naming strategy	Patronimic/one name	Patronimic/many names	Pseudonym	Pseudonym
Value chain control	Very high	High	Low	High
Target	Elite	Wide	Medium	Widest
Main product	Leather goods	High-end ready-to-wear	Womenswear	Mass market clothing
Main critical factor of success	Heritage	Lifestyle	Value for money	Cheap/trendy/fast
Brand example	Hermès	Giorgio Armani	Max&Co.	Zara

Source: author's elaboration.

- the *"Made in" industry*[4]: is it a company with French (Chanel) or Italian (Armani) origins that make a great value-add for the company? Or does it have British or American roots, which also add value but not as much as the previous cases cited? Or is it a company whose origins don't add any value, at least for the moment?
- the *type of founder and the image role he or she plays*: is he or she a couturier (Coco Chanel) or a designer (Giorgio Armani) that is recognised or recognisable to most consumers as playing a fundamental role when it comes to positioning? Or is he or she an industrialist and thus only plays a marginal image role, or perhaps doesn't play any role at all, such as for the industrial and fast fashion brands?
- *unspecialisation in price range*: is it a company that mainly competes in one price range (e.g. very high for Chanel, mid-range for Liu Jo and medium/low for Zara)? Or is it in many price ranges, from very high to medium, like with many contemporary brands, such as Armani?
- the *naming strategy adopted*: is it a company that uses only one patronymic name on all of its products and lines, such as the historic brands (Chanel)? Or does it use different names that all refer back to the main house, as with the majority of the contemporary brands (Armani, e.g., with Armani Privé and Emporio Armani)? Or does it use both strategies in that the naming strategy isn't all that important in terms of positioning, such as, for example, with some of the fast fashion brands (Inditex, Zara, Zara Home and Bershka)?
- *control of value chain*: is it a company that has a high level of control over the value chain (from upstream, production, all the way downstream and distribution) like the leaders

of historic brands, contemporary brands, fast fashion brands? Or does it have a low level of control like the majority of the industrial brands?

- *target market*: is it a company that reaches a well-defined target, that is an elite target market such as the historic brands or "medium" as in the case of industrial brands, or does it have a (very) large target market, as in the cases of Zara and Armani, respectively?

By combining the above-listed variables – summarised in the following chart (Table 1.2) – it is possible to identify four groups, each one adopting a specific business model, which will be analysed in the following chapters:

1. historic brands (Chapter 3);
2. contemporary brands (Chapter 4);
3. industrial brands (Chapter 5);
4. fast fashion brands (Chapter 6).

The first two were founded by a couturier and a designer, respectively, in different periods of history. The historic brands were founded between the beginning of the 1800s and the first part of the 1900s, while the contemporary brands were mainly founded in the twentieth century from the end of the 1960s and beginning of the 1980s. For both, the historic origins of the company, type and image role carried out by the founder and "Made in" characteristics are fundamental elements in determining positioning. The third group, the industrial brands, was "created" by an industrialist, and the variables we've just mentioned – specifically, the historic origins and type and role carried out by founder – have almost no importance since they leverage on other factors of success. The fourth group is the fast fashion brands, the newcomers of the new century. These were also founded by an industrialist, and the variables mentioned previously also have no relevance for them since they leverage on other key factors of success.

1.11 Specialised companies

The fourth macro cluster, the specialised companies, as previously maintained, is made up of companies that have two characteristics: the first and most important is that they have focused their strategy on a specific product, such as casualwear, underwear, formalwear, bags, shoes, etc.; the second, which is a result of the first, is that they are perceived in the market as being strongly focused on that specific product. As a result, those companies generate almost their entire overall sales in a specific product category, and any potential diversification into other categories has a merely marginal function. As stated by David Pambianco in his interview available at the end of the chapter, these enterprises can also offer a total look; nonetheless, around 70% of their turnover is made thanks to the product/market combination in which they're specialised. The majority is also specialised in a specific price range and very few compete in many or all price ranges. Some focus on a specific, given target market, while others have a larger, more wide-ranging target market. Specialised companies, therefore, offer a certain brand image and specialisation in a product or price range (and often within the target market as well) that doesn't allow them to successfully diversify into other products, and/or price ranges, and/or target markets. The specialised companies' macro cluster, as I mentioned before, can in turn be broken down into as many

TABLE 1.3 Specialised companies

Specialised Companies					
Clothing				Bags	Shoes
Formalwear	Casualwear	Activewear	Underwear		
Kiton, Zegna …	Levi's, Diesel, …	Nike, Adidas, …	Victoria's Secret, Intimissimi, …	Coach, Valextra, …	Louboutin Zanotti, …

Source: author's elaboration.

business subsets as there are categories of fashion products. There are specialised companies in clothing, footwear, leather goods, jewellery, watches, fragrances, cosmetics, eyewear, etc. Within the clothing industry, it is also possible to identify as many business subsets as the many sub-industries that make them up. Therefore, there are specialised companies in formalwear, with still others in underwear, etc.

By applying this approach, we have identified the following sub-groups of companies, and a specific chapter is dedicated to each of them:

1. emerging ready-to-wear-specialised brands (Chapter 7);
2. formal menswear-specialised brands (Chapter 8);
3. casualwear-specialised brands (Chapter 9);
4. underwear-specialised brands (Chapter 10);
5. activewear-specialised brands (Chapter 11);
6. streetwear-specialised brands (Chapter 12);
7. footwear-specialised brands (Chapter 13);
8. bags-specialised brands (Chapter 14).

We need to specify that, within this fourth macro cluster, we could have identified specialised companies also for an even more specific product category – trousers rather than shirts or hosiery – which, for the sake of conciseness, was not considered. Moreover, we could also identify companies specialised in high-end women's shoes or men's luxury shoes or medium-price footwear for both genders. Therefore, the sample of companies for the footwear and bags industry was chosen so as to give an exhaustive picture.

Interview with David Pambianco, CEO at Pambianco

What are the successful strategic models of the fashion industry?
There are several successful models; first of all, we have big luxury groups: LVMH, Kering and Richmont. Except for the fact that the latter is specialised in the jewels/watches segment, they adopt similar logic: a buy strategy, they compete in luxury. A successful luxury model is adopted only by "foreign" companies.

What is the minimum turnover to be part of this cluster?
I would say that the minimum threshold is about €8–10 billion per year.

Are Italian companies competitive in the luxury industry?
They belong to another mega-cluster that is not as successful as the previous one because the turnover is a pivotal factor. There are no Italian luxury groups, but only small independent businesses that haven't adopted a buy strategy: Ferragamo, Zegna, Dolce & Gabbana, Armani, Tod's and Prada.

In the accessible luxury segment, do we find successful business models?
It is a segment where we do not find big groups and where there is no consolidated successful model; however, the segment has great potential, most of all in Asia. It is characterised by specialised companies like Furla, and other unspecialised brands such as Liu Jo, Pinko, Patrizia Pepe and small groups like Capri Holdings; a cluster where Italian companies are smaller than foreign ones.

What about the medium-low segment?
It is dominated by fast fashion brands. Vertical integration, trendy style, accessible prices and very high brand awareness are their factors of success.

What about companies specialised in a specific product?
Specialised companies are suffering because they can't be economically big enough to be competitive. Many of these brands offer a total look, but most of their turnover – about 70% – is generated by one product. They are very specialised companies that are not able to emotionally involve the consumer; nowadays, young people recognise themselves in lifestyle brands and want to be surprised and involved. Only activewear-specialised brands have achieved excellent results.

What are the main reasons?
Adidas, Nike and Puma have achieved results similar to LVMH and Kering – but with one brand – thanks to the casualwear phenomenon and in particular to sneakers and to the effectiveness of omnichannel and customization; and they still have a huge potential, thanks to the crucial role of endorsers. In the last few years, we have assisted to the development of niche brands, specialised in streetwear, whose success is due to their ability to intercept the new generations with effective online communication strategies.

What are the most important topics in the fashion system?
There are themes such as sustainability, digital and e-commerce platforms, as well as customization and omnichannel. Sustainability is simply connected to brand reputation. Fashion companies have become sensitive to this topic because they have been encouraged by the consumer who is not very willing to purchase non-sustainable brands. However, in the short term, almost all the players have had to adopt sustainable conduct; therefore, being sustainable won't represent an added value for the brand anymore, but a prerequisite of the product. The same applies for digital and e-commerce: initially, they were considered an innovation and a factor of competitive advantage; shortly all companies will be equipped with these tools, and they won't be a differentiating aspect anymore. It is important to emphasise that innovations do not substitute "past rules", they complement them. An example is the evolution of distribution. The mono-brand and later the omnichannels complemented the wholesale one. The complexity of the fashion system has increased if compared to the past.

What innovations will be included in the close future?

Artificial intelligence is emerging and will become more important; it is less evident because it is transversal. As I mentioned earlier, omnichannel is a big challenge for the future, I've read an interesting annual report stating how difficult and useless it is to separate offline and online sales since the latter influence the former. Another important trend is customization that furtherly increases complexity; companies will have to be able to offer a very high degree of customization organising their logistics and production in order to offer such a service.

Can you summarise in a few words what the successful business models are?

In luxury, the most successful is the buy model, whereas in fast fashion, the make one.

Fashion is focusing on the two extreme segments: is the medium one losing competitiveness?

The medium segment has now been "included" by Zara.

And what about the medium-high segment?

It represents that middle world that, on the one hand, has great potential, but on the other hand, we need to understand how sustainable it is. In the premium segment, there are no groups that can reach a turnover of at least €10 billion yet: they are all smaller businesses.

Student activities

- determine the variables to identify the sub-sectors in the business of watches (or jewels);
- by applying the variables you have defined, identify the different strategic groups of the above-mentioned sector and sub-sector;
- identify the main players of each strategic group and the applied strategies they share.

Notes

1 This chapter is based on the one described in the book *Fashion Business Model* (Golizia, 2016).
2 The authors exclude companies that only concentrate on production.
3 Luxottica has an assortment constituted by both acquired and licensed brands.
4 By this I mean where the company started and not where it manufactures.

2

LARGE UNSPECIALISED FASHION COMPANIES

Reading: The CEO

The Chief Executive Officer (CEO) defines the brand strategy, its positioning and the message that is to be conveyed to the market. Moreover, this figure strategically organises the company by coordinating all the departments – in particular, the creative, productive, marketing-communication and sales ones – with the aim to reach the economic and social goals set. The task of the creative department, managed by the director of the style office, or Creative Director, is to coordinate the stylistic development of the collection and to creatively interpret the storytelling. The function of the production department is to transform the creative dream into a product to be delivered, in the right time, and with the right qualitative standards, to the distribution network and, finally, to the end consumer. The role of the marketing department is to contribute to the creation of a story and message in support of the product and to amplify the storytelling and the emotional aspect. The function of communication is to coordinate traditional and digital communication activities to make sure the message reaches several targets, from influencers to customers. Finally, the sales department collects the results of the storytelling through the coordination of the distribution network and with the aim to reach the sales budget.

2.1 Who are they?

As mentioned in Chapter 1, big unspecialised groups are characterised by a diversification that embraces many categories of merchandise and that is primarily based on a buy strategy. LVMH and Kering are the main representatives of this cluster and are the subject of analysis of this chapter. Both public companies, they compete in numerous sectors and own plenty of brands, all positioned in the luxury segment. LVMH, established in 1987 and boasting, in 2019, revenues of €53.7 billion as well as 163,000 employees, is the leader of this cluster and of the entire fashion industry. It controls 75 brands gathered in five main divisions (see paragraph 2.5): from Moët & Chandon champagne, to Sephora, a chain of cosmetics shops, from historic lifestyle brand Louis Vuitton, to the emerging Fenty, designed by Rihanna. Kering was founded in 1963 as Établissements Pinault when François Pinault established a wood trading business. Until 1999, the year in which it diversified into fashion by acquiring the Gucci Group, the core business had been rooted in distribution: in the last few years the group has sold all its shares in this sector to focus on only the fashion luxury.

2.2 Style, by Daniela Guariento and Antonio Patruno

The creative process cannot disregard strategic positioning, the brand identity as well as – in the short term – the decisions on the marketing mix (Ironico, 2014).

In order to maximise their market share, the brands belonging to LVMH or Kering have to (or should) be complementary to each other. Complementarity is achieved not only through accurate marketing strategies but also by means of style differentiation. We hereby observe and compare the creativity of some brands belonging to Kering: Gucci, Bottega Veneta, Alexander McQueen and Brioni. On the one hand, we find Gucci, best representative of contemporary fashion maximalist aesthetic, whose new Creative Director's language has become part of our daily life and has been enriched with embroidered tigers and bees, as well as by big glasses and must-have white socks to be worn with classic shoes. Its aesthetic is not "ugly" but an experiment that travels through the history of styles and contaminates them; the result is a fashion that goes beyond the concept of excess. On the other hand, we have Bottega Veneta, a luxury brand of very high manufacturing quality and specialised in leather goods, whose philosophy is mirrored in its name – BOTTEGA VENETA. In fact, the latter underlines its craftsmanship that, thanks to the weaving of leather technique, has become an identifying element. To the same group belong, among others, Alexander McQueen and Brioni. The former is experimental, avant-garde and unconventional. The latter, instead, stands out for opposite features: men's tailored, classic and timeless suits.

2.3 Supply chain and sustainability, in collaboration with Celeste Corso

In the past, fashion companies used to produce almost exclusively in their own plants. In the last two decades, the productive strategy has changed considerably. Most companies outsource the production of finished garments to external suppliers that are in charge of the whole productive chain. Only top-level companies, which feel the need to control the quality of the production process, manufacture those items whose price can compensate for the higher cost of in-house production (Bini, 2011). Furthermore, in the last few years, the consumer has become more and more sensitive to the social and environmental impact of production, thus convincing fashion companies to apply sustainable policies (Rinaldi and Testa, 2013). The purpose of this paragraph is to examine how the 13 different clusters – analysed in this book – structure their production policies and handle sustainability.

Considered the importance of the whole strategy (only) for this cluster, the manufacturing strategy is considered in a more comprehensive context, the value chain, that is the set of separated "activities a firm performs in designing, producing, marketing, delivering, and supporting its product" (Porter, 1985, p. 33).

The LVMH and Kering groups boast the highest control of the value chain in the fashion system.

The former is described below as a representative example. As confirmed by Antonio Belloni, General Manager of LVMH, the degree of control varies according to the category of product: the typologies of merchandise diversify for their different levels of vertical integration. High-end brands privilege a strong integration of the whole value chain, from ateliers to shops. Wines and spirits, watches and cosmetics mainly rely on third-party distribution. Le Bon Marché and Sephora are distributors (Sacchi, 2020). If we analyse high-end brands (belonging to the "fashion and leather" division), the French group applies an extremely high control thanks to two connected factors:

1. in-house management of the main value chain activities;
2. very high control on the work of third-party suppliers.

Speaking of the first factor, the principal activities that constitute the value chain – style, production, marketing and communication, and distribution – are internally supervised by the company; they are not entrusted to third parties. For this reason, each brand is controlled by its own Creative Director in charge of the collection. Most of the items are manufactured in the production plants of the holding and sold through their own distribution network; the marketing and communication function is organised and managed by the company. This strategy is applicable thanks to the conspicuous financial resources that allow for investments in directly owned production and distribution. Hence, the second factor.

The final and remaining activities delegated to external suppliers are strictly controlled by LVMH. The financial and economic solidity of the group is crucial for imposing rigorous rules on partner companies. When the actual quality of products is superlative (see paragraph 2.5), total control of the value chain – and in particular of the supply chain – becomes pivotal.

Finally, the very high resources allowed LVMH (and Kering too) to directly produce and sell their eyewear lines, which are generally manufactured and sold by licencing.[1] LVMH, which in the past had collaborated with several licensees, has recently established Thelios, a specialised joint venture with Marcolin, whose 51% is controlled by LVMH and the remaining 49% by the partner. This strategy is aimed at directly producing and selling the corporate brands to increase value chain control and be more cost-effective.

For a long time LVMH and Kering have invested many resources in sustainability, in ethical labour and in the environment. LVMH has organised many initiatives among which we find LIFE (*LVMH* Initiatives For the Environment), a programme that is an integrating part of its corporate industrial plan. The goal is to reduce CO_2 emissions and to monitor the supply chain and reduce the environmental impact of production (LVMH, 2020). During the Covid-19 pandemic, the General Manager, Mr. Belloni, declared that the group tried to contribute by making donations to those territories where the brands of the group are distributed (Sacchi, 2020). For instance, Bulgari and Dior Fragrances produced hand sanitisers. Louis Vuitton, Dior, Celine and Fendi manufactured masks and protective overalls.

Like LVMH, Kering committed to sustainability by signing the *Fashion Pact*, an agreement for safeguarding the planet. Its President and CEO, François-Henri Pinault, declared that to be a successful entrepreneur, you must be socially and environmentally responsible, most of all when you lead a big company. In order to give back something to society and to be consistent, it is necessary to promote causes that are close to the interests of employees (Sacchi, 2017). Together with LVMH, the group drew the regulations for the work conditions of models, taking a direct responsibility that in the past had been delegated to agencies.

2.4 Segmentation strategies

2.4.1 Premise

Abel's model (1980), based on the combination of product/market and five strategies – which focuses on both segment and product, product specialisation, market specialisation, selective specialisation and total market coverage – is rarely applicable in its "pure" form to fashion businesses. This is due to three reasons.

First, as explained in Chapter 1, the fashion system is not represented anymore – as in the 80s – by a single product, clothing, but it is the sum of several sectors that are in turn composed of different sub-sectors. As a consequence, a company may compete only in the clothing sector/underwear sub-sector; another in clothing but in two sub-sectors (casual-wear and activewear); another only in footwear and in the women's shoes sub-sector – the number of options is extremely high.

Second, "the customer is ever more transversal in terms of age, lifestyle, and income bracket" (Corbellini and Saviolo, 2009, p. 150) and "in real life, different groups move from one segment to another" (Corbellini and Saviolo, 2009, p. 137). As a consequence, the product-market combinations that may define a company's segmentation strategy – by applying the above-mentioned model – are (almost) infinite and not always clearly distinct from one another. Of course, one of the five options is the main one for most companies, which are analysed below and in the following chapters. Nonetheless, a company rarely applies one of the five mentioned options in its "pure" form.

The third, and maybe most important reason, and also the focus of this analysis, is the recent affirmation of a new segmentation model that falls outside, but at the same time is connected to, a product/market combination. This is the most adopted model by successful companies and can be defined as a lifestyle strategy. Lifestyle strategy means that the company, despite having a very extended product range and despite satisfying many different micro-needs, is able to convey the same stylistic and identity message, in one word a lifestyle (Fabris and Minestroni, 2004).

Until the arrival of streetwear brands (see Chapter 12), it was believed that the necessary steps to design this strategy were the following (Pambianco, 2008):

1. to debut and to concentrate resources on a product/market strategy in order to acquire a high degree of brand awareness, a distinctive brand identity based on strong speciali-sation and consequently obtain excellent economic results;
2. to later on diversify in many other product/market combinations;
3. to contextually transform the initial wholesale distribution policy in a mainly (or exclu-sively) direct retail strategy in order to market the whole merchandise offer and improve economic results;
4. to turn the image that in the past was focused on product characteristics into one based on symbolic and emotional values related to the brand first and to the corporate lifestyle later.

This strategy, due to its high degree of complexity, has required several decades to be put into practice, and only a few companies have been able to apply it. This strategy boasts an undisputed advantage compared to the five above-mentioned traditional ones: the choice of the consumer is not based on the product benefits or a difference from competitors, but is driven by the company behind the product, its symbolic and emotional values evoked by the reputation of the parent brand (Fabris and Minestroni, 2004). Apparently, this strategy could be applied only by those companies established by couturiers/designers and having a strong heritage. Nevertheless, a few bright examples in streetwear, casualwear and formal-wear have proven that decades of heritage (in the former) or a couturier/designer founder (in the latter) are not always a prerequisite.

We now proceed with the analysis of the segmentation strategies adopted by a sample of companies for each of the 13 clusters.

LVMH and Kering, whose aim is to maximise the market share of each industry they compete in, adopt a similar scheme based on the complementarity of brands: there are brands that apply a lifestyle strategy, others an undifferentiated one, and others a target-focused methodology, or a product-focused one. For this reason, we first consider two brands for each group: Gucci and Alexander McQueen for Kering and Louis Vuitton and Stella McCartney[2] for LVMH – which are mainly examined in the following paragraphs[3] – and, finally, Brioni and Berluti.

We may notice that Gucci and Louis Vuitton – historic brands with an extended product portfolio – apply the same strategy: lifestyle. For instance, over the years, Louis Vuitton has created a very extensive product range aimed at satisfying different targets, yet all sharing the same concept: to represent the most refined qualities of Western *Art de Vivre* in the world; it is synonymous with elegance and creativity, it blends tradition and innovation and it lights up dreams and fantasy. In this context, the main product, leather goods, does not lose importance, but, on the contrary, it is strengthened by the strong values of the brand Louis Vuitton and of the corporate, LVMH.

Conversely, Stella McCartney and Alexander McQueen are not endowed with such a strong identity and values as Louis Vuitton and Gucci; for this reason, they implement an undifferentiated strategy. Undifferentiated does not have a negative connotation as in classic marketing theories; on the contrary, it means offering many products to many targets differentiating them. Stella, in fact, has always concentrated its efforts on sustainability and social responsibility, proving the will to create a green and conscious lifestyle strategy. Likewise, Alexander's offer stands out for its experimental, gothic and artistic content.

We conclude by explaining two more cases for each group: Berluti and Brioni. They both adopt a strategy that does not belong to any of the five above-described options, but is a hybrid of the two: product and market specialisation. Both brands address a similar target (market specialisation) – elegant men with a very high income – to whom they offer a set of products among which shoes and suits, respectively (product specialisation), are pivotal.

2.5 Brand

2.5.1 Premise

The literature about the brand and its importance in the fashion industry is very rich. Let's begin by defining what a brand is and why it is so important:

> branding is all about creating a difference. Branded goods are distinguished from un-branded goods by their intrinsic and symbolic value …; the intrinsic value is tangible an associated with product attributes. The symbolic value is intangible and associated with the emotional value the brand is able to communicate.
>
> *(Corbellini and Saviolo, 2009, p. 155)*

Krishan (1996) stresses the importance for a brand manager to design a unique image, impossible to copy or imitate. Kapferer and Bastien strengthen the above-mentioned concepts even more by maintaining that "there is no luxury without a brand" (2009, 2012 reprint, p. 141); to then underline the importance of factors like personality, iconic products, service and dream, for a luxury company.

We now describe the branding policy of the analysed clusters by studying the following aspects:

1. the original business (product);
2. the eventual diversification strategy applied;
3. the current assortment;
4. if the brand is endowed with iconic products, heritage and a recognised *made-in*;
5. the relation between perceived and actual quality;
6. the applied productive techniques;
7. the naming strategy;
8. the designer's role;
9. customisation and made-to-measure service.

We begin by investigating the original business of a brand and by analysing if it diversified into other product categories. This aspect is essential since the most successful companies are those whose brand identity was built on the original business and whose eventual diversification was made consistently. At the same time, this allows for an analysis of the current assortment to understand whether it comprises iconic products, legendary items, which made the brand's history, and that are worshipped by consumers, and add an extraordinary value to the brand. Heritage is also a crucial variable because "like a living being, the brand has ancestors, a history…; it is anchored, not invented" (Kapferer and Bastien, 2009, 2012 reprint, p. 143); *made-in* is also important since many brands tend to take back the positive associations connected to a specific country of origin (Ironico, 2014).

Also, the (product) effective and (brand) perceived quality have a pivotal role in defining the brand identity: it is important to do research not only on their level (high or low), but also if they coincide or one prevails on the other; as well as if in the same company, we (may) find several product lines characterised by different levels of actual/perceived quality. Speaking of actual quality, production techniques – artisanal, semi-artisanal or industrial – are as important to define the brand identity.

"The name remains the first sign of recognition of a brand. It is never neutral" (Chevalier and Mazzalovo, 2012, p. 103); so it is a further characterising element for the branding of fashion companies. The same can be said for Creative Directors because "Designers are useful figures because they incarnate their brands" (Tungate, 2005, p. 49).

In this analysis we observe how the importance of the above-mentioned variables changes according to the cluster of reference.

Moreover, do not forget that capsule collections have an essential role in the characterisation of a brand; nevertheless, this topic is so pivotal that, in addition to being cross-analysed in all the paragraphs dedicated to communication, it is also discussed in a specific paragraph (co-branding, from 2.7.7. to 13.7.7).

In this section, in order to offer a general vision, we first analyse the brand portfolio of LVMH and Kering with a specific focus on the former. Subsequently, four brands, two for each group, are examined to highlight their diversity and, at the same time, complementarity.

LVMH includes 75 brands grouped into six divisions:

1. wine and spirits;
2. fashion and leather goods;
3. perfumes and cosmetics;
4. watches and jewellery;
5. selective retailing;
6. other activities.

The first encompasses the most prestigious wine, cognac and champagne brands like Moët & Chandon and Hennessy; the second, the subject of analysis in the chapter, comprises historic lifestyle brands like Louis Vuitton and Dior, emerging and niche labels like Fenty, a brand specialised in cashmere like Loro Piana, a label specialised in luggage (Rimowa), a company specialised in men's footwear (Berluti). The third division boasts specialised companies like Guerlain and Acqua di Parma, as well as Parfums Christian Dior, the result of a brand extension; the fourth includes only specialised brands such as Bulgari; the fifth encompasses retailers specialised in cosmetics and fragrances like Sephora, as well as the historic and most prestigious "department store", Le bon Marché Rive Gauche. The last division includes activities that "share a passion for lifestyle, culture and the arts" (LVMH, no date) The main business is fashion and leather that, in 2019, represented 41.3% of the total turnover.

Kering is active in the fields of fashion and leather goods, watches and jewels with "only" 12 brands as compared to the previously described group. In the fashion division we find Gucci, a lifestyle brand, emerging and niche labels like Alexander McQueen, as well as companies specialised in formal menswear like Brioni. In the second division, the fashion conglomerate comprises specialised companies like Boucheron and Pomellato.

We hereby proceed with the analysis of two brands for each group, pointing out how both Kering and LVMH adopt similar strategies for their historic lifestyle brands – Louis Vuitton and Gucci – and for niche brands – Stella McCartney and Alexander McQueen.

The original businesses of the first two brands are luggage and luxury leather goods, on which they have built their values. Despite leather goods being the most significant business, in years, they have extended their offerings to ready-to-wear (both womenswear and menswear), footwear, jewellery, watches, eyewear, fragrances, home décor and hotels. The decision to offer a very extended product range is founded on the need to satisfy the requests of many micro-targets and to achieve very high turnovers. These brands applied a horizontal diversification strategy by extending to other product categories, whereas in order to preserve their exclusivity – a typical characteristic of luxury brands – they did not choose vertical diversification by adding other lines of the same product and brand (Corbellini and Saviolo, 2009). At the root of this strategy, there's a specific corporate choice: the acquisition of different brands to compete in the same business area. Hence, in the segment of high-price bags, we find Louis Vuitton, Fendi, Dior and Celine – just to mention a few – as representatives of LVMH.

Conversely, Stella McCartney and Alexander McQueen, which debuted in ready-to-wear, have diversified by reaching a less extended range. This choice originates from a focused strategy that leverages on a sophisticated-style product for an ultra-selective target. Among the listed brands, the former is the only one that in 2004 penetrated the activewear market thanks to a long collaboration with Adidas (Stella McCartney, no data). Adidas by Stella McCartney and McQ Alexander McQueen – the second focused on the jeanswear segment – are two examples of limited vertical diversification.

Louis Vuitton and Gucci have made their heritage an essential factor; the former stresses it through its place of origin by embossing "Louis Vuitton Paris" and "Made in France" on its leather products. Stella McCartney and Alexander McQueen have a much shorter history and, as a consequence, cannot rely on heritage. Hence, the choice of leveraging is based on other differentiating elements (Porter, 1980), the former on a universal concept of sustainability, which makes it unnecessary to emphasise the "made in", and the latter on English tailoring tradition and on "Made in Britain".

As asserted by Chevalier and Mazzalovo (2012), stylistic codes are crucial for positioning, and Louis Vuitton and Gucci possess several; for instance, the respective logos – the LV monogram and the double G – that contributed to the creation of their legendary stories and of numerous iconic products. Also, the latter play a crucial role in the branding policy and, for both labels, belong to the original category of leather goods. Gucci boasts the legendary Jackie and Bamboo bags. Louis Vuitton's symbolic product is the Speedy, the quintessential trunk designed in the 30s and dedicated to globetrotters of any age. To appeal to new generations, timeless iconic products are redesigned with seasonal colours that allow for sophisticated customisation (Golizia, 2016). Gucci, in addition to leather goods, is renowned, but also recognisable, for its moccasins and floral pattern, both constantly reinterpreted and updated according to seasonal trends. Even though Alexander McQueen and Stella McCartney have established their business in ready-to-wear, footwear and bags – resulting from a diversification – have become their most representative products. However, in this case, these items cannot be defined as iconic, but rather as representative. In fact, despite playing a crucial role in the definition of the brand image, the impact is not as significant as that of iconic products that involve brand heritage and a higher degree of recognition. In 2015, accessories for Stella McCartney represented almost one-third of total sales mainly thanks to Falabella bag. Alexander McQueen's representative products have gained this status thanks to their distinctive design, rather than for their sales. Armadillo boots are a cult object because they were presented in the last collection designed by the founder before his death (Stansfield, 2015); the stylistic codes of the brand are rooted in the English tailoring tradition and in the skull pattern.

Louis Vuitton and Gucci boast a high perceived quality which also coincides with the actual one. The latter is guaranteed by superlative raw materials and by artisanal techniques handed down from generation to generation. Louis Vuitton has always stood out for the perception of "durability" of its canvas bags (Keshni, 2015).

Both leader brands apply a naming strategy attributable to historic brands (Corbellini and Saviolo, 2009), using the name of the respective founders and extending it to every category of product. Their name is their heritage: treasured and preserved, year after year, decade after decade, it has generated a very high awareness and a clear and exclusive image (Golizia, 2016). However, it is important to stress that in common thinking, the two founders, Louis Vuitton and Guccio Gucci, are not associated to the brand. Hence, the marketing strategy is to give these companies the "face" of current personalities in order to compensate for this "lack". In 2018, Louis Vuitton appointed Virgil Abloh – star and symbol of luxury street culture – Creative Director of menswear collections (Cochrane, 2018). Even the art director of the womenswear division, Nicolas Ghesquiére, is recognised as one of the most important professionals of the industry. Likewise, in 2015, Gucci appointed Alessandro Micheli as art director, who started the so-called "high-fashion-sweater era" (Long, 2018). Concerning the remaining two brands, both designers contribute with their name as well as with their personality. Even after Alexander McQueen's death, Sara Burton is carrying on the tradition of the brand, with the founder remaining the main point of reference for the market. The same goes for Stella McCartney who does not only sign all the products with her name, but who is keep also its symbol thanks to the incorporation of the values of veganism and animal and environment protection.

Among the examined brands, Alexander McQueen is the only one that does not offer any form of product customisation. In contrast, Luis Vuitton and Gucci have been pioneers in this sense. They both offer the opportunity to engrave one's own initials and customise a limited number of items, mainly made of leather. Moreover, Gucci supplies a made-to-measure service for knitwear (Gucci, no year) and has been a precursor of in-store customisation by introducing the possibility to customise the product with the *DIY Patch* (patches for knitwear) (De Klerk, 2016).

2.6 Pricing, in collaboration with Benedetta Breschi

2.6.1 Premise

Literature is rich in texts that examine the pricing of the fashion industry. Two in particular are functional for this analysis. The first is by Corbellini and Saviolo, who affirm that "moving from the ready-to-wear segment to the mass market, the importance of elements such as stylistic creativity, product innovation and the 'dream factor' decreases in favour of aspects such as the price, volumes, efficiency of the supply chain" (2009, p. 105).

The second is by Kapferer and Bastien who underline the importance of product perception in the pricing process: "the more is perceived by the client to be a luxury, the higher the price should be" (2009, 2012 reprint, p. 74). We proposed a model (Golizia, 2016), which allowed to distinguish, for each price segment, companies specialised in a specific product, from unspecialised ones. In this book, the analysis has been enriched with a research aimed at defining and justifying the positioning among the 13 clusters; the characteristics of the research are the following:

1. eight categories of merchandise were analysed: the shopper, women's blazer, women's sneakers, flared and high-waist jeans, the hoodie, the silk nightgown, pumps and men's suits[4];
2. observed price: medium[5];
3. four price segments were considered: absolute luxury, aspirational luxury, accessible luxury and medium/low;
4. (minimum) number of observed companies per category of merchandise, eight: four unspecialised (one per price segment)[6] and four specialised (one per price segment).[7]

Speaking of this cluster, we must consider both the positioning of some brands in the corporate and that of a reference brand, Dior, compared to other clusters.

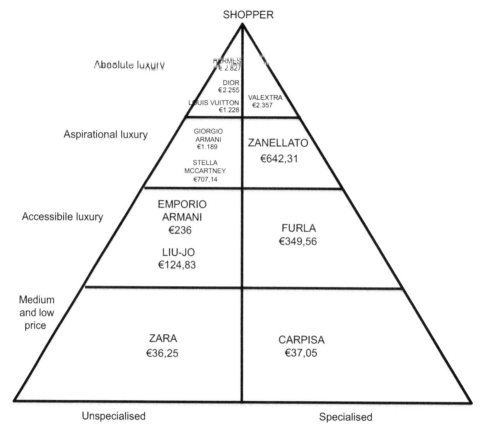

SHOPPER

Absolute luxury — HERMÈS €2.827

DIOR €2.255

LOUIS VUITTON €1.228

VALEXTRA €2.357

Aspirational luxury

GIORGIO ARMANI €1.189

STELLA MCCARTNEY €707,14

ZANELLATO €642,31

Accessibile luxury

EMPORIO ARMANI €236

LIU-JO €124,83

FURLA €349,56

Medium and low price

ZARA €36,25

CARPISA €37,05

Unspecialised   Specialised

FIGURE 2.1 Golizia's pyramid of shoppers
Source: Prepared by Dario Golizia.

Concerning the first, two are the main aspects: first of all, both LVMH and Kering own a set of brands that compete exclusively in luxury; the former has always applied this strategy, the latter, which in the past used to encompass brands operating in other price segments (see Puma and Volcom), in the last few years, has modified its approach by focusing on only luxury. The second aspect refers to the different positioning of single brands in the same group, as proven by the research. If we consider leather goods – a key category for luxury – average prices (and as a consequence the positioning) of Dior, Louis Vuitton and Stella McCartney (LVMH group) are different: Dior and Louis Vuitton are positioned in the absolute luxury segment (the former higher than the latter), whereas Stella McCartney belongs to aspirational luxury. This proves that the group intends to reach different targets in the luxury perimeter: more exclusive for the first, more extended for the second, more niche for the third.[8] Furthermore, we can observe that, horizontally speaking, the first two, Dior and Louis Vuitton, stand in between unspecialised and specialised companies; despite having a product portfolio that encompasses all the categories of merchandise, leather goods represent the core business for both.

Concerning the positioning in relation to other clusters, only one brand from LVMH was considered, Dior, whose price was compared to brands from two clusters: specialised brands competing in a higher price segment and an unspecialised brand, Giorgio Armani,[9] competing in the lower price segment, aspirational luxury. These are the results.

Dior, as compared to the specialised brands belonging to the above-described eight categories of product, shares with two of them a substantially similar positioning, whereas with five, a clearly superior one, and with one an inferior positioning. The positioning of two products, the shopper and the men's formal suit, is essentially similar. In both cases, the two specialised companies, Valextra and Ermenegildo Zegna, respectively, have been able to build a brand image in their sectors, which has given them the possibility to impose prices similar to those of the renowned fashion house.[10] Concerning other products, Dior boasts a significantly superior price positioning: for blazers the price is 115.3% higher compared to Margiela's, a specialised ready-to-wear brand. In fact, the latter (see Chapter 7) does not enjoy the same brand awareness and power of the famous French fashion house. Speaking of sneakers and hoodies, the scenario is the same: the price is, respectively, 171.9% and 381.6% higher that Y-3 and Off-White's. Luxury sneakers and streetwear are relatively young segments and product categories; for this reason, these companies haven't had the time to build, and convey to the market, an image that could allow aligning the price to that of historic brands. The price of jeans is even higher (+ 299.7%) as compared to that of 7 for all mankind. What permits Dior (but, in general, all historic brands) to have such a higher price positioning? We hereby report some considerations concerning historic brands, and made in the previous book (Golizia, 2016), where we had underlined the essential role of price in reflecting their absolute luxury positioning (Allérès, 2003). Their positioning had been explained through an integrated set of the following factors: intangible elements such as heritage, the mythical personality of the couturier and founder evoked by the brand name and legendary iconic products; tangible direct elements like the quality of raw materials and artisanal production techniques; and tangible indirect elements such as the very high distribution and communication costs. Conversely, for opposite reasons, Dior has a lower price positioning for pumps, whose price is 19.9% inferior than Jimmy Choo's (see 14.6), a brand that has been able to build a trendsetter and co-leader image in its industry. In the lingerie segment, the French company has a limited product range that does not include nightgowns.

Concerning its positioning, compared to a contemporary brand (Giorgio Armani or Dolce & Gabbana),[11] Dior boasts a decisively superior price positioning for (almost) all product categories thanks to a higher brand image: 89.6% higher for the shopper, 76.7% for the blazer, 50.7% for sneakers, 52% for jeans, 263.6% for the hoodie and 44.8% for pumps, but only 6.8% higher for men's suits. In fact, thanks to its superlative brand image, Giorgio Armani has transformed the suit into an iconic product sold for a substantially similar price.

The purpose of the above-described research was to prove that the brand image is the real price positioning driver for absolute or aspirational luxury brands, as stated by Kapferer and Bastien (2009, 2012 reprint). The products of these companies all feature a very high effective quality and are made with the best raw materials and by the most skilled craftsmen; nevertheless, price is chiefly determined by the intangible attributes evoked by the brand rather than by tangible product characteristics.

In addition to the naturally superior brand image, among the reasons that justify Dior's more expensive price compared to the one of brands from lower price segments – accessible luxury and mass market – we find the higher the actual quality of the product, the higher the creative content. Dior's price is superior in all product categories if compared with Liu Jo and Zara, but it is interesting to notice the ratio. For example, the price of Dior's bag (€2.255) is 18 times higher than that of the former (€236) and 62.2 times higher than the latter's (€36.25); concerning footwear, instead, the ratio is 14.5 and 20.1 times higher.

2.7 Communication

According to Posner (2011), communication has to aim at defining the brand identity, strengthening its perception, increasing brand awareness, persuading consumers to buy and support sales. In order to achieve these goals, a (fashion) company applies the so-called communication mix (Anouti and Graham, 2018), that is, a set of integrated and consistent tools, aimed at reaching its target.

Corbellini and Saviolo (2009) have already accurately identified the distinguishing characteristics of both high-end and mass brands. Nevertheless, we believe that each of the 13 clusters deserves its own specific analysis. We proceed as follows:

1. we summarise the image of the cluster, that is, the characteristics shared by its most representative brands;
2. we then proceed with the description of how (only) one company from the same cluster organises and manages the marketing and communication function;
3. finally, for each cluster, we identify and outline the communication mix applied by a sample of companies:

   a. fashion shows and trade fairs;
   b. advertising, editorials and advertorials;
   c. influencers, gifting and endorsements;
   d. social media;
   e. sponsorships and co-brandings;
   f. museums, foundations and leisure time activities.

2.7.1 Cluster image

Only for this cluster, in addition to summarise the brand image, we proceed with the representation of the corporate image, that is, how the company is perceived. In the fashion industry, there are no organisations having such a strong and defined reputation like the big luxury groups. The characteristics associated with LVMH and Kering are the following: being innovation leaders, solidity, luxury, being global, heritage, and being socially responsible. We are now describing the most successful fashion conglomerates (in particular, LVMH), which adopted an innovative and winning business model, achieved superlative economic results, implemented avant-garde social responsibility policies, aggregated tens of luxury brands, some of which, are, in turn, leaders of their sector.

Speaking of the cluster image, considering the high number of brands (75 only for LVMH), it is impossible to define one (brand) image that can represent them all. We can proceed with the division of the brands into several groups, each one with their own characteristics: from mega-brands like Louis Vuitton and Gucci, to emerging brands like Stella McCartney and Alexander McQueen, just to mention some. The former share the following peculiarities: they are global and historic brands with a very comprehensive product portfolio, boasting iconic products and a specialisation in leather goods; they are also lifestyle brands characterised by Made in France and Made in Italy. The latter, notwithstanding having few peculiarities, share the following factors: they are avant-garde, they address a niche target and they are contemporary and non-conformist.

2.7.2 Marketing function and communication, in collaboration with Michele Leoni

2.7.2.1 Premise

How is such an articulated and complex function organised and managed in a fashion company?

The press or communication office, reporting to the marketing office, if any, is in charge of managing most of the communication aspects of the brand. Usually, it can be internal and supervised by the company's employees or external and composed of a team of consultants that work on the communication strategy of brands. Sometimes, we can have a mix of the two situations with an internal press office supported by external professionals.

The following analysis studies the organisation of the marketing and communication function of the 13 different clusters. For each, one sample company is analysed.

We now proceed with the analysis of a brand from the LVMH group, Kenzo. It would have been relevant to describe the organisation of one of the two mega lifestyle brands of the group – Louis Vuitton or Dior; however, the information was not available. Nevertheless, we may hypothesise that these brands have a structure similar to Prada's and, as described in paragraph 3.7.2, their structure is based on the direct management of every communication activity, none of which is delegated to external consultants.

Kenzo, a brand established in Paris by Japanese designer Kenzo Takada, was acquired by LVMH in 1993. Kenzo's press office is incorporated in the marketing department of the brand and is managed by the Director of Marketing and Communication reporting to the Creative Director and to the CEO of the company. The headquarters of the press office are located in Paris, in the historic domicile of Rue Vivienne. The Global Director of the Press Office and Public Relations manages and coordinates all the consulting communication agencies based in those countries where the business is more expanded. These agencies, in turn, deal with the collection management: they take care of the sending of samples for shootings and of the communication of news about the brand corporate, directly supplied by the headquarters.

The digital marketing office reports to the marketing and communication department, which supervises all the social media channels of the brand for content creation directly. The VIP office which is in charge of the relations with VIPs' stylists and of events organisation – mainly fashion shows and stores openings – and the graphic-creative department which is responsible for the creative contents and design both report to the above-mentioned division.

2.7.3 Fashion shows and trade fairs, in collaboration with Andrea Doroldi

2.7.3.1 Premise

Fashion shows and trade fairs are two important means to present collections. In general, companies participating in the former do not take part in the latter and vice versa.

The fashion show is mostly employed to obtain media visibility, but it also has a crucial role in dictating new trends. There are two main fashion weeks – fall-winter and spring-summer – where fashion shows are organised, "by invitation only to buyers, fashion editors, journalists and influencers" (Anouti and Graham, 2018, p. 176). In the last three years, we have witnessed an increase in the number of bloggers and influencers– important final consumers, and not traditional "fashion professionals" – in the parterre of the main fashion shows. Paris and Rome are where haute couture brands showcase their collections, while New York, London, Milan and also Paris are a window for ready-to-wear lines.

In addition to traditional fashion shows, fall-winter and spring-summer, brands also organise the event for their pre-collections, the most important being the pre-spring or Cruise or Resort. These, unlike the main collections, take place in several cities of the world (Anouti and Graham, 2018).

Only very few fashion brands participate in the fashion weeks; if we consider the examined cluster, we find the designer labels of big luxury groups (Dior, Louis Vuitton, Gucci, etc.), historic "independent" brands (Chanel, Hermès, etc.), the first and second lines of contemporary brands (Giorgio Armani, Emporio Armani, etc.), very few industrial brands (Max&Co.), very few casualwear-specialised brands (Diesel Black Gold), some streetwear brands (Vetements and Off-White), some formal menswear brands (Ermenegildo Zegna) and some underwear brands (Victoria's Secret). Except for some cases, these brands were mostly established by a couturier or a designer, having their own creative process and competing in luxury.

Almost all industrial brands, casualwear and streetwear-specialised brands, formal menswear and underwear brands do not participate in fashion weeks; fast fashion companies do not participate in either (expect for some very rare cases such as H&M that in some occasions designed a specific line), as well as activewear, footwear and bags-specialised labels. This trend is confirmed by both Anouti and Graham (2018) and Ironico (2014).

The former state that for "premium brands, mass and mid-market brands, however, to show at a trade fair offers a more economical and direct way of engaging with potential buyers" (Anouti and Graham, 2018, p. 181). The latter underlines that trade fairs are important mainly for some targets (men, kids, brides, etc.) and specific categories of merchandise (sportswear, activewear, underwear, footwear, bags, etc.) (Ironico, 2014).

The reasons why these companies attend trade fairs are several: the acquisition of credibility, the collection of orders, to the acquisition of more visibility, but also to create contacts with new potential clients and to preserve the existing business relationships. The number of trade fairs in the fashion industry is extremely high. Ironico (2014) highlighted how only in Italy 43[12] main fairs are held in one year. Among them, Milan's Salone del Mobile (Milan's Design Week) was not – rightly – included: in fact, some fashion companies, for visibility reasons, attend this trade fair (with events that are not held in the fair pavilions) independently from their price positioning and given that they have an interior design line.

In order to present a correct and homogeneous analysis of fashion trade fairs, we have studied a sample of companies from the following clusters: big luxury groups, historic and contemporary brands, industrial brands, fast fashion, casualwear and formalwear-specialised brands that participated (or did not participate) in two editions – one in 2019 before the Covid emergency and the other in 2020 in the post-Covid era – of the following fairs:

- Mipel, Milan's international leather fair; editions n. 116 of 2019 and n. 118 of 2020;
- Pitti Immagine, Florence's fair for menswear (Pitti Uomo), womenswear (a small area in Pitti Uomo) and kidswear (Pitti Bimbo) trends: editions of January 2019 and Pitti Connect, July–October 2020.

For underwear, activewear, streetwear, footwear and bag-specialised companies, we considered the specific trade fairs for the sector listed in the respective chapters.

After this premise, for each cluster we will:

- verify whether they participated in the fashion weeks or not, and, if they did, we examine the typology of the fashion show following the model proposed by Vilaseca (2010);
- verify whether they participated in the above-mentioned fairs;
- finally, if companies have ever participated in the Salone del Mobile.

In the big luxury groups, most of the brands rely on fashion shows organised by the press office which, with the Creative Director, organises the concept. Among the several typologies of fashion shows (Vilaseca, 2010), many are defined as theatrical, that is, they are endowed with narrative and scenic structures similar to those of operas (Alexander McQueen's stands out for the use of theatrical lighting and models that, instead of modelling, play a role). Speaking of cruise collections, a significant example is Dior's fashion show organised in Marrakech and inspired by the themes of inclusivity and multiculturalism (Curci, 2019). For this show, the brand collaborated with local artists and producers in order to gain the attention of the media. Choosing and preferring the fashion show to promote collections, none of the studied designer labels – Gucci, Luis Vuitton, Dior, Fendi, Givenchy, Alexander McQueen and Stella McCartney – has participated in the above-mentioned trade fairs. Some companies have participated in the Salone del Mobile with the so-called *Fuori Salone* events: in 2019, Fendi presented *Back Home,* a special installation celebrating the iconic Pequin pattern presented for the first time in 1987 (Tortora, 2019). Conversely, Brioni, a company specialising in menswear, participated in the 2019 Pitti Uomo (but not in the digital edition of 2020), a global point of reference for the sector.

2.7.4 Advertising, editorial, advertorial, in collaboration with Benedetta Breschi

2.7.4.1 Premise

"In general, advertising involves the use of a medium such as TV, print, radio, billboard or web, which is paid for by the brand to communicate a message to the desired consumer" (Anouti and Graham, 2018, p. 60). Its main advantage is the possibility to reach a broad audience; among the disadvantages, we find the impossibility to interact with the recipients, and to create customised messages.

In the previous book (Golizia, 2016), the author had carried out a research with the aim of comparing the different advertising investments and their "return" in terms of advertorials and fashion editorials[13] for four clusters: historic brands, contemporary brands, industrial brands and fast fashion brands. In this book, the research was extended to nine more clusters: 4 companies for 12 clusters and 3 for the remaining 1, leading to a sum of 51. Except for the different period of analysis (September 2019 instead of September 2015), the same research methodology was applied, in detail:

- measured data: number of advertising pages, advertorials and fashion editorials;
- studied magazines: Italian publications of *Vogue, L'Officiel, Vanity Fair, Elle* and *Glamour;*
- period of study: September 2019;
- examined categories of product: apparel, shoes, bags, fragrances and cosmetics.

2.7.4.2 Double objective

First of all, to compare the results of the two research studies carried out on the four clusters analysed in both 2015 and 2019 and to verify if, in 2019, companies invested more, less, or the same amount as in 2015.

Second, to compare the results of the 13 groups and to verify what groups purchased the highest amount of advertising pages in 2019.

We hereby proceed with the analysis of the results of the above-mentioned research for the group of companies considered in this chapter.

Even if this cluster had not been included in the previous research, it is possible to proceed with a comparison – albeit partial – with the research done in 2019, as both samples include Gucci.[14] Given that one single company is not indicative of an exhaustive comparison, it is relevant to highlight how the Florentine brand – despite a growth in turnover by 146% compared to 2015,[15] and even though it could have purchased more advertising pages – in the analysed period, bought eight pages, the same quantity as in 2015. Therefore, we can assume that the strategy applied even by top performers does not contemplate more investments in traditional press: fashion magazines are, in fact, giving way to campaigns on social media and, generally speaking, online.

If we refer to the total ranking of 2019, this cluster – compared to the total 13 – is second in ranking for the number of advertising, 19, for fashion editorials, 36, and for advertorials, 6. It is relevant to notice that the magazines from which they purchased the highest amount of advertising are *Vogue* and *L'Officiel*, consistently with the core target represented by high-spending-power adults.

TABLE 2.1 Advertising, fashion editorials and advertorials of unspecialised big groups

Unspecialised Big Groups	*L'Officiel*			*Vogue*			*Vanity Fair*			*Elle*			*Glamour*			*Total*		
	A	*FE*	*AD*	*A*	*FE*	*AD*	*A*	*FE*	*AD*	*A*	*FE*	*AD*	*A*	*FE*	*AD*	*A*	*FE*	*AD*
Gucci	4	7	1	1	3	0	2	2	0	1	3	1	0	1	2	8	16	4
Louis Vuitton	2	5	0	2	2	0	1	0	0	0	1	0	0	1	1	5	9	1
Bottega Veneta	2	5	0	2	0	0	0	0	0	0	1	0	0	1	0	4	7	0
Stella McCartney	0	3	0	2	0	0	0	0	0	0	0	0	0	1	1	2	4	1
Total	8	20	1	7	5	0	3	2	0	1	5	1	0	4	4	19	36	6

Source: Authors' data processing on the basis of fashion magazines published in Italy in September 2019. A, FE and AD stand for advertising, fashion editorial and advertorial, respectively.

2.7.5 Influencers, gifting, endorsement, by Lavinia Biancalani

Social networks and mobile devices have overturned fashion companies' communication and their relationship with consumers. Initially, traditional media and organisations resisted this revolution. Nowadays, the scenario has changed and the most successful influencers are well-integrated in the fashion system. In fact, companies are relying more on ads to gain visibility (Misani and Varacca Capello, 2017).

According to Lea-Greenwood (2012), a celebrity is someone who is publicly known; the field is rather diverse and heterogeneous and encompasses athletes, actors, models, musicians, bloggers, etc. From the brand point of view, there are two typologies of involvement:

- "by celebrity gifting: this occurs when a celebrity is photographed in an item that appears to have been chosen by them";
- "by celebrity endorsement: is a contractual agreement between a label and a celebrity or their management, for them to appear publicly wearing the brand" (Anouti and Graham, 2018, pp. 98–99).

The biggest world luxury conglomerates, LVMH and Kering, have been able to apply very effective digital marketing strategies. They both planned a strategy for corporates and for each brand, respectively. The analysis begins by considering the groups LVMH and Kering, and then examines the single brands: Louis Vuitton and Stella McCartney for LVMH, Gucci, and Saint Lauren for Kering.

Since the beginning, LVMH felt the need to adopt a digital marketing strategy. In the course of time, the group increased its digital investments and has recently shown a great interest for personalities with global audiences on social networks.

The experience with Fenty Beauty – make-up line of singer Rihanna – had already highlighted the considerable advantages and the potential of having a *celebrity brand* in the group. Rihanna is famous for her remarkable voice, but thanks to the partnership with Fenty Beauty, LVMH had the opportunity to also appreciate her entrepreneurial spirit and her extraordinary leadership. In 2019, the success of the beauty line encouraged the conglomerate to launch an apparel line, Fenty, signed by the same artist (who is also a celebrity, mega-influencer and social icon with 86.7 million followers on Instagram). LVMH's interest in personalities with many followers was reemphasised by choosing Chiara Ferragni, probably the most famous influencer worldwide. In 2019, she was among the judges of a contest for young talents, *LVMH Prize for Young Fashion Designers.* Amidst the judges were Aimee Song, Instagrammer and blogger, as well as representatives of traditional media with a strong online presence.

Even Kering supported *endorsement* initiatives for corporate projects, often following the wave of innovation promoted by its brands. In 2017, Alessandro Michele, Gucci's Creative Director, launched the *White Ribbon for Women* campaign to fight violence against women; the hashtag #ICouldHaveBeen was promoted by the group's Creative Directors and also by some male influencers like Leonardo Decarli in Italy and Z. Tao in China. They posted on their social profiles a series of video clips to raise awareness on the topic. The core objective of the campaign was to involve younger generations, specifically Generations Z and Y, to cause a deep and sustainable change in mentality, culture and behaviour.

Moving on to the analysis of the digital strategies of some brands of the two groups, we can observe the peculiar case of Louis Vuitton: established as a retailer and leather goods brand in 1854, it debuted in ready-to-wear only in 1997 under the creative direction of Marc Jacobs. The characteristics of this evolution influenced the brand identity that leverages on two competitive advantages: *heritage* for leather goods and trend-driven fashion for ready-to-wear. This is a key factor to specify that the implemented digital marketing strategies are formulated keeping in mind the different targets of the two categories of product.

Speaking of ready-to-wear, Louis Vuitton addresses groups of personalities that have to reach different targets: fashion influencers to communicate with experts of fashion, looking for the latest seasonal trends; celebrities, for a more mainstream target.

The first group, famous trend-driven fashion influencers, such as Grey Yambao, Tamu McPherson, Susanna Lau, is essential to promote fashion shows and collections and to gain visibility. The second includes celebrities in the strict sense (singers, actors, etc.), including Willow Smith, Laura Harrier and Emma Roberts – some of whom are also brand ambassadors sitting in the front row during fashion shows. The goal of this collaboration is to position the brand as a point of reference for international celebrities both on- and offline. The most structured endorsing activities involve celebrities, most of all for their offline popularity. For instance, on the occasion of the 2019 Met Gala, Louis Vuitton collaborated with Sophie Turner and Chloë Grace Moretz – actresses and social media personalities with, respectively, 15.3 and 16.7 million followers on Instagram – to post two videos on Instagram TV[16] showing their preparation for the event in which they participated as guests of the brand.

At the same time, it is crucial for Louis Vuitton to constantly nourish its brand awareness as a leather goods company, a category of products that is part of its heritage, as well as the most profitable. The goal of social media marketing for leather goods is to reach a wider and more mainstream target that associates the brand to its historic tradition, a target of potential leather goods customers, yet less interested in the fashion content. In addition to intense activities of seeding and gifting, which included the launch of the Capucine bag, local influencers, targeted towards different markets, were involved in several experiences. For instance, in July 2019, for the opening of the store in Porto Cervo, the brand organised a travel experience with some Italian fashion influencers including Valentina Siragusa, Filippo Fiora, Filippo Cirulli coining the #LVPortoCervo hashtag. Involving local influencers with a wide loyal audience is fundamental to grow engagement conversion and to encourage purchases.

The British designer Stella McCartney was one of the first to promote eco-fashion on social networks. McCartney not only promotes her sustainable collections, but discusses the theme of sustainability as well. Her true commitment is documented and supported on social media, a perfect means to spread these values. Stella conceives social media as viral "diffusion" tools and, for this reason, the brand posts ad hoc photos (and many videos) speaking the language of the "green" community. Its target is attracted not only by the design of the collection but mainly by the values it portrays: for this reason, social media contents are always accompanied by a detailed caption. For instance, in 2017, for Earth Day, the brand conceived the *Clevercare* campaign to inform consumers about the carbon footprint of garments whose 25% is generated by their care. Videos were posted featuring models that explained how to clean the iconic Falabella bag. For Mother's Day, to mention an Italian case history, the brand organised an influencer marketing activity to support the

#MotherEarthMotherDay for Stella McCartney Eyewear campaign, in order to stress the bond between a mother, her children and the planet; the materials of the collections came from renewable sources. Among the influencers who were asked to post pictures with their children were the Italian Beatrice Valli and the Instagram profile Likemiljlan.

Gucci, property of Kering, made significant investments in social media and influencer marketing, most of all since the hiring of Alessandro Michele. Before observing its digital communication strategies, we start by saying that Michele's approach was all-inclusive and involved not only creativity, but also communication and retail. And, as it often happens when undergoing a radical transformation, the brand also underwent an evident renewal. So, the new digital marketing plan not only aimed at increasing conversion on sales, but was also conceived as a tool to build the new identity. As a consequence, even this approach was all-inclusive for all categories of merchandise and leveraged on a strong and consistent identity language for ready-to-wear, accessories, fragrances and the make-up line launched in May 2019.

Unlike other fashion houses, since 2018, Gucci has started decreasing its gifting activities to influencers, so as to underline a new strategy directed to having a stricter control on the online image. The strategy is confirmed by the choice of social media stars, who become *friends-of-the-house* for several projects and products. Among the names frequently associated with the brand we find Bryan Grey Yambao, Veronika Heilbrunner, Tina Leung – all boasting great credibility in the world of fashion influencing – who were involved in a series of initiatives during the travelling shows like the launch of new products. For the presentation of the make-up line, Bryan Grey Yambao was hired, among others, for a storytelling about the party held in New York and followed by the posting of advertising contents bearing the hashtag #GucciBeautyNetwork. The collaboration was repeated on the occasion of a resort 2020 fashion show in Rome. The same influencers, involved in the first New York chapter, were invited to the show in Rome and asked to post contents about the beauty line and to include them in the storytelling of their experience of the ready-to-wear fashion show. A cross-pollination strategy is thus evident in the digital marketing plan for the product range of the brand.

A particularly innovative endorsement strategy is also worth mentioning: even though collaborations between brands and artists are not recent in fashion, Gucci focused more and more on not-necessarily-established personalities in the field of art, but who could leverage on both their creativity and their numerous online followers. It is the case of the launch of a clothing and accessories capsule collection by British artist Helen Downie, known as Unskilled Worker, who boasts 279,000 followers on Instagram; of the creation of memes with William Ndatila, Alec Soth and the group of photographers of @meatwrek for the launch of *Le Marche des Merveilles* watch collection in 2017.

Saint Laurent is an exemplifying case, not only because it allows an understanding of the different approaches to influencer marketing between the two brands, due to their different positioning, heritage and approach, but also because it highlights a relevant aspect of the fashion industry. Compared to Gucci, Saint Laurent – generally associated with the concept of Parisian elegance – in 2016, under the creative direction of Anthony Vaccarello, renewed, also online, its bond with the international jet set through a marketing strategy based on celebrities and *friends-of-the-house* endorsements, gifting, seeding and events participation. Unlike Gucci, the brand doesn't often involve actual influencers in the promotion of apparel and accessories which is mainly entrusted to celebrities who are also popular online.

Moreover, it is relevant to emphasise the aggressive strategy that Saint Laurent has adopted in the last five years in terms of influencers and digital marketing for its fragrances and beauty line, Yves Saint Laurent Beauté, produced by licencing with L'Oréal. Luxury brands owning a cosmetics line invest more in social media personalities for this category, rather than for fashion products, due to the following reasons: it is more profitable, the budget is higher (as a result of the joint efforts of the brand and the licensee – L'Oréal for YSL) and, finally, because it's an entry-level product addressed to a wider target. This strategy is widespread among many brands having a beauty/fragrances/make-up licence and is applicable to all the analysed clusters, independently from their positioning.

2.7.6 Social media

The most used social media among fashion brands are Instagram and Facebook, the former being their favourite and also the main subject of the analysis of the 13 clusters. Twitter and YouTube are less employed and are examined only when relevant. Weibo and WeChat are utilised chiefly in Asia and are not considered in this book, in order to make the analysis more concise.

We begin with the study of the key social media for the observed cluster.

First, it is worth underlining how the success of social media contributed to the visibility of the two fashion giants, even among those who are not "fashion insiders". The two big groups communicate with their audience with regular posts.

The official profiles of both groups are characterised by a formal attitude: they speak with an impersonal and impartial tone. However, we can highlight a difference in their approach: most of Kering's contents are institutional and show the initiatives of the corporate, whereas LVMH focuses on single brands.

Speaking of Kering, for instance, they create videos – specifically for social media – emphasising their logo. Contents are often about Kering or the Pinault foundation and showcase their commitment to the training of employees, to sustainability, to women's rights, as well as to exhibitions about art, music and food. Moreover, they post the victories achieved by the group in competitions, the awards received and the recognitions gained by single brands. Publications often follow the format of news and are mainly posted on Twitter, the most suitable social media for the valorisation of contents. On Facebook and Instagram, the group generally communicates the same news with video- and photo-based contents.

LVMH applies a diverse approach: it privileges contents that tell about single brands rather than the group as a whole. Publications are about seasonal fashion shows, new collections and campaigns, as well as the opening of new shops. The profile looks like an assembling of the main news about the principal brands like Dior, Louis Vuitton, Celine, etc. Less attention is dedicated to corporate initiatives: group achievements, sustainability recognitions, awards, etc. The logo of LVMH is almost never used, a confirmation of the strength of its brands individually. Concerning contents differentiation according to social media, this group is more selective: we rarely find the same content in different platforms.

As a consequence of the above-described characteristics, the two groups pursue different goals by means of their social media strategy.

Kering exposes itself directly, communicating its social responsibility policies, sustainable decisions, charity and humanitarian initiatives. The latter are not addressed to an elite audience, but they are promoted in every platform through constant reminders and posts, thus making them accessible and democratising luxury. While LVMH has silently faced sustainability challenges, Kering and Pinault – its CEO – have decided to openly speak about them. The group created an "environmental profit and losses" section where everyone can see how and where their supply chain impacts on the environment: for instance, the intensive use of soil for cashmere farms in Mongolia and the water pollution generated by Bolivian mines that provide silver for jewels (Bof, 2019). Moreover, the corporate encourages inclusion and communicates it through its social media. In one of its official posts (published on the analysed platforms), the group has stated that Kering has accelerated its commitment to diversity by appointing Kalpana Bagamane Denzel Chief Diversity Inclusion and Talent Officer. The decision results from the belief that diversity of gender culture, origin, disability and sexual orientation is a value.

Conversely, LVMH pursues a different scope: the strengthening of brand awareness and the conversion into sales of the users' visits to their pages. Each post contains the link to the official website, to the profile of one of the used platforms and to the e-commerce. The group (like Kering) is committed to promoting initiatives like *Life*, which has already been discussed. Another example is the agreement signed with UNESCO for the preservation of biodiversity, an issue that requires long-term programmes. However, these initiatives are not much promoted on social media; the Director of the Environmental Department Sylvie Bénard affirms that the group prefers to act, rather than to sign agreements (Kent and Guilbault, 2019).

2.7.7 Sponsorships and co-branding

Dahlén, Lange, and Smith (2010) state that the aim of sponsorships is to build lasting long-term relationships, which create mutual value.

Among LVMH and Kering groups, we can identify different sponsorship and co-branding strategies.

Louis Vuitton and Gucci, consistent with their DNA, sponsor a few exclusive events. For many years, the former has supported the *Louis Vuitton Cup*, the official selection of the most exclusive international sailing competition (Golizia, 2016). The latter, like many historic brands (both independent and not independent), has created *Gucci Masters*, one of the most important indoor competitions worldwide.

Stella McCartney supported an inclusive event strongly based on the values and territory of the brand. The designer offered a scholarship to the neediest students of Central Saint Martins, the same London-based school that she had attended. The project focused on sustainability.

Unlike sponsorships, co-branding is often applied by big brands. Louis Vuitton particularly stands out for being one of the pioneers of collaborations with musicians, architects, designers and artists (Golizia, 2016). For instance, the company collaborated with Jeff Koons who applied to the most iconic bags of the brand – Speedy, Keepall and Neverfull – the images of the *Gazing Ball Paintings* series. The series included the masterpieces of Leonardo da Vinci, Tiziano, Rubens. However, the partnership doesn't always involve symbolic products; for example, the one between Gucci and Coco Capitán, a young Spanish artist, gave birth to a collection comprising unisex garments like T-shirts and sweaters, all bearing hand-written writings by the artist. In other cases, the goal of the collaboration is to intercept a different target. This is the case of Louis Vuitton x Supreme and Louis Vuitton x Air Jordan addressed to a younger audience. In other cases, the objective is to strengthen the relationship with important retailers: Gucci x Saks Fifth Avenue and Gucci x Harrods. Co-brandings with mainstream brands are rare; see Gucci x Fiat. Even Alexander McQueen and Stella McCartney have relied on co-branding with sports companies; these collaborations stand out for their longer duration. Alexander McQueen and Puma, for instance, initially teamed up only for the footwear line to then extend their partnership also to accessories and clothing. Same for Adidas and Stella McCartney. Brands sometimes also collaborate on products that are "far" from their core activity: in this case, the aim is to either increase brand awareness (e.g. Alexander McQueen and American Express) or strengthen their positioning (e.g. Stella McCartney and environmental associations like Parley for the Oceans).

2.7.8 Museums, foundations and leisure time activities, in collaboration with Andrea Pittana

2.7.8.1 Premise

Fashion companies have proven to be very innovation-driven in their communication by introducing "atypical tools" such as museums, foundations and leisure time activities. Museums are generally rich in documents, drawings, garments and other items that tell the story of the fashion house and its founder. Foundations include a space dedicated to the exhibition of contemporary art, but they are also the favourite means to donate money. Among leisure time activities we can consider hotels, restaurants, bars and clubs where consumers can fully experience the brand; this business has been implemented by companies endowed with a very wide and differentiated product assortment aimed at satisfying several needs and that feel the necessity to communicate the brand lifestyle.

The scope of this paragraph is to verify what, among the above-mentioned activities, have been implemented by the examined clusters and to understand the underlying strategic reasons. The scheme proposed by the authors is based on three factors: contents, relation and touch points.

Contents are those elements of meaning that describe the brand and its world. An example may be a document preserved in a glass case and displayed in a museum to certify the company establishment, a donation made by the foundation to an institution, the choice of a specific style for the interiors of a hotel property of the brand. Contents aim to create a relation between the company and its target to make people discover, understand and love it. Finally, touch points include physical factors that allow a concrete and real encounter between the brand and its target. Traditionally, in the fashion industry, they are embodied in the store; however, companies have conceived alternatives such as museums, foundations and leisure time activities, whose purpose is to spread the brand identity and to develop a constructive and positive relationship with its public.

Through the analysis of these three factors, it is possible to describe and study the underlying marketing strategy applied by brands in order to strengthen their symbolic contents, expressed by their values. Values are intangible elements of meaning that characterise and describe the world of a brand. For example, a made-to-measure suit created by the designer and exposed in a museum is the content that epitomises the typical value of some categories of labels, in this case, tailoring in the modern world. To interpret the model, the time variable, represented by either the heritage or contemporary age, must be considered. By using its heritage, the brand intends to consolidate its future relationship with the target by telling about its past. For this scope, museums and foundations are the main tools or contents. By describing contemporary age, the brand aims at reinforcing its future relationship with the target by telling about its present; leisure activities, which include hotels, restaurants, clubs and bars, represent the main instruments or contents. By leveraging on both heritage and contemporary age, customer experiences create a bond with the company and become a common thread that generates values for the brand and, as a consequence, for the consumer.

We now proceed to apply the above-described concepts to the analysis of unspecialised big luxury groups. These groups, thanks to their economic strength, and to the multiplicity and specificity of controlled brands, have worked on all the described factors: they own museums, foundations and leisure time businesses. A difference may be pointed out. On the one hand, we have mega-brands like Louis Vuitton and Gucci that need to convey both the heritage – through museums and/or foundations – and a contemporary message, by means of leisure activities. On the other hand, we have Stella McCartney and Alexander McQueen, more recent and niche brands, that need to construct their heritage because they're not naturally endowed with it.

At *Fondation Louis Vuitton* (Louis Vuitton Foundation), more than 1 million visitors participate in contemporary and modern art exhibitions, in events such as concerts, shows and conferences, films, ballets and others. At the beginning of 2020, in Osaka, Japan, the first Louis Vuitton café and restaurant was opened on the top floor of the homonymous store.

The other big French luxury group opened the Kering Foundation to promote diverse initiatives. Among the most important, the campaign against cyberbullying with the hashtag #IDon'tSpeakHater was mainly addressed to Generation Z. Concerning historic and artistic valorisation, the new headquarters of the group hosts a space dedicated to the communication of an innovative perspective on art and fashion. Among the brands of this group, it is worth mentioning *Gucci Garden* in Florence, offering a holistic and immersive experience: a three-level space, a few steps away from the Uffizi Gallery, where visitors can admire a boutique proposing exclusive accessories and garments, a museum and the Gucci Osteria.

On the contrary, the most recent brands feel the need to valorise their recent past to build the future, proposing a direct experience to the consumer. In 2018, Stella McCartney launched a charity platform in two areas: the first, *Green*, to support sustainability; the second, *Pink*, to sensitise on the topic of breast cancer prevention. The other British brand, instead, organised *Alexander McQueen: Savage Beauty*, an exhibition hosted by the Victoria and Albert Museum in London.

2.8 Distribution, in collaboration with Andrea Doroldi

2.8.1 Premise

Distributive choices are one of the crucial aspects for fashion companies, striving to maintain a consistent market positioning.

Until 20 years ago, in the fashion industry, distribution was exclusively offline and in the previous book, this topic was extensively discussed. In the last few years, the system has undergone a radical evolution characterised by two main changes: the growth of online channels and the birth and development of the omnichannel system. Adopting an omni-channel approach means connecting all communication and sales channels in a way that makes the brand be perceived as one. The topic is so relevant that it has also been discussed in a dedicated paragraph and supported by further research.

The growth from 1.1% in 2004 to 12% in 2019 of online fashion sales evidences this transition. Since this book is based on a practical approach, research was carried out to verify whether a group of sample companies for a specific cluster:

- sells through its e-commerce, and, if it does, whether this option includes the whole or a partial product assortment;
- sells through the following nine digital platforms/marketplaces/multi-brand online stores: Farfetch, Luisaviaroma, Yoox, Net-à-Porter, Matches Fashion, MyTheresa, Amazon, Ssense and Browns, and, if it does, whether it proposes the whole or a partial product assortment;
- allows also for mobile devices purchases;
- has the power to check the prices of online-sold items.[17]

The above-mentioned nine e-tailers belong to the categories below and have the following characteristics:

- *multi-brand digital platforms* (e.g. Farfetch): they chiefly sell goods property of other stores hosting their full or partial assortment (anonymously) on their platform upon payment of a fee (around 30%);
- *marketplaces* (e.g. Amazon): they are actual multi-functional markets offering both directly purchased products and goods presented and sold by brands/retailers;
- *purely multi-brand e-tailers* (e.g. Yoox, Net-à-Porter): created as online stores and having no brick-and-mortar spaces;
- *online multi-brand shops* originating from multi-brand traditional stores (e.g. Luisaviaroma, Matches Fashion, MyTheresa, Browns);
- *omnichannel platforms* (e.g. Ssense): originally online multi-brand stores that also extended their business offline.

Nevertheless, the offline channel was not overlooked and an analysis was carried out to verify the following aspects:

- the total number of mono-brand stores;
- the percentage of turnover deriving from the direct retail;
- the location of mono-brand stores in Milan;
- the eventual presence of a wholesale channel.

As for (most of) the other paragraphs of this chapter, we start by examining the distribution policy of Louis Vuitton and Stella McCartney for LVMH and Gucci and Alexander McQueen for Kering, underlining, once again, the similarity between the strategies applied by on the one hand, Luis Vuitton and Gucci, and, on the other, Stella McCartney and Alexander McQueen.

We now proceed with the analysis of brick-and-mortar distribution first and then move to online distribution.

The distribution adopted by legendary fashion houses like Louis Vuitton and Gucci is selective, global and accurately controlled. The former relies exclusively on directly managed mono-brand points of sale, as well as shops-in-shops located in department stores. The latter mainly applies the same formula, together with the usage of franchising partners, for retail, and independent multi-brand stores. Both brands locate their shops in the most prestigious areas of the trendiest worldwide fashion cities and they are designed and decorated by famous architects. The choice of having few stores (few in relation to their global size) is justified by the desire to preserve their exclusivity and heritage. The fact that they are direct mono-brands and shops-in-shop allows for an increase of their already strong brand awareness and to consistently convey the identity. The management is exclusively or chiefly direct (DOS – directly operated stores) because it gives the opportunity to control every single detail without – or with a limited – intermediation of the franchisee.

We hereby consider some figures. In 2018, Louis Vuitton, the only fashion luxury brand to be exclusively distributed in a direct retail channel (mono-brand stores and concessions in department stores), boasted 460 direct mono-brand shops. Gucci, which has also franchised some shops, counts on a similar amount (487), inclusive of DOS and direct concessions.

Therefore, the percentage of direct retail on the total turnover is 100% for the former and 85% for the latter.

As a consequence, the number of franchising stores is null or low and is mainly concentrated in emerging markets (Chevalier and Gutsatz, 2012); in the latter, it is pivotal for companies to have a business partner able to attract and convince the consumer whose characteristics differ from those of a traditional clientele. Whether they are in franchising or directly operated, mono-brand stores are located in exclusive and strategic areas.

In Milan, Louis Vuitton and Gucci both have a boutique in the very central Via Montenapoleone, one of the most prestigious European shopping streets, another in the famous Galleria Vittorio Emanuele II, where we find designer labels like Prada, Giorgio Armani, Chanel, as well as a shop-in-shop in the most important Italian department store, La Rinascente.

The percentage of turnover deriving from wholesale is low or null, since very few categories of merchandise are sold through this channel; for instance, for Gucci only, beauty and make-up products are distributed in specialised chains of shops like Douglas and Sephora, and eyewear is sold by chains like Salmoiraghi & Viganò.

Only in the case of Gucci, the other product categories are available in very few historic shops, like Adani in Modena, or the more recent Gaudenzi 11 in Riccione, whose merchandising choices are made by the respective buyers according to the type of customers.

Unmistakably different are the distributive choices of Stella McCartney and Alexander McQueen: while the locations of their mono-brand stores are similar to those previously examined, the strategy concerning the number of mono- and multi-brand stores is the opposite. Stella and Alexander, respectively, own 52 and 64 mono-brand stores; 863 is the number of multi-brand stores of the former (the data about the latter is not available). The main reason is that they are niche brands addressing a more sophisticated target and offering a less extensive product range. There is no official data of the direct retail percentage on the total turnover; however, we hypothesise that, for both, it is almost (or slightly superior to) 50%.

We now proceed with the study of the online distribution strategy of the above-mentioned companies.

We can observe that both Gucci and Vuitton have their own e-commerce (independently managed, without external partners like Yoox) where the whole product assortment is available (except for some limited editions). Gucci can be found on all the nine above-listed platforms which, on the whole, propose a wide product range giving priority to leather and small leather goods – pivotal products – and, second, to ready-to-wear and footwear. The price of a Gucci product on the company's website coincides with the one on Farfetch, a sign that the brand can control the pricing strategy. Conversely, Louis Vuitton is not sold in any of these nine platforms for the same reasons it chose to prefer direct offline distribution, that is, to maintain total control on the brand distribution and positioning. The only online store where Louis Vuitton is sold is the multi-brand 24sevres.com (the online shop of the famous department store Au Bon Marché, part of LVMH).

Furthermore, both brands have leather goods as their core business, that is, most of their turnover derives from bags, accessories and small leather goods (a typical characteristic of other luxury leaders like Dior, Hermès and Chanel).

Both brands allow for the purchase of products with mobile devices thanks to a responsive design that adapts to the chosen device.

Also, Stella McCartney and Alexander McQueen are available on the nine platforms we mainly find their ready-to-wear and footwear (for Stella also bags). Price on their e-commerce and on Farfetch coincide, as a confirmation of their control of the pricing strategy.

2.9 Omnichannel, in collaboration with Sabrina Pomodoro and Benedetta Breschi

2.9.1 Premise

This research aims at supplying a descriptive picture of the different forms and levels of integrated communication in order to explain how and how much fashion companies co-ordinate strategies, contents and communication tools to convey a consistent and integrated message. In particular, the purpose of the analysis is to understand how the synergy among the aesthetic and seasonal elements of a collection, the communication themes and the four communication tools – fashion show (if any), social networks, shop windows of mono-brand stores and advertising campaigns – is generated.[18] The qualitative analysis was made on the communication campaign for fall-winter 2019/2020 for a sample of 51 brands, 4 for 12 clusters and 3 for the remaining 1. An interpretative and descriptive model (Pomodoro, 2017), based on five different integrated communication levels, from the highest, to the total absence of integration, was applied to carry out the study. The levels are the following:

*   *brand concept orchestration*: this category expresses the highest degree of integration as a result of a complex and consumer-oriented strategic process. Such a level is reached through an integrated system proposing a concept of a unique and distinctive brand, whose heritage and intangible values go beyond the single collection, time, and the different seasonal campaigns, generating a long-term narrative path. Integration takes place by means of an "orchestration" process among channels, messages and tools;

- *creative-idea-led integration*: this category represents a high degree of integration, although inferior to the previous one. Integration is based on a communication theme/concept, originating from different sources – films, theatre, literature, art – which inspires and leads both the style of the collection and the whole communication imaginary consistently and with synergy. Contents, ideas and messages are integrated, even though a communicative concept which goes beyond the single season is lacking;
- *collection-led integration*: this category involves a medium degree of integration; communication is consistent with the style of the collection whose distinctive element or elements – prints, colours, decorations, fabrics – inspire the communication theme which expands to the set of promotional activities. The leitmotif of the fashion tale is, therefore, a stylistic topic and not an actual communication concept;
- *visual and iconic integration*: this category expresses a low degree of integration; the contents and forms of communication are repeated in a superficial and standardised manner; top models in fashion shows are the same chosen for advertising campaigns, and the text of the campaign is also displayed in the background of shop windows. Integration with a clear message and a defined concept to be conveyed is missing;
- *absence of integration*: in this category, despite the use of several communication tools, no degree of integration is observed.

The results of the application of the above-described model have been subdivided according to the 13 clusters, where the 51 brands belong.

We proceed with the analysis of the integration degree of unspecialised big luxury groups.

Gucci can be categorised in the *creative-idea-led integration* group for the fall-winter 2019/2020 collection: the concept of the mask – the core of the whole fashion tale – was in fact consistently applied to all the communication tools analysed in the fashion tale: invite, fashion show, shop windows, digital communication and advertising campaign. The collection was presented on social media with a mask that recalled the head of a classical Greek statue. The fashion show invite was characterised by a papier mâché mask of a Hellenic-inspired hermaphroditic. Models on the catwalk as well as in advertising campaigns were wearing a mask; the same theme inspired the shop windows.

Belonging to the same group (Kering), Bottega Veneta can be considered as characterised by an *absence of integration*. In fact, it is not possible to identify a leitmotif integrating the different communication tools applied for fall-winter 2019 collection. While the advertising campaign portraits an avant-garde, trendy, confident woman with a passion for sports cars, the same message is absent in the other media: social media are poor in information; they display neither the fashion show, nor its invite, nor the advertising campaign. Likewise, the store does not recall the fashion show or the campaign: by observing the windows, there is a clear reference to the brand but not to its fall-winter 2019/2020 collection.

Louis Vuitton, if we consider fall-winter 2019/2020 collection, can be included in the *collection-led integration* group: the common thread that connects all the analysed media is, in fact, the style of the collection. Louis Vuitton uses for its garments strong primary colours such as yellow, blue and red, as well as the black and white chess pattern. The same colours are found in the setting of the fashion show as well as in the background of shop windows in their big red, blue and yellow steel pipes. The invite of the fashion show posted on Instagram represents the same colourful steel structure. Louis Vuitton, in fact, reconstructed the well-known Centre Pompidou in the Louvre. The background of the advertising campaign, despite not recalling the steel pipes, evokes the yellow and green and the black and white chess pattern of the garments showcased during the fashion show and displayed in the shop windows

Stella McCartney boasts the highest degree of integration: brand concept orchestration. The brand has always supported environmental sustainability. In the fall-winter 2019/2020 collection, Stella McCartney demonstrates once again the will to promote a more ethical, animal friendly and sustainable world. The brand thus dedicated all its campaign to the future of the planet, choosing the unpolluted Coast of Wales as its setting.

The theme of sustainability develops throughout the four elements of the fashion tale: fashion shows, advertising campaigns, social networks and the shop windows of mono-brand stores. The fashion show invite, posted on Instagram, contains the hashtag #ThereSheGrows that encourages guests to dedicate a tree and a message to a special someone. In the Instagram stories highlights, as well as in the page feed, the images of the fashion show and advertising campaign backstage are available, together with explicit references to the show. Even the collection is rich in connections to the topic of sustainability, embodied by the recycled materials used for certain clothes. All communication tools applied by Stella McCartney to promote the fall-winter 2019/2020 collection are fully consistent with one another.

Interview with Edoardo Sabbadin, professor of Fashion and Design Marketing at the University of Parma

What characteristics define the Big Luxury Groups?
As you have underlined, LVMH and Kering are conglomerates, which have grown remarkably (mainly the former), thanks to a strategy founded on the acquisition of many luxury brands.

Who are their funders and what was their role?
LVMH was established by Bernard Arnault, whereas Kering by François Pinault: the former is still President and CEO of the group; the latter was succeeded by his son, François-Henry. Thanks to their innovative vision, they had a crucial role in the establishment and development of their respective groups. Despite coming from other industries, they both believed in the great potential of fashion luxury, the first at the end of the 80s, the second a decade after. However, most of all, they shaped a new acquisition-based business model, which represented an absolute innovation for that time.

Are they the only entrepreneurs who adopted such a model?
Of course not. Yet very few people remember that from 1998 to 2002, the acquisition rush had generated what Pambianco (2008) defined as *paper holdings*: groups that, in 2–3 years, had grown considerably, but that, as fast, disappeared from the market.

What led them to failure?
The owners, who had mainly a finance-driven vision, had insufficient knowledge of the fashion field and had not designed a serious industrial plan that could allow for swift development of the acquired brands.

While Arnault and Pinault…
While Arnault and Pinault, from the beginning, had understood that fashion companies, despite their peculiarities, had to be *managerialised*.

It is a rather complex business model to implement.
As you have described in the previous paragraphs, they are groups that compete in many sectors (mostly LVMH), and with many brands positioned in the top segments. Hence, an elevated risk of mutual cannibalization; for this reason, it is paramount to apply product, communication and marketing policies aimed at differentiating brands. Furthermore, to compete in such different industries, you must have specific know-how for each of them.

So it is not enough to hire the best Creative Directors of the fashion system, is it?
Absolutely not. Differentiating brands competing in the same industry and in the same price segment is one of the hardest tasks of marketing, and it requires extremely talented and skilled managers.

To summarise, what are the key factors of success of these groups?
Implicitly we have already listed them: to operate in many fields (for LVMH) with a balanced brand portfolio, to be endowed with significant financial resources handled by the best managers and to have the highest control of the value chain in the fashion system.

What about creativity?
It is the core of every fashion company. You may have conspicuous financial resources and the best managers, but without product innovation, you do not perform outstandingly. Arnault and Pinault agree on this: heritage and craftsmanship are not enough anymore, new generations ask for emotions and they are nourished mainly through creativity.

Student activities

Choose a brand and based on your choice:

- define the sustainability actions to be applied in the future;
- identify the combination product/price segment/target where to diversify;
- identify a social media and the content typology to be developed;
- define which of the following formats – brick-and-mortar mono-brand store, brick-and-mortar multi-brand store, shop-in-shop in department stores, online mono-brand shop and online multi-brand platform – need to be developed the most;
- verify the degree of synergy among the aesthetic elements of the latest collection: the fashion show, social networks, mono-brand store windows and the advertising campaign.

Notes

1 A licencing production agreement is based on the collaboration between licenser and licensee: the licenser (brand owner) gives the licensee (producer) the licence to manufacture and sell specific products in return for a fee (Giannelli and Saviolo, 2001).
2 Actually, Stella McCartney is not 100% controlled by LVMH, buy it signed a partnership with the French group in July 2019 to accelerate growth (lvmh.com).
3 We have chosen these brands because the comprehensive strategies applied by, on the one hand, Gucci and Louis Vuitton and by Alexander McQueen and Stella McCartney, on the other hand, have many similarities. These two brand pairs, Louis Vuitton-Gucci and Stella McCartney-Alexander McQueen, are taken as an example for most of the paragraphs of this chapter.

4   Even though the product, whose price was compared, has homogeneous characteristics among brands, the analysis does not consider variables like materials or manufacturing details

5   Prices were taken from the institutional e-commerce of brands (spring-summer 2020 collection and carryovers).

6   Unspecialised companies are the same for the eight categories of product: Zara for the medium/low segment; Liu Jo for accessible luxury; Giorgio Armani for aspirational luxury and Hermès for absolute luxury. If one of these brands did not have the product subject of the analysis, it was substituted by another from the same cluster. For some categories, Emporio Armani was added, to explain the pricing policy of contemporary brands.

7   Specialised companies vary according to product category; for instance, Jimmy Choo was considered for absolute luxury footwear, while for absolute luxury men's suit, Ermenegildo Zegna was studied.

8   A similar consideration can be made for Gucci and Alexander McQueen whose prices are, respectively, €1,673 and €830.

9   If Giorgio Armani did not have the product subject of the research, then Dolce & Gabbana was considered.

10 Actually, Dior's bag price is 4.35% lower, while that of a formal suit is 5.9% higher; however, these differences are irrelevant in absolute luxury.

11 The comparison was made with Giorgio Armani for the following products: shopper, women's blazer and sneakers, men's suit and pumps; with Dolce & Gabbana for jeans, hoodies and nightgowns.

12 The number also includes trade fairs that are held twice a year like Pitti Immagine Uomo Pitti Bimbo, Pitti filati, Milano Unica, Micam and White Milano.

13 An editorial is a promotional page, in a magazine, which displays a series of products sharing a characteristic and a style inspiration; in editorials we normally find a still life of garments, accompanied by captions that specify name, price and brand (Ironico, 2014). A fashion editorial is a shooting made for a magazine using both models and still life techniques (Ironico, 2014).

14 In the previous research, Gucci had been included in the historic brands chapter because the author had not distinguished between the independent ones and those controlled by unspecialised big luxury groups. In this book, the Florentine brand is discussed in this dedicated chapter.

15 The turnover in 2019 was €9.6 billion, against €3.9 billion in 2015.

16 Instagram TV is an accessory Instagram platform that allows the sharing of videos lasting more than 60 seconds.

17 The price of the company's e-commerce and that of Farfetch were compared.

18 Fashion shows were taken from the *Vogue* Italia website; the studied social network is the official Instagram page of the brands; shop windows are those of Milan's mono-brand stores observed from 26 September until 10 October, where fall-winter 2019/2020 collections were displayed; advertising campaigns were taken from different sources: official Instagram page and the website of the brands as well *Vogue*, *L'Officiel* and *Pambianco Magazine*.

3
HISTORIC FASHION BRANDS

Reading: the Creative Directors[1]

Today, Creative Directors are mostly image-makers. They show a point of view, mould an ideology for the brand and mostly direct other talents. Creative direction involves anything that relates to the vision of a brand, the aesthetic and the narrative behind everything that communicates the codes of the house. The Creative Director tries to bring their point of view, taste and handwriting, but always keeping in mind the DNA of the brand. They look back at the company heritage and try to move things forward. In the last few years, the role of the Creative Director has changed a lot. Once they were directly focused on designing a range of products, but today a Creative Director doesn't necessarily need to have formal training as a designer. In the past, it was more about making clothes, whereas, today, the attention is shifting towards image-making. In contemporary fashion, Creative Directors are more involved in branding and communication. He or she interacts with other figures of a fashion firm, for instance, with the design team, with the Production Department to coordinate the work of suppliers and also with craftsmen. The degree of collaboration depends on the company's structure and size. The Creative Director has a crucial relationship with the CEO or the Managing Director. A successful fashion house relies on both creative and business skills. The outbreak of Covid-19 has changed the rules of the game. During the lockdown, creatives working in design studios faced the challenge of an unprecedented "together-apart" process. A slow motion and confinement only interrupted by Zoom-Teams meeting that gave time to stop and think. Today, the new imperative is to restart and reset following a "go for good" approach where inclusion and sustainability help to reinvent the future.

3.1 Who are they?[2]

The historic brands represent the quintessence of luxury created by a single, enlightened fashion designer or entrepreneur and devoted to the sale of splendid objects of the very best artisanship (Rocca, 2011). They were founded by a couturier (Coco Chanel), by an artisan (Thierry Hermès) or by a shoemaker (Salvatore Ferragamo) between the beginning of the

1800s and the first half of the 1900s. For them, "history is much more than a mere collection of the past. It is about being remembered in the future" (Ricca and Robins, 2012, p. 112). They are *maisons*, even before they are firms, the fashion houses who have created the most beautiful apparel, shoes, bags and accessories of all time. The French Hermès and Chanel are the undisputed leaders in this category. The distant roots and the coherence of the strategies adopted have allowed them to acquire a fame that has made them renowned in every corner of the globe. Their "reputation" is strictly tied to the genius and the creativity of their founders, who gave their name to the original atelier, workshop and shoe factory: Coco Chanel, Salvatore Ferragamo, just to cite a few. In some cases, the heirs still manage the creative and/or business side of the firm: Prada is headed by the niece Miuccia, a third-generation heir. In others, such as Gucci, Louis Vuitton and Dior, as discussed in Chapter 2, the property now belongs to big luxury groups, LVMH and Kering, while the values and ideals of the label have been passed on to the designers who followed one another as head designer. We now examine Hermès, Chanel, Prada and Ferragamo, underlining that we do not intend to analyse all the brands of this cluster.

3.2 Style, by Diana Murek[3]

The style of bags and apparel varies from iconic and traditional, as in the case of Hermès, to experimental and irreverent as in the case of Prada. However, for this cluster, it is worth stressing that creativity is influenced by the heritage and the creative vision of the founder designer and of the current Creative Director. Styles vary according to the debut product of the company. In the case of Hermès, its historic identity is strongly rooted in accessories and less in clothing. Consequently, the style is defined by leather goods inspired by the horse-riding and saddlery world where the brand made its debut. In apparel lines, on the contrary, the style relies on the interpretation of the Creative Director. In the last few years, Hermès has witnessed the different styles of several Creative Directors, from Martin Margiela, and Jean Paul Gaultier, to Christophe Lemaire, to Nadège Vanhee-Cybulski, each one expressing their own vision. The first proposed a conceptual vision, the second a feminine and sensual style, Lamaire a minimal fashion, while the latest director a more contemporary look.

3.3 Supply chain and sustainability, in collaboration with Celeste Corso

The whole value chain is directly managed as in the case of historic brands – Louis Vuitton and Gucci – controlled by big groups. None or very few steps of the supply chain are outsourced. As a result, the level of integration is very high, mainly for bags manufacturing. For instance, Hermès boasts total control thanks to the direct ownership of crocodile breeding farms that supply the raw materials as well as of the tanneries and workshops that produce them.

The productive process in Hermès is managed and controlled directly by the company that owns 40 out of 45 production units; 34 of them are based in France. Three hundred employees, specialising in leather selection and processing, work in the new offices of Pantin, a few kilometres away from Paris (Rocca, 2011).

Prada's products are manufactured by 12 directly owned companies, 11 of which are based in Italy and 1 in the UK. The brand also collaborates with a network of external sub-producers that are accurately selected to guarantee strict control on artisanal quality and reliability. Each step of the productive process is carefully and directly monitored: from the supply and purchase of raw materials (external suppliers included), to the production of prototypes, up to the planning and coordination of production which is both in-house and with the support of sub-suppliers.

Sustainability has become a leading trend among fashion brands. We are currently witnessing a historic revolution that leverages on the concept of "being" and that goes beyond the so-called "green-washing" based on the idea of "appearing". Hermès, Chanel and Ferragamo are some of the names that signed the *Fashion Pact*, only one of the many initiatives.

In 2018, Chanel abandoned the usage of exotic leather and acquired part of the Finnish start-up Sulapac, specialising in the production of recyclable and biodegradable materials.

Finally, Ferragamo, which named its sustainable vocation *Responsible Passion*. The brand commits to protecting the environment by reducing power consumption – with the usage of Leed lighting systems and Forest Stewardship Council (FSC) packaging: moreover, the *Orange Fiber* collection, launched for 2017 *Earth Day*, was made out of orange waste from the food industry.

3.4 Segmentation strategies

The examined brands debuted with a target and product-driven strategy; the product was mainly constituted by leather goods for an elite customer. The strategic evolution described in paragraph 1.10 has led them to currently adopt a lifestyle strategy as defined in paragraph 2.4. In fact, the concepts explained for Gucci and Louis Vuitton may also be extended to the brands of this cluster that made very similar strategic choices – except for the fact that the two above-mentioned brands are controlled by big luxury groups. While in paragraph 2.4 – besides defining the lifestyle strategy – we pointed out the complementarity of the brands belonging to the same group, in this section we aim at stressing the essential role played by some of their "particular" customers in their transformation into legendary companies. Customers are in fact essential for brand reputation: and what reputation can a fashion house (e.g. Hermès) acquire if it boasts of Grace Kelly among its customers, who was the incarnation of charm, fame, sensuality, wealth, simplicity, and had her name associated with one of the most desirable and imitated (and expensive) bags in history? (Rocca, 2011).

3.5 Brand

The branding strategy is very similar to the one described in Chapter 2 for Louis Vuitton and Gucci.

The diversification process is extensive: many new categories of merchandise were added to the original product (high fashion for some, leather goods for most of the players). The current product portfolio includes not only bags, shoes and ready-to-wear, but also watches, jewels, *art de table*, furniture, home decoration, as well as accessible products such as fragrances, glasses and cosmetics. Some companies even extended their business to hotels, for instance, Ferragamo opened *Hotel Lungarno* in Florence, while others like Hermès did not contemplate diversification. As in the case of Louis Vuitton and Gucci, and for the same reasons, diversification is only horizontal (product-based) and not vertical (line-based) and leverages on the heritage and on the concept of *made-in*.

Notwithstanding the wide diversification, leather goods are still the core business and some products of this category have even made the history of fashion.

When talking about Hermès' two iconic bags, Kelly and Birkin must be mentioned; the latter has become the forbidden dream of almost every woman. While the Kelly bag is more suitable for an adult target, the Birkin is appreciated by a transversal consumer without age distinction. Another iconic bag is Chanel's 2.55: the first truly stylish bag of the brand, suitable for every type of outfit; a mothers' bag also loved by her daughter who wears it with jeans. Among timeless products, we also find the more accessible Chanel N°5, the first successful perfume of the brand, also considered the most famous in history. Prada is recognised for iconic materials rather than for products. The first are the result of great experimentation and of the ennobling of raw materials, which have given birth to the successful *saffiano* leather invented by Mario Prada. This material has become iconic thanks to the restyling by her granddaughter Miuccia. Moreover, in the middle of the 80s, Miuccia designed a black nylon backpack – one of her first successes – transforming the perception of nylon forever.

The quality of products (mainly leather goods, haute couture and ready-to-wear) is extremely high. They are hand-made by talented craftsmen in workshops controlled by the company. The legendary status of Hermès is (also) due to the craftsmanship of its products; artisanship reveals its proximity to art (Rocca, 2011). For instance, every Kelly is totally hand-made by one craftsman who needs 24 hours of work and 2,500 saddle stitches to assemble it. Raw materials are of absolute prestige, supplied by excellent producers, sometimes owned by the fashion house (mainly for leather goods).

Historic brands have kept the same original name for all the products added in the following phases of their evolution to preserve and protect their heritage. Chanel signs all its clothing lines with the same name; no suffix has been attached to the name. This aspect differentiates from many contemporary brands that, instead, have chosen the opposite strategy; e.g. Armani Privé for high fashion and Armani Exchange for casualwear. The brand name is strengthened by the concepts of Made in France (mostly) and Made in Italy, meant as places of origin of the company, of materials, of production, and that add further value to the already excellent label.

To Hermès and Ferragamo we can apply the same considerations made for Louis Vuitton and Gucci: their founders are not associated to the brand in the consumers' mind. In contrast, in the case of Prada, Miuccia epitomises the company; speaking of Chanel, this aspect is even more evident: the Creative Director, Karl Lagerfeld, represented the brand world until his death.

Customisation plays a crucial role in communicating the symbolic values of the brand and to make its perception legendary. To explain this concept, we consider the Lady D(ior) bag: it is available in different colours and sizes to satisfy all the needs of the sophisticated clientele of the fashion house.

3.6 Pricing, in collaboration with Benedetta Breschi

To elaborate the pricing strategy of this cluster, we analyse Hermès, whose prices of bags and sneakers are available on the website, and Prada for the remaining products.[4]

As in Chapter 2, we proceed by comparing the price positioning with that of two clusters, taking into consideration a specialised brand competing in the highest price segment and an unspecialised brand competing in a lower price range, aspirational luxury.[5]

From the analysis, we observe that Hermès' and Prada's strategies are very similar to the one discussed for Dior in Chapter 2.

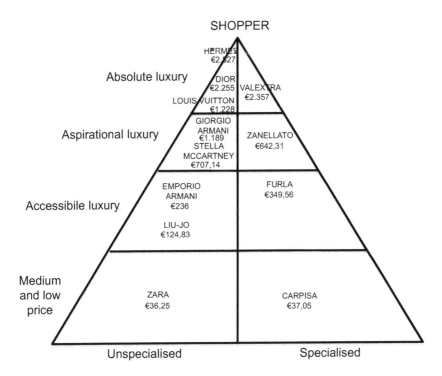

FIGURE 3.1 Golizia's pyramid of shoppers

Source: Prepared by Dario Golizia

In fact, from the comparison with specialised companies, we notice that the two brands have a similar positioning for a product – superior for most of them – and a slightly inferior positioning for others.

The price positioning of Prada's formal men's suit is similar[6] to Ermenegildo Zegna's for the reasons explained in Chapter 2.

Taking other products into consideration, the above-mentioned brands have a higher price positioning: for the shopper, Hermès' price is 19.9% more expensive than Valextra's. The difference is due to the legendary status of Hermès – seen as the most prestigious brand by the consumer – because of its iconic products like Kelly and Birkin bags.[7] Likewise, the price of sneakers is higher (59.2%) as compared to Y-3.

Concerning other categories of merchandise, Prada has a higher positioning for blazer and jeans (8.4% and 136.3% higher, respectively) compared to specialised companies from the same price segment, Maison Margiela and 7 for all mankind, for the reasons explained in Chapter 2.

On the contrary, Prada's positioning for pumps is inferior (−57.4%) as compared to Jimmy Choo: even in this case, the rationale was explained in.

Also, in comparison with a contemporary brand,[8] we see a similarity with Dior: Hermès (or Prada), thanks to a superior brand image, has a higher price positioning in (almost) all categories of product: the French brand has a 137.7% and 33.9% higher price for the shopper and the sneaker, respectively; the Italian brand a 10.2% higher price for pumps and a 3.5% % higher price for formal men's suits. As already mentioned, and as explained below and also in Chapter 4, historic brands can count on a superior brand image compared to contemporary ones, and this allows them to impose a premium price. Prada's positioning for women's blazer (-12.3%) and jeans (-11.2%) is slightly interior; these products are iconic, respectively, for Giorgio Armani and Dolce & Gabbana. Furthermore, consumers do not usually associate jeans with Prada. This proves how even a strong image connected to a specific product (not to a brand) can be relevant for the positioning.

3.7 Communication

We now proceed with the definition of the image of the cluster; afterwards we study how the marketing and communication function is organised and managed by a company from the same group. Finally, we outline the communication mix applied by some brands.

3.7.1 Cluster image

The image of historic brands can be associated with the following keywords: luxury quintessence, couturier, craftsmanship, heritage, Made in France, bags, iconic products and in-house production.

3.7.2 Marketing function and communication, in collaboration with Michele Leoni

Prada, a historic brand that competes in numerous markets with a comprehensive and high-price product range, owns its marketing and communication office. This choice is due to the need to fully control every communication activity: in fact, none of these tasks is entrusted to an external consultancy agency. This department of the company is very complex and organised as follows.

The Director of Marketing and Communication is in charge of the Press Office and directly manages the marketing area, and the Director of Communication is responsible for communication and in turn supervises the work of three key figures: the Corporate Communication Manager (business and finance), the Product Communication Manager as well as the Manager of Public Relations. The latter is responsible for the supervision of the editors in charge of each product line – whose task is to promote the collections with the press – and of stylists who are responsible for all the global shootings to be published in magazines. Moreover, the Press Office also includes the following roles: the VIP and Celebrities Communication Manager taking care of the relationships with celebrities, the Media Buying Manager in charge of the purchase of advertising spaces, the Digital Department Manager who is responsible for online communication. Finally, there are two specific offices: one takes care of events organisation, and the other works on the production of images, catalogues, look-books and other items for communication activities.

3.7.3 Fashion shows and trade fairs, in collaboration with Andrea Doroldi

Historic brands share the greatness and the spectacularity of their shows that always boast a great visual impact. Their fashion shows take place during traditional fashion weeks and are organised by the Press Office that, together with the Creative Director, designs the concept.

If we apply Vilaseca's (2010) methodology, we can examine Chanel that organised in Paris a theatrical fashion show for its ready-to-wear spring-summer 2019: for the occasion, the brand had recreated a beach resort with real sand and sea waves. In 2016, the cruise collection fashion show was held in Havana, the city that had inspired the collection and its Cuban mood.

For the same reason explained in Chapter 2 – the fashion show is the main occasion to showcase collections – none of the brands considered – Hermès, Chanel, Prada and Ferragamo – participated in Mipel and Pitti Immagine in 2019 and 2020.

Speaking of Salone del Mobile, it is worth remembering the participation of Salvatore Ferragamo in 2019: in La Rinascente department store, the brand had decorated its corner with paper flowers in line with its *The Green Life* theme.

3.7.4 Advertising, editorial, advertorial, in collaboration with Benedetta Breschi

The sample of brands, Chanel, Hermès, Ferragamo and Prada, is partially the same as the one used in 2016: Gucci is not included in this section because it was analysed in Chapter 2, dedicated to LVMH and Kering, whose cluster had not been studied in the previous book (Golizia, 2016). The research highlights how, in 2019, the four brands purchased 20 advertising pages compared to the 41 in 2015, a decrease by 51%. However, while in 2015, among the four examined clusters, they were second in ranking for number of bought advertising pages, in 2019, they bounced to the first place, leaving the 13 remaining clusters behind. They are first in ranking also for the number of fashion editorials, 37, and advertorials, 8, thanks to their investments and persuasive power. The selection of magazines in which they invested the most, *Vogue* and *L'Officiel*, is suitable for historic brands – property of unspecialised big luxury groups – if we consider the target similarity – adult, with a very high spending power – and the brands' positioning. This group of companies, despite being first in ranking, halved the number of purchased advertising pages.

3.7.5 Influencers, gifting, endorsement, by Lavinia Biancalani

For a long time, the digital communication of historic brands had been inactive and based on their heritage, built without 2.0 communication and social networks; this explains their late approach to this new tool. Among the marketing functions of social networks and influencers, brand awareness was considered the only goal of digital communication, conveyable by

TABLE 3.1 Advertising, fashion editorial and advertorials of historic brands

Historic Brands	L'Officiel			Vogue			Vanity Fair			Elle			Glamour			Total		
	A	FE	AD	A	FE	AD	A	FE	AD	A	FE	AD	A	FE	AD	A	FE	AD
Chanel	6	7	1	4	4	0	0	0	0	1	1	0	0	3	2	11	15	3
Ferragamo	0	3	0	2	1	0	0	0	0	1	1	1	0	1	0	3	6	1
Hermès	2	6	0	0	0	1	0	0	0	0	1	1	0	0	0	2	7	2
Prada	0	5	0	4	3	0	0	0	0	0	0	0	0	1	2	4	9	2
Total	**8**	**21**	**1**	**10**	**8**	**1**	**0**	**0**	**0**	**2**	**3**	**2**	**0**	**5**	**4**	**20**	**37**	**8**

Source: Authors' data processing on the basis of fashion magazines published in Italy in September 2019. A, FE and AD stand for advertising, fashion editorial and advertorial, respectively.

means of traditional communication methods. In the field of influencer marketing, the brands belonging to this cluster selected personalities who were influential on traditional media and, at the same time, could interpret the brand values. More frequently than other clusters, these brands collaborated with socialites, representatives of traditional media, celebrities and fashion experts who, besides having a conspicuous number of followers on social networks, could validate the brand's importance with their social and professional role. Consequently, their collaborations rely on brand ambassadors, even if unofficial, and *cross-media-friends-of-the-house*, and transcend the digital medium to extend to the most traditional endorsements.

Model Cara Delevingne, belonging to the 2010–2015 supermodels generation, has built her reputation online and has been one of the muses of Chanel and Creative Director Karl Lagerfeld, as well as the face of the brand since 2012. Even though she had never been a brand ambassador for the fashion house, with 44 million followers on Instagram, she exposed the brand to considerable visibility on social networks. In 2017, she was the protagonist of a fashion film for the launch of Chanel's *Gabrielle* bag and walked on the Met Gala red carpet totally dressed in Chanel and with a silver hairstyle that would become viral.

Prada may be considered as a *latecomer* of the cluster. The pushing of digital media, contextual to the appointment of Bertelli Junior, as Head of Digital Communication in September 2017, is evident at the opening of their fashion shows to influencers and web personalities aligned with their positioning. While some of them, most of all those famous in the Asian market such as BryanBoy and Susie Bubble (Susanna Lau), had already been invited to the show, others like designers Gilda Ambrosio and Giorgia Tordini, or the celebrity influencer Chiara Ferragni have started to participate only recently. Ferragni also collaborated with the brand for an outfit worn during her pre-wedding party in September 2018. For the fall-winter 2019/2020 menswear campaign, the brand chose to team up with Chinese pop star Cai Xukun, known as Kun (22 million followers on Weibo), to showcase its interest in the Chinese market and its digital frontmen.

The role of content creators able to speak to a younger and social media-friendly target is evident in Salvatore Ferragamo's strategy. In July 2018, after the arrival of the new CEO Micaela Lemmi Le Divelec, the company began to rationalise its digital communication. In January 2019, to celebrate the *gancini* (hooks), the iconic symbol of the fashion house, the brand hired fashion influencer Bryanboy (585,000 followers on Instagram) to direct a series of clips and short movies to be posted on social networks. Among their protagonists, we find Caro Daur, Tamu McPherson, Aureta, Susie Bubble (Susanna Lau) and Carlo Sestini.

Hermès without doubt represents a more emblematic case of this cluster's "resistance" towards digital and influencer marketing. Even today, the brand does not collaborate or sign endorsement agreements for its accessories and apparel lines. While, in July 2019, for the launch of the new fragrance, Twilly *d'Hermès Eau Poivrée*, influencers and content creators Sophia Salaroli Caniaux, Carlotta Rubaltelli, Claudia Ciocca and Elen Ellis were invited to the fashion house to discuss the product's creative process and to participate in the promotional party.

3.7.6 Social media

The most used platforms by these brands are mainly Instagram, followed by Facebook.

Hermès' online image, the emblem of luxury, has remained consistent over time, finding an accurate balance between history, tradition and avant-garde in digital communication

(Golizia, 2016). Its digital strategy and planning can be defined as platform- and geo-specific: the brand almost never designs one content for all social media, but a specific one for each of them; moreover, contents also vary according to geographical area. The topics discussed on social media by Hermès – but also by other historic brands – focus on lifestyle, craftsmanship, iconic products and exclusivity.

Hermès has designed a harmonious Instagram profile whose consistent contents lead the user through the brand narration. Craftsmanship and iconic products are communicated in videos showing the backstage of the *Carrè* production, while the brand lifestyle is portrayed by displaying the whole product range in photos and videos of fashion shows and of the homewear line. Exclusivity is a key topic of each content, not just for elite products like watches and jewels, but also in images that portray, for instance, a salt grinder: an apparently ordinary product is "celebrated" to emphasise the uniqueness of the brand.

On Facebook almost all Hermès' contents are video-based: publications are similar to TV spots that in a few seconds conquer the heart of the spectator involving their five senses. The product is not presented with a claim: the video has no text and its editing encourages the viewer to look for more information.

Even YouTube and Twitter deserve mention: with the former, Hermès comprehensively informs the user by showcasing the "behind the scenes" of the posts published on other platforms. An example is the *Hèrmes Documentaries* series describing the artisanal techniques applied in the creation of iconic products like bags and horse-riding saddles, or the bond between the company and local communities. For instance, the video tells about how the acquisition of a leather manufacturer contributed to the repopulation of a town in the south of France. With Twitter, the Parisian fashion house communicates news that is consistent with its image: results of horse-riding contests, exhibitions or installations in collaboration with artists, as in the case of the travelling exhibition *Species of Spaces* in Seoul, Taipei or Dubai, or *Hermès Heritage* in Shanghai, Jakarta or Singapore.

For every brand of this group – be it Chanel, Hermès or Prada – another characteristic aspect, besides exclusivity, lifestyle, iconic products and craftsmanship, is the uniqueness of social contents. Only a few images are taken from advertising, fashion magazines or other media; these labels prefer to publish close-ups of products or of their details. Items are always accurately chosen according to their symbolic value for the brand: Prada, for instance, selects accessories, while Ferragamo selects shoes; other products, instead, are portrayed because they epitomise the brand dream as in the case of Chanel's jewels or high fashion lines.

Brands employ social media for diverse purposes.

Unlike other clusters, they don't just need to interact with users, or convert them into buyers, but they also have to showcase the brand world to emotionally involve them. Their scope is to contextually reach an elite target and a more extended audience; to do so, they post more affordable contents (e.g. Chanel's beauty line) without losing their exclusivity status (in fact, the majority of these brands do not reply to users' comments). These labels mainly target Millennials who represent the present and the future of luxury and whose expectations are different from those of other generations (Danziger, 2018). This is the reason behind the choice of brand ambassadors like Lily-Rose Depp who boasts millions of followers, as well as a famous family (Sherman, 2017). Another crucial topic is sustainability, which is not just a trend, but a driver for purchases. Prada has organised *Shaping a Creative Future*, a conference whose purpose is to explore new possible connections between sustainability and innovation (Pambianco, 2017).

Inclusivity is another recent – yet not always implemented – topic. Despite organising initiatives like the *Diversity and Inclusion Advisory Council* – organised by Prada and chaired by Ava DuVernay and Theaster Gates, both Afro-Americans – aimed at supporting talents, mainly among black people, companies do not seem to invest much of their attention in them.

3.7.7 Sponsorships and co-branding

Historic brands apply co-branding and sponsoring strategies similar to Gucci and Louis Vuitton (analysed in Chapter 2). These initiatives stand out for their hyper-exclusivity. Hermès sponsors the Saut Hermès competition, a prestigious event reserved for professional horsemen, in order to strengthen its identity, which has always been bound to the equestrian world. Likewise, Prada used to sponsor the Luna Rossa team during its participation in the most prestigious sailing event, *Challengers Selection Series*. Later on, Prada would also replace Louis Vuitton as a sponsor of the event. For both Prada and Hermès, the sponsoring gave birth to two lines named after the contests.

Still with the aim of stressing its exclusivity, Hermès signed a co-branding with Bugatti, a prestigious artisanal automotive brand. In other cases, by signing partnerships with some artists, co-branding was chosen to promote the iconic product. An interesting example is *Hermès Carré Club*, a travelling event that exhibits the personal interpretation of the iconic *carré* by some artists like Gianpaolo Pagni. The purpose is twofold: to approach the youth, who are the future, and to convey a surprising institutional image (Mffashion, 2020). A similar case is *Prada Invites* where famous architects and designers like Rem Koolhass reinterpreted nylon. However, the collaboration is not always aimed at promoting an iconic product; sometimes the goal is to push a "secondary" product as in the case of Chanel x Pharrell Williams x Adidas sneakers, only available for a month at Colette, Paris.

3.7.8 Museums, foundations and leisure time activities, in collaboration with Andrea Pittana

For these companies, the heritage is an essential element of their brand identity.

Hermès and Prada have chosen to focus on their foundations to construct a relationship with their target, incorporating in their brands the classic values of art. On the contrary, Salvatore Ferragamo has adopted a more integrated approach communicating its heritage through its museum, strengthening its image with its foundation and promoting a brand lifestyle with leisure activities.

Hermès focuses on the field of artistic creation with its *Fondation D'Entreprise* (Company Foundation) established in 2008 and whose exhibitions have inspired and moved thousands of visitors.

The Prada family relied on their passion for art to establish Fondazione Prada (Prada Foundation) in 1993. It is a space dedicated to contemporary art exhibitions, architecture projects, cinema and philosophy whose new futuristic location was opened in Milan in 2015 and designed by Office for Metropolitan Architecture (OMA) architecture studio.

Speaking of leisure time activities, the Milanese company controls Pasticceria Marchesi 1824, one of the oldest and most famous pastry shops in Milan: located in the fashion district, in Via Montenapoleone, it represents a unique and special experience; however, the connection with the world of Prada is not explicit, at least for non-fashionistas.

Ferragamo Museum, located in the old town centre of Florence, headquarters of the fashion house, aims at informing the public about the fundamental role played by the company in the history of shoe-making. Moreover, Ferragamo, in order to stress its bond with the territory of origin, has made several donations to support art and architectonic beauty in Tuscany. Concerning leisure time activities, the brand has opened both hotels and restaurants that offer a refined, "made-to-measure" and exclusive atmosphere.

3.8 Distribution, in collaboration with Andrea Doroldi

We hereby examine the studied cluster and its brick-and-mortar[9] and online distribution.

For the first aspect, we confirm what was earlier stated about Gucci and Louis Vuitton, that is, the distribution strategy adopted by these two legendary fashion houses is selective, global, controlled in each single detail and (almost) exclusively relying on directly managed mono-brand stores and shops-in-shop.

Some figures are as follows. Chanel, Hermès, Ferragamo and Prada own, respectively, 360, 310, 398 and 654 including mono-brand stores and direct concessions. For Hermès out of 310 stores and concessions worldwide, 219 are direct, which corresponds to 70.6% of total number of stores. So, considering the higher average size and turnover of Directly Operated Store (DOS) stores, if compared to franchising ones, we estimate that the percentage of DOS revenues is about 80% on the total revenues. We hypothesise that the same percentage may be higher than 90% for Chanel. For the Prada Group[10] and Ferragamo, the percentage is, respectively, 81.7% and 65.3%. Like Gucci, the percentage made by franchising sales is small and the locations of the stores are equally prestigious: in Milan, Prada, Ferragamo and Hermès chose to open their points of sale in Via Montenapoleone (e.g. Gucci and Louis Vuitton), and Chanel in the adjacent Via Sant'Andrea; as well as in the most important Italian Department store, La Rinascente (it's not the case for Hermès and Prada). Prada also owns two stores in the prestigious Galleria Vittorio Emanuele II where the brand first debuted, while Chanel owns only one.

Very few are the categories of merchandise sold through the wholesale channel: beauty products, make-up, fragrances and eyewear, as stated in Chapter 2, are mostly sold by specialised retailers, in addition to directly operated "boxes" in department stores. The remaining items are not marketed through wholesalers, except for The Webster in Miami for Chanel and Ratti in Bologna where Hermès has its dedicated corner. In both cases, these exceptions are due to the personal relation with the store owner.

The choices of Prada and Ferragamo are more flexible as they allow a higher number of stores – still exclusive and selected – to sell a more extensive merchandise offer.

The online distribution strategy of the same companies has strong similarities with what was observed in Chapter 2 for Louis Vuitton and Gucci.

The four brands have their e-commerce where the entire assortment is available (except for some limited editions). Chanel and Hermès (like Louis Vuitton) are not available on the nine platforms (except for some rare cases mainly connected to the vintage sector, for instance, on Farfetch), thus proving the will to have a higher control over distribution. Prada and Ferragamo, instead, are available: the first on all nine platforms; the second on seven (not available on Ssense and Browns); they offer a comprehensive assortment privileging the same categories highlighted for Gucci: first of all leather and small leather goods, followed by footwear and ready-to-wear; the product price on their e-commerce and on Farfetch coincide, as a confirmation of their control of the pricing strategy. Moreover, they allow for the use of mobile devices thanks to a responsive design.

3.9 Omnichannel, in collaboration with Sabrina Pomodoro and Benedetta Breschi

Prada and Chanel are the only designer brands included in the *creative-idea-led integration* category.

For Prada, the key concept of the whole fall-winter 2019/2020 collection is romanticism. The same idea is stressed in the advertising campaign where models are surrounded by flowered meadows as well as in the shop windows which display mannequins embraced by flowers. Even the garments showcased during the show and in the shop window have flowers as the key element of the collection. Moreover, the Instagram page promotes the fashion show to enhance the theme of the collection.

Chanel's fall-winter 2019/2020 collection is inspired by the idea of "winter", which we find in the shop windows, where reproductions of pieces of ice are displayed next to mannequins. The same concept is expressed on the catwalk where snow is the protagonist of a mountain village set in the Paris Grand Palais, the usual location for Chanel's fashion shows. However, due to the exclusion of advertising, integration is only partial; publicity, in fact, does not recall the above-mentioned theme and the model is photographed wearing the same outfits as in the shop window, but in an aseptic setting, probably a photo studio.

Unlike Chanel, Ferragamo adopts a "stylistic" integration, definable as *collection-led integration*: the outfits on the catwalk are the same as those in the advertising campaign and in the shop windows, and the recurring colours are red, orange and fuchsia; however, no repeating key theme is identifiable. Also, the Instagram page posts only the videos of the fashion show without a creative concept that goes beyond the stylistic identity of the collection.

Finally, analysing Hermes, no degree of integration was identified. The boutique windows, where the iconic Kelly stands out together with the classic use of orange, recall neither the garments showcased on the catwalk nor the collection theme. Even the advertising and the fashion show are totally inconsistent in terms of communication.

Interview with Mauro Ferraresi, director of the Made in Italy Master at IULM (International University of Languages and Media) University

What are the characteristics that define historic brands as "independent"?
As you highlighted in this chapter, they are not just fashion houses, they are also actual businesses, because since their establishment, they have felt the need to apply a strong entrepreneurial spirit. The owners and often the management are still part of the founding family. The "family property" entrepreneurial formula succeeds in the difficult task of combining creativity and business skills.

What are the main choices of their business model?
The main businesses are leather goods; for instance, 50% of Hermès' 2019 turnover was generated by the "leather and saddlers" division. To consolidate their exclusive brand identity,

they have implemented a comprehensive product diversification, thus becoming lifestyle brands, able to convey a way of living. A product range, at the centre of which emerges the craftsmanship with which the products have been made.

Is craftsmanship an important asset for their strategy?
Yes, Hermès defines it as "the first pillar of its strategy, with nearly 5,200 craftsmen in France"; the motto "a craftsman, a bag" means that, to create a Kelly, 24 hours of work are required.

What are the other important strategic choices?
They exercise the greatest control over the value chain. For instance, "the majority of Hermès production take place in France, at 43 production sites"; their exclusive distribution, boasting more than 300 mono-brand stores, "is the second pillar of Hermès strategy". Differently from the big luxury groups, always looking for new brand acquisitions, these brands tend to buy small artisanal production workshops in order to exercise a more and more complete control on the value chain.

They look like the antithesis of marketing.
It is yet another peculiarity of these labels whose purpose is to generate desires rather than following existing ones: they are the opposite of a certain type of marketing that privileges the "signified" to the "signifier".

When speaking of historic brands, we cannot refer to positioning in a classic sense of the term.
Exactly, it is difficult to develop an effective positioning map, since they tend to create and tell "unique" stories, rather than identifying variables through which they can differ from competitors. If you think of Hermès, it boasts many characterising factors such as artisanship, luxury, exclusivity, exquisite leather goods, carré, equestrian world, Birkin and Kelly bags; therefore, it has a classic, elegant, discrete, distinct personality and a cultural reference evoking Paris, and the French aristocracy; a set of tangible, intangible and emotional characteristics, which allowed it to acquire a unique and inimitable positioning.

An essential factor of their positioning and therefore of the brand identity is Heritage.
Yes. Their historic identity is closely tied to artisanship, to heritage, to the legendary figure of the founding couturier, and to the symbolic and emotional values that cult products can communicate. Their identity is so well-defined that one element is enough to evoke the label.

They belong to a very exclusive club.
Exactly. It is a very concentrated group by far given the very high, and almost insurmountable, barriers to entry, mostly represented by their long-established historical significance.

How has COVID affected luxury brands?
It has led to a better understanding of the opportunities offered by the web. In general, we have realised that luxury can exploit websites to improve the direct customer relationship and to market its products online. Many events and presentations, in fact, can be enjoyed directly on the web and the *click and mortar* is effective also in the luxury sector.

Student activities

Choose a brand and based on your choice:

- define the sustainability actions to be applied in the future;
- identify the combination product/price segment/target where to diversify;
- identify a social media and the content typology to be developed;
- define which of the following formats – brick-and-mortar mono-brand store, brick-and-mortar multi-brand store, shop-in-shop in department stores, online mono-brand shop and online multi-brand platform – need to be developed the most;
- verify the degree of synergy among the aesthetic elements of the latest collection: the fashion show, social networks, mono-brand store windows and advertising campaign.

Notes

1 Thank you Massimo Nicosia – Design Director for an international men's luxury group – for collaborating in the writing of this book.
2 This paragraph is based on the one described in the book *Fashion Business Model* (Golizia, 2016), chapter 2, paragraph 2.1.
3 This paragraph is based on the one described in the book *Fashion Business Model* (Golizia, 2016), chapter 2, paragraph 2.9.2.
4 The hoodie and the silk nightgown are not available on the two companies' websites.
5 Giorgio Armani's prices were analysed for the following products: shopper, women's blazer, women's sneakers, men's formal suits and women's pumps; Dolce & Gabbana was considered for jeans, hoodie and silk nightgown.
6 Actually, Prada's price for men's formal suit is 2.8% higher; however, such a difference is irrelevant in the segment of absolute luxury.
7 The same considerations made for Dior and Louis Vuitton in paragraph 2.4, about their positioning being in between specialised and unspecialised companies, are applicable to Hermès.
8 The comparison was made with Giorgio Armani for the following products: shopper, women's blazer, women's sneakers, men's formal suits and women's pumps; Dolce & Gabbana was considered for jeans.
9 The analysis of the offline distribution channel was adapted from the book by Golizia D., *Fashion Business Model,* Franco Angeli, 2016, chapter 2, paragraph 2.9.6.
10 The percentage refers to Prada Group including the brands Prada, Miu Miu, Car Shoe, Church's and Marchesi.

4

CONTEMPORARY FASHION BRANDS

Reading: the fashion stylist

The fashion stylist is a key figure in terms of style and image. The fashion stylist has a crucial, yet behind-the-scenes, role since they define and often anticipate the trends that we will see on fashion magazines. Their task is to valorise the collection, organising all the steps of the shooting: the concept, the location, the choice of models, their make-up and the selection of outfits. The fashion stylist may work for a brand or for a magazine. In the first case, they closely collaborate with the designer and try to mitigate their artistic and visionary touch to create more realistic and usable outfits. In the second case, the stylist takes care of all the aspects involved in the making of a photo shooting. The goal, in both cases, is to create a storytelling, and an experience that is conveyed through the evocative power of images and pictures. For this reason, this figure is endowed with a comprehensive culture of history of fashion and photography, as well as innate creative and team-work skills (Zinola, 2011).

4.1 Who are they?[1]

Contemporary brands, whose leaders are Giorgio Armani and Ralph Lauren, embody a generation of multi-talented creative designers endowed with management skills. The key-words defining these brands are designer, contemporary, prêt-à-porter, lifestyle and the crucial role of their founder. The first is shared with historic brands in the sense that they were founded by a "creative personality" too.

The second keyword, contemporary, differentiates them as they were mainly established between the end of the 60s and the beginning of the 80s of the past century. The third is prêt-à-porter: a garment made in series with a very high stylistic content and in contrast with the fashion of couturiers. However, the main distinctive element is lifestyle, as defined in paragraph 1.10; these brands have created a lifestyle under their name, as well as a culture, and a social message that communicates the brand essence. These companies, despite having diversified in numerous product categories, preserve a consistent image and style identity. The image is essentially bound to their founder, the last but essential keyword. The founder, in contrast to most historic brands, is (except for some cases) alive and has had, and still has, an essential role in the characterisation of the company. For instance, it's Giorgio Armani himself, at the same time founder, designer and manager, who builds the connection among company, style, products, brands and consumers. All these peculiarities have allowed young designers from the 70s to build a strong, unique and distinctive brand image, not based on the heritage, as for historic brands, but on the opposite strategy: strong designer personality, specific style content, democratisation of their offer and extended communication (Golizia 2016).

Some founders (Dolce & Gabbana and Giorgio Armani) are still owners and strategic and creative leaders of their companies; others (Ralph Lauren), despite having gone public, still hold a crucial role in their management; whereas Tommy Hilfiger and Calvin Klein preferred to sell their own companies (both to PVH). There is also the case of those (Michael Kors) that acquired a company of the same cluster (Versace), the premature death of whose founder (Gianni) had left the hard task of managing the strategic and creative heritage to his successors.

The above-mentioned companies are studied in the following analysis, even though, as premised in Chapter 3, not all the brands of the clusters are observed.

4.2 Style, in collaboration with Diana Murek and Antonio Patruno[2]

The style of contemporary brands strongly depends on the founder designer who approaches the creative process in their own way to shape the brand image. By considering some designer brands, we may identify well-defined and original styles.

Ralph Lauren's style is representative of American culture and roots and epitomises some of their aspects such as the country lifestyle – most of all in the Double RL line – and the refined and sophisticated fashion of New England. Since the beginning, its style has interpreted the past with a touch of romanticism: the traditions of English aristocracy – mostly inspired by the impeccable Duke of Windsor – and the old-generation Hollywood stars like Cary Grant and Fred Astaire. The brand conceives its collections with an eye on sport, African safari and holidays in New England. The company targets WASPS (White Anglo-Saxon Protestants), the white American upper-middle class, but its style is appreciated worldwide (Vergani, 2010).

Dolce & Gabbana's stylistic codes, instead, originate in Sicily and address a very feminine, sensual and Mediterranean woman. The style is endowed with recognisable traits that detach from the fashion panorama of those years in which the manager woman was the dominating character. Dolce & Gabbana designs a sexy, seductive, but at the same time, strict woman, who is also devoted to religion and to family. A mix of glamour and verismo, a celebration and rediscovery of Mediterranean culture (Vergani, 2010).

The factor that has made Giorgio Armani immortal is time. The latter is not identified with a season or a trend: its cuts and silhouettes are clear and defined, classic, but never anachronistic; they are inspired by the shapes and patterns of faraway cultures.

Even though contemporary and historic brands respect the same timing and qualitative standards in ready-to-wear production, the former stand out for their individual and unique style, which in a few years, when they are perceived as historic, will constitute the brand heritage.

4.3 Supply chain and sustainability, in collaboration with Celeste Corso

Concerning control of the supply chain, due to the very high number of products, contemporary brands are not as stringent as historic brands.

The majority of them directly produce ready-to-wear first lines, but outsource the manufacturing of the most accessible apparel collections. On the PVH website we read:

> We have an extensive established network of worldwide sourcing partners… Our products were produced in over 1,200 factories in approximately 50 countries during 2019. All but one of these factories were operated by independent manufacturers, with most being located in Asia.
>
> *(PVH, 2020)*

All brands license the production and selling of cosmetics, fragrances and watches to partners.

Greenability is the new frontier of sustainable thinking, a new way of conceiving and producing but also a means to generate a new business model. It is a training that every brand should do in order to develop the necessary competences to change the economy: from linear – based on the exploitation of resources to gain profit – to circular – virtuously rooted in the principle of self-regeneration, re-integration and valorisation. This is a challenge that brands can win only by training and daily committing to it at a cultural and practical level: sustainability is also, and mainly, a cultural issue that must transform into targeted actions. *Greenability* finds its highest application in the cluster of contemporary brands. It is important to stress that contemporary brands, like historic brands, are investing considerably in sustainability.

Giorgio Armani announced that a sustainable positioning is essential and that it is first a matter of ethics rather than strategy. Armani also stressed the necessity to educate the consumer about this aspect through product quality and transparency. Moreover, Armani, thanks to its history, and to the celebration of values based on local Italian production, is in itself a manifesto of sustainability. Its style, translated into durable products, is a tangible evidence of it: Armani, in fact, declared that the use of sustainable materials is not the only evidence of sustainability, the timeless style of a garment is also sustainable (Pambianco, 2018a). Armani, like Chanel, Hermès and Ferragamo, signed the Fashion Pact in favour of the planet. In 2016, the brand also banned the use of animal fur in its collections and respects social and environmental codes of conduct (Armani, 2020).

4.4 Segmentation strategies

Contemporary brands debuted with a target and product-driven strategy; in most cases, their product consisted of ready-to-wear collections in womenswear (even though Ralph Lauren differentiated for its men's ties production). However, due to the diversification process, this methodology turned into a lifestyle strategy (defined in paragraph 2.4). What had begun, more than 40 years ago, with a ties collection, has transformed into a world that redefines style and innovates a lifestyle communication. These companies offer a copious quantity of merchandise categories (see following paragraph) addressing many micro-targets, but communicating the same stylistic identity and image: there is a leitmotif that connects the young who buy an Armani Jeans tricot hat and a young couple choosing furniture by Armani Casa; the love for tradition and for timeless fashion, both representatives of Armani's world.

4 · Brand[3]

In this sector, the main business is apparel, with the exception of Michael Kors, which mainly operates in the segment of bags. However, these brands, Armani and Ralph Lauren in particular, have adopted a more extended diversification strategy in the fashion industry: horizontal (different product categories) and vertical (different lines in the same category).

Concerning horizontal diversification, their offer is very exhaustive and includes apparel, bags, footwear, eyewear, fragrances, cosmetics, watches and jewels. It also comprises products that are not strictly connected to the fashion system like hotels (see Versace), flowers and sweets (see Armani), furniture (see Ralph Lauren). This typology of items is not always produced to increase sales, but rather to create a lifestyle and/or to achieve other results: for instance, a hotel may be an excellent starting point to access/penetrate new geographical markets. For example, Ralph Lauren boasts one of the most extensive product portfolios in the fashion industry achieved through the development of a series of brands, all connected to each other (Aaker and Joachimsthaler, 2000). In the same cluster, we find brands that applied a different strategy; the Sicilian company preferred to incorporate the D&G line (the last collection was spring-summer 2012) in the Dolce & Gabbana line. Many believe that the decision was due to the desire to strengthen the brand image, which is now only associated to the main line and not affected by the "mechanism" of second lines.

Contemporary designers are also characterised by the maximum vertical diversification in the apparel sector. In most cases, it extends to all occasions of use: from high fashion to ready-to-wear, from casualwear to activewear and underwear, from an adult target to kids. For this reason, the brand portfolio of many companies is constituted by numerous brands, each one aiming to satisfy the needs of different targets and reaching a very expanded market.

Over the years, this vertical diversification strategy has taken two different directions, trading down and trading up. In the first phase, contemporary brands had added only casualwear lines (e.g. Versus or Versace Jeans) – addressed to younger targets and with more accessible prices – to their classic expensive ready-to-wear line for an adult target (e.g. Gianni Versace). In the following phase, some also included a high fashion line (e.g. Versace Atelier).

The branding policy is not based on heritage as in the case of historic brands, but it leverages on a series of recognisable elements that constitute the brand's values and lifestyle: timeless style and *greige* for Armani, Sicily and lace for Dolce & Gabbana, the *medusa* for Versace and the horse and preppy style for Ralph Lauren.

These companies have their iconic products too, even though not as many as historic brands; for instance, Armani is remembered for its unstructured jacket and for the perfume Acqua di Giò, while Ralph Lauren for its Polo T-shirt. However, none of them has been able, despite the many attempts, to become renowned in the field of accessories.

Speaking of actual quality, which in the other groups is homogeneous (very high for historic brands and medium-low for fast fashion), in this cluster, it varies from line to line. The actual quality is excellent and resulting from top materials and an (almost) exclusive tailoring production for high fashion and first lines of ready-to-wear; while it is medium-low in informal lines due to the choice of lower-quality materials and often outsourced industrial production. However, the perceived quality of all lines is high thanks to corporate respectability, the prestige of the designer, the reputation of first lines and very high investments in communication.

The naming strategy differs from the one of historic brands. Most contemporary labels applied a different methodology based on giving another name to each line. Nevertheless, the name is almost always connected to the one of the designer/owner or to another recognisable element. Ralph Lauren, for instance, encompasses many brands: from luxury and sophisticated labels like Ralph Lauren Collection for women and Purple Label for men, to sporty lines like RLX and Polo, up to the most "democratic" like Lauren by Ralph Lauren. However, it is worth remembering the peculiar choice of Dolce & Gabbana that, as stated before, merged the second line, D&G, into the first.

As we have already stated, the Creative Director is an essential figure for these companies; they also coincide with the founder and, in most of the cases, and unlike historic brands, they are still alive.

Customisation, which has now become a recurring trend, has been well implemented by Dolce & Gabbana. From the very beginning, the brand has embraced this trend and it is still possible to directly customise sneakers on the brand's official platform (Dolce & Gabbana, 2020).

4.6 Pricing, in collaboration with Benedetta Breschi

Price is a strategic element of paramount importance for contemporary brands, yet for different reasons, as compared to the two previously discussed clusters. While the primary objective of the latter's pricing strategy is to legitimate their superior brand image in order to justify a higher price – for the same tangible product characteristics – and to position themselves in the segment of absolute luxury; for this cluster, the main purpose is to validate their status of lifestyle brands.

There are two dominant features of the examined companies: they have the most extended price range in the fashion system and they operate in several price segments within the same product category (most of all in leather goods and apparel).

Concerning the first, the price changes according to the product and can vary from a few dozen euros for a chocolate box, to hundreds of euros for a night in a "branded" luxury hotel.

However, the peculiarity of these companies is represented by the second characteristic: the price of the same product varies according to line/brand. It is worth observing how these labels have reached this structure. At the outset, they offered ready-to- wear garments that were exceptionally styled for a high, yet lower than French couturiers', price: this was their main competitive advantage (Porter, 1980). In the second phase, they first lowered the entry price, creating new and more accessible lines for a target having less resources. Afterwards, some of them increased the maximum price and penetrated the segment of high fashion with specific brands.

This is the case of Giorgio Armani S.p.A. which, in the apparel/adult segment (except for EA7 specialising in activewear), offers different lines, each one with its own positioning.

The first is Armani Privé, a high fashion line comprising bespoke garments having the highest price and being positioned in absolute luxury; the second, Giorgio Armani, the heart of the company, is positioned at the top of aspirational luxury: the positioning is justified by the preciousness of materials, by the excellent production and by the image evoking style and sophistication. Emporio Armani is positioned at the top of accessible luxury: it is the bridge line characterised by a younger-looking, formal, yet informal style, in particular since the encompassing of Armani Jeans, not available anymore. Lower in positioning – between accessible luxury and mass market – stands Armani Exchange addressed to a younger target with even lower prices and cooler and less formal products. As stated by Corbellini Saviolo (2009, p. 108), second and third lines are the result of "a balance between a good product (trendy/fashion) and a good price (economies of scale)".

Even in the case of contemporary brands, price reflects the positioning and is compared, on the one hand, to historic brands, and on the other, to industrial brands.

Concerning the comparison with the former, we reiterate what was stated in Chapter 2 (for Dior) and Chapter 3 (for Hermès and Prada), that is, in (almost) all categories of merchandise, contemporary brands are lower in positioning.[4] They are perceived as "inferior" by the market due to their weaker heritage, and, consequently, cannot position themselves at the same level.

Concerning the comparison with the latter (Liu Jo is the chosen company), these brands boast a (much) higher positioning in all product categories. For instance, Giorgio Armani's shopper costs 852.4% more, the women's blazer costs 795.5% more and the formal men's suit 678.8% more. In this case, both intangible product characteristics (see paragraph 4.7.1) and

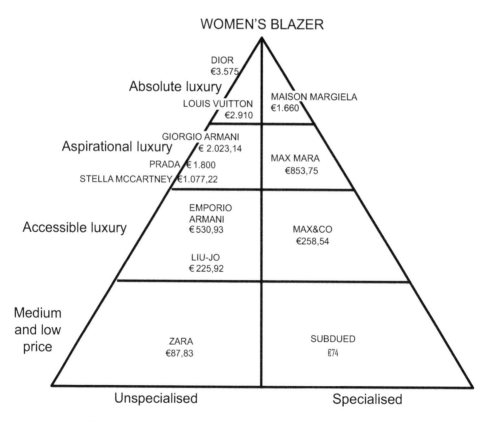

FIGURE 4.1 Golizia' pyramid of women's blazer
Source: Prepared by Dario Golizia

the actual product quality are superior (very high raw materials and artisanal manufacturing quality and outstanding stylistic content) and justify a higher price.

However, as discussed before, contemporary brands, in order to reach a very extended market, offer several lines for the same product category, all having relevant price differences. For instance, the prices of Giorgio Armani's shopper, women's blazer and formal men's suit are higher than Emporio Armani's: plus 403.8%, 281% and 144.9%, respectively. It is necessary to observe that in the same product categories, the prices of Emporio Armani (see second lines) are 89%, 135% and 217.7% higher compared to Liu Jo's (industrial brands). The typical factors of success of second lines – style and image consistency with the first line (Corbellini and Saviolo, 2009) – justify the higher positioning.

4.7 Communication

We now proceed with the definition of the image of the cluster; afterwards, we study how the marketing and communication function is organised and managed by a company from the same group. Finally, we outline the communication mix applied by some brands.

4.7.1 Cluster image

Lifestyle, cult brands, founder seen as a mythical figure, designer, ready-to-wear, Made in Italy, style/trend, omni (product, brand, channel, price, communication and target) are the peculiarities of these brands.

4.7.2 Marketing function and communication, in collaboration with Michele Leoni

Versace has its own marketing and communication office. The Chief Brand Officer (CBO) is the head of the department and takes care of the brand strategy development in terms of communication, brand image and experience. This figure closely collaborates with the CEO and the Creative Director. The directors of the different departments report to the CBO: the Global Communication Director, to whom report the Directors of Italian and International Corporate Communication; the Director of Product Communication and their teams; the Global Media Director, to whom reports the Media Planner; the Social Media Manager, to whom reports the Social Media Coordinator; the Global Events Director, to whom reports the Events Manager; the Global Customer Relationship Management (CRM) Director, to whom report the CRM Business Analyst and the CRM Specialist; the Product Marketing Manager who is in charge of coordinating the marketing activities with the priorities of the merchandising department; the Heritage Manager who is in charge of the archive of the company and the Creative Services Director who deals with the creation of all the contents of the marketing activities and to whom reports a team comprising the Art Director, copywriters, producers, graphic designers and video makers. Marketing and Communication Directors for the APAC (Asia Pacific) and US regions and their respective teams complete the organisational chart.

After the acquisition by the Capri Group, the chart has remained the same, except for the Creative Services department that, in the past, used to rely more on the work of external suppliers.

4.7.3 Fashion shows and trade fairs, in collaboration with Andrea Doroldi

Contemporary brands showcase their collections in the same fashion weeks as historic brands: the two "traditional" collections – fall-winter and spring-summer – the cruise and the high fashion for those which have this line. Even in this case, the office in charge of organising the event is the PR office. Unlike historic brands, these companies can showcase more ready-to-wear collections as they include different lines (e.g. Giorgio Armani, Armani Privé and Emporio Armani).

By applying the scheme used in the previous chapters (Vilaseca, 2010), we observe that some prefer a classic approach with a minimal and basic scenography to allow for a more objective and focused vision of the collection (Ironico, 2014), while others a theatrical one, as defined in Chapter 3.

In the first category we find Armani that, for spring-summer 2020, chose to stress the creative content of the collection rather than the scenographic location. Conversely, in the second group stands Dolce & Gabbana that, for 2020 High Fashion collection, opted for memorable scenography and locations to offer its guests a unique experience. The event consisted of three different shows held over three days and places: one for the jewellery line, one for women's high fashion and another for men's high fashion.

Also, the analysed brands have included a cruise collection: we mention, for instance, Giorgio Armani's 2020 cruise collection whose fashion show was organised in the National Museum of Tokyo, a city loved by the Milanese designer.

Like the brands examined in the two previous chapters and for the same reasons, Armani, Ralph Lauren, Calvin Klein Dolce & Gabbana and Versace did not participate in the following trade fairs: Mipel and Pitti Immagine in 2019 and 2020.

Like historic brands, some of them participated in the Salone del Mobile, organising some events for the *Fuori Salone*: in 2019, Armani hosted a collection dedicated to Architect Tadao Ando in its Armani/Silos, while Versace presented its new Versace Home collection.

4.7.4 Advertising, editorial, advertorial, in collaboration with Benedetta Breschi

For the 2019 edition, the brand Michael Kors was added to Giorgio Armani, Dolce & Gabbana and Gianni Versace, subject of the previous research (2016). By comparing the two studies, we can observe how, in 2019, for the three brands, the purchase of advertising pages

TABLE 4.1 Advertising, fashion editorial and advertorials of contemporary brands

Contemporary Brands	L'Officiel			Vogue			Vanity Fair			Elle			Glamour			Total		
	A	FE	AD	A	FE	AD	A	FE	AD	A	FE	AD	A	FE	AD	A	FE	AD
Giorgio Armani	0	2	0	2	6	0	0	0	1	0	0	0	0	0	1	2	8	2
Dolce & Gabbana	0	1	0	4	7	0	0	0	0	0	0	0	0	0	0	4	8	0
Versace	1	2	0	2	2	0	0	1	0	0	3	0	0	0	0	3	8	0
Michael Kors	0	1	0	1	1	0	0	1	0	0	0	0	1	0	1	2	3	1
Total	**1**	**6**	**0**	**9**	**16**	**0**	**0**	**2**	**1**	**0**	**3**	**0**	**1**	**0**	**2**	**11**	**27**	**3**

Source: Authors' data processing on the basis of fashion magazines published in Italy in September 2019. A, FE and AD stand for advertising, fashion editorial and advertorial, respectively.

decreased by 64% as an evidence of the decline of investments in print media. In 2019, the group is fourth in ranking behind industrial brands (see next chapter) with the purchase of 11 advertising pages. However, despite purchasing 27.3% less pages compared to industrial brands, they dedicated 70.3% more to fashion editorials, thus proving the "persuasive power" of these famous fashion houses.

4.7.5 Influencers, gifting, endorsement, by Lavinia Biancalani

The arrival of contemporary brands on social media follows that of historic brands. Thanks to the constant update of their platforms and the evolution of different targets, they were able to dictate communication trends, creating a strong sense of belonging for their fan base. Particularly interactive communities, including consumers as well as celebrities and influencers, contributed to expanding the success on social media of many companies of this group. Instagram has proven to be the perfect window to the world to describe the story of the brand, its collections, atmospheres and events. Among the first to take advantage of the web, we find Dolce & Gabbana who created "Instant"[5] campaigns. They represent actual benchmarks and precursors of social media strategies that are still applied by other fashion labels. Contemporary brands were among the first to transform the catwalk into a system of interaction with digital consumers, so much so that fashion shows – in the past very exclusive events – have become global phenomena to be commented live and challenging boundaries and time zones. The "event show" considered an opportunity for global visibility, together with influencer marketing campaigns for the launch of products and capsule collections, and with seeding and PR activities, has defined an almost always successful pattern of social communication.

Dolce & Gabbana has always embraced innovations in digital communication. It was among the first to involve influencers in its fashion shows and events, with the aim of surprising Millennials, the new generation of consumers. In January 2017, they hired an "army" of celebrities and influencers to replace models on the catwalk. From famous YouTuber Cameron Dallas, with more than 20 million followers on Instagram at that time to Presley Gerber (son of Cindy Crawford) and Rafferty Law (son of Jude Law). In the same year, during the February fashion week, the brand repeated the experiment with an even more flamboyant show with Pyper America Smith, Pixie Lott, Isabel Getty, famous influencers who modelled wearing outfits inspired by Sicilian nature. Their hiring impressively increased the buzz around the brand thanks to a storytelling that also involved the fitting and the post-show phases, using the hashtag #DGMillennials and #DGFamily. Moreover, influencers and celebrities asked to represent the apparel line were often involved for accessories, cosmetics and fragrances lines.

A more thought-out, but impactful approach characterised Armani, which landed on social networks thanks to the first social endorsement with Leonardo Di Caprio who, in 2016, won an Oscar for *The Revenant* and attended the ceremony wearing a Giorgio Armani tuxedo. The post dedicated to the actor registered a good result in terms of interactions (more than 85,000 for the Armani profile which, at that time, already boasted 4.2 million followers). In 2017, the brand became the fashion week leader with more than 404,000 interactions in one day, thanks to the publishing of about 20 posts for a very detailed storytelling. One of the most interactive contents had as a protagonist Spanish influencer Gala Gonzalez and, among the most used hashtags, #armanistars. As for the other brands of this cluster, Armani considers the show the perfect occasion for a social storytelling and in 2018 the Emporio Armani fashion show became emblematic – 2,300 guests and an audience worthy of a rock concert in an unexpected location: Milan Linate Airport. From Leona Lewis to Cameron Dallas, as well as the most famous Italian social media stars, everyone documented not only the garments, but also the exclusive performance of Robbie Williams. In this context, endorsement strategies are evident and they prove Armani as one of the protagonists of the most important red carpets.

Calvin Klein, the symbol of daring and progressive ideals, in addition to its seductive aesthetic, aims at inspiring and motivating its fan base through social media. Unlike the previously considered brands, it did not leverage totally on the spectacularity of its show, but it mainly focused on the design of digital communication campaigns, developing a new language. This was a strategy that had its turning point in 2016 with #mycalvins campaign interpreted by Justin Bieber and with the participation of international influencers (more than 600 worldwide). #mycalvins was the most powerful influencers campaign of the year, a success replicated by the following Our Family #mycalvins focused on the values of family and community (with the participation of Solange, A$AP Rocky and the Kardashian sisters, among many), which reached an outstanding engagement. Calvin Klein chooses to experiment with new languages and formats on social media: *I speak my truth in #myCalvins* is the 2019 campaign that gives a voice to some of the most influential personalities of the world, inviting them to tell their stories in episodes; each episode is launched in a video on all the digital platforms and social media of the brand. Artists like Billie Eilish, Bella Hadid and Kendall Jenner participated in the campaign.

4.7.6 Social media

The observed brands employ the same social media analysed in the previous chapters: Facebook, Instagram, Twitter and YouTube.

Speaking of contents, we observe three characteristics: the first two highlight substantial differences from the previous cluster, while the third shows an analogy. The first feature is related to contents which do not differ from platform to platform, and are contextually posted on every social media: Instagram Facebook, Twitter and Pinterest. Moreover, if the content is a video, it is also published on YouTube. This strategy is opposed to that of historic brands.

The second element that characterises contents is the choice of individuals or groups of people – often famous – rather than products. In those cases, in which the content includes the product, the latter is always recognisable, and, consequently, can be traced back to the brand and its values.

The last characteristic is shared with the previous cluster and is stressed even more. We can observe inspirational contents with images of interiors, flowers and not necessarily fashion subjects that help create and live the brand lifestyle. The variety of contents is very high as to prove the ability to satisfy any need at any time, thanks to the most extended product offer in the fashion system.

The goals are numerous.

The first is to consolidate the image of a lifestyle brand, interacting with the audience and involving them in the life and development of the company. The second is to reach many different targets focusing on new ones. Ralph Lauren, in order to conquer the heart of the youngest, signed a collaboration with Palace, a streetwear company. The products were sold in some selected stores through the Polo app, which substituted its traditional retail network. The new "requests" of the fashion scenario, sustainability and inclusivity, have become another goal and object of great attention. Unlike the brands of the previous chapter, which implement green actions but do not stress them in their communication, contemporary labels have promoted multiple digital initiatives in favour of the environment. For the launch of its *Earth Polo* line, Ralph Lauren posted two videos on its social profiles: the first informed consumers that for each produced *Earth Polo*, about 12 bottles less ended up in the oceans and in landfills. The brand also stated that its commitment was to recycle 170 million bottles by 2025. In the second video, the company affirmed that *Earth Polo* is more than a T-shirt; it is the witnessing of their constant commitment to innovation (Bhasin, 2019).

However, social media are changing the fashion scenario, offering visibility and a voice to those communities that had always been ignored by the industry. In this sense, inclusivity is another topic dear to these labels: being "less historic" they need to discuss more contemporary issues and with more confidence. With regard to this, Dolce & Gabbana has extended its womenswear size range to size 54, since the pre-fall 2020 collection. For years, Dolce & Gabbana has supported curvy models and, with this project, they intended to stress the brand commitment to feminine diversity. The spokesperson of the brand affirmed that beauty is not a matter of size and that the company has always emphasised women's silhouette independently from their measures (Pambianco, 2019).

4.7.7 Sponsorships and co-branding

Contemporary brands apply the sponsorship tool differently from historic companies (both controlled and not controlled by big luxury groups). While the latter mostly promote elite events (e.g. horse-riding and sailing events), the former, consistent with their more transversal brand and product portfolio, organise more "ordinary" events with more "ordinary" personalities. For instance, Hugo Boss sponsors the Formula 1 team Mercedes and the German national football team. These sponsorships anchor the brand to its territory, Germany, even more, and communicate its values to millions of sports discipline spectators.

Armani is an excellent example. Over the years, the brand has signed several sponsorships with different purposes. Olimpia is an interesting case: Armani first became the sponsor of the Milanese basketball team, then, its owner. The example is fascinating for two reasons: first, the sponsorship created a bond between the brand and Milan, the territory where it was founded; second, because the team is sponsored by more than one brand belonging to Armani. We hereby consider the strategic reasons. Armani Exchange's purpose is to strengthen the value of informality; Armani Exchange Watches focuses on raising brand awareness; EA7 stresses the technical component of the line. However, the team is also sponsored by Nike, with which the Milanese brand intends to share the status of leader.

Another interesting case is Emporio Armani's sponsorship of the team that was supposed to participate in the Olympic and Paralympic games of Tokyo 2020 (postponed to 2021). This strategy allows to associate the brand to the country of origin, Italy, to a global sports event, the Olympic Games, and to exclusivity by dressing disable athletes.

Speaking of co-branding, different objectives and typologies were identified. Versace to raise sales and brand awareness – inferior than those of the other brands of the cluster – has signed limited editions by H&M. These collections combine the creativity of designer labels with the low prices of the Swedish giant (Golizia, 2016). Emporio Armani, Tommy Hilfiger and Versace have partnered with sports and streetwear brands – with Reebok, Vetements and Kith, respectively – in order to reach a younger target who appreciates an urban style. The same purpose is at the root of the collaboration Tommy Hilfiger x Zendaya.

Collaborations with super-exclusive brands like Giorgio Armani for Bugatti or with mainstream brands like Emporio Armani for Piaggio, Tommy Hilfiger for Coca-Cola and Dolce & Gabbana for Martini are yet another evidence of the versatility of these companies, which can reach different targets with different products and brands. In order to appeal to (partially) different groups of customers, collaborations with several typologies of retailers have been implemented by some companies: for example, Dolce & Gabbana teamed up with LuisaViaRoma and MyTheresa as well as with the classic department store Harrods. Finally, to witness the need to convey a universal social message, we may consider the collaboration between FEED – an association committed to fighting children's malnutrition – and Ralph Lauren, which, for each sold bag, offers a meal to children in need.

4.7.8 Museums, foundations and leisure time activities, in collaboration with Andrea Pittana

The brands belonging to this group have adopted different strategies. On the one hand, we find Armani, one of the pioneers of the fashion system that invested many resources in leisure activities and that has recently invested just as many in its heritage. On the other stands Dolce & Gabbana that developed only leisure time activities and with a smaller effort. American brands like Calvin Klein and Michael Kors, to mention others, have adopted a more cautious approach and have only established their foundations.

There would be no need to explain why Armani implemented leisure time activities, simply because it has been one of the pioneers that inspired many players of the same industry to do the same, as well as many authors to coin the concept of lifestyle (Fabris and Minestroni, 2004). Armani is, in fact, the quintessence of lifestyle (Golizia, 2016). Its leisure time activities are embodied by two hotels in Milan and Dubai where two *Armani/Privé Clubs* are also located, clubs that mix both music and Armani style. Moreover, the brand has opened some restaurants, the first in Paris in 1998, awarded with the prestigious Michelin Star, and followed by 20 more scattered in the most renowned international locations (Armani, 2019).

Speaking about heritage, the need to be considered a historic brand and to increase sales of accessories encouraged the Milanese company to organise initiatives that, in the past, had only been a prerogative of historic brands. For this reason, in 2015, Milano Armani/Silos was opened: this location tells the brand story with 400 garments and 200 accessories. In 2016, Fondazione Giorgio Armani was established with the goal to carry out projects of public and social utility.

As mentioned above, less efforts were made by Dolce & Gabbana, which, thanks to a partnership with Martini, opened the Dolce & Gabbana Martini Bar and Bistrot. Overseas, Michael Kors (Kors, 2019) and Calvin Klein focus on donations to support charity projects.

4.8 Distribution, in collaboration with Andrea Doroldi

Analogously and consistent with other marketing policies, distribution is also a very differentiated variable. In fact, contrary to historic brands that apply a selective distribution strategy, exclusively and chiefly mono-brand, the companies of this cluster – whose product/brand portfolio is the most extended of all – adopt the most complex and widespread distribution strategy of the entire fashion system.

For instance, Ralph Lauren with its 426 mono-brand stores worldwide (of which 121 are full-price and 305 outlets), 653 direct concessions in the main department stores and 12.230 multi-brand stores epitomises the current situation. As a consequence, in the case of contemporary brands, the percentage of turnover made through direct retail is inferior than that of historic companies: for Ralph Lauren, it corresponds to 64.3%, thanks to a high percentage of outlets; for Tommy Hilfiger and Armani, whose data is not available, we hypothesise a percentage less than 50%.

Even though the distribution strategy still employs a mix of channels, even for these brands, the mono-brand store has a crucial role, since it allows increasing the brand awareness and presenting a more comprehensive product offer than in other channels. The mono-brand stores of this cluster, unlike historic brands, adopt a specific strategy for each label.

For instance, Armani Privé, purchased by an elite clientele that can afford very expensive garments, is available in only very few mono-brand boutiques worldwide (also because it is an haute couture line it is made to measure upon order). Giorgio Armani, the first ready-to-wear line, is sold in only few mono-brand boutiques – mainly directly owned – and very few selected multi-brand stores. Emporio Armani and Armani Exchange, the accessible and causal lines, are found in multiple channels: from mono-brand to multi-brand stores, from department stores to online shops, to allow for a more capillary distribution.

Also, for these brands, beauty products, fragrances, eyewear and make-up are available in specialised chains of stores.

The store location varies according to brand. In Milan, for instance, Giorgio Armani's boutique is located in Sant'Andrea, a very central location; Giorgio Armani Accessori is found, and it's not by chance, in Galleria Vittorio Emanuele II, next to Louis Vuitton and Gucci and opposite Prada, three important brands for leather goods; a shop-in-shop of Emporio Armani can be found at La Rinascente. In the same city, in 2000, the Milanese company opened one of the first megastores in history, *Armani Manzoni 31*. Armani Casa, at first located in *Armani Manzoni 31*, now owns its own store in Corso Venezia.

Conversely, Dolce & Gabbana, which has merged all the brands into one, differentiates its stores according to various criteria such as product typology, target or a combination of both. Still in Milan, we find the men's tailoring boutique, as well as the womenswear and women's accessories boutiques in Via della Spiga, in the fashion district and in the adjacent Corso Venezia.

Let's observe the online distribution strategy of Giorgio Armani, Ralph Lauren, Dolce & Gabbana and Versace. They all have their own e-commerce where the entire assortment is available (the first two also have the home collection). They are all present in the considered platforms: Versace and Dolce & Gabbana on all nine; Armani on six and Ralph Lauren on only three.[6] Also, in this case, the product range is wide, yet the main categories are not leather and small leather goods but ready-to-wear, the main product of the assortment. By comparing prices on companies' websites and Farfetch, we see that only Dolce & Gabbana can impose the same price; for Giorgio Armani and Ralph Lauren the price on Farfetch is slightly higher, while for Versace, barely inferior: this is a symptom of an inferior control on positioning. They all allow for mobile purchases thanks to a responsive design.

4.9 Omnichannel, in collaboration with Sabrina Pomodoro and Benedetta Breschi

From the analysis of fashion tales emerges a weak degree of integration among contemporary brands Armani, Dolce & Gabbana, Michael Kors and Versace. The core is the stylistic identity of the collection that inspires the whole communication and fashion tale, according to a *collection-led integration* model.

Armani is characterised by a scarce integration based on some stylistic elements of the collection such as velvet, transparencies and little sequins applied on blue and black. The advertising campaign is inspired by the same stylistic codes of the fashion show. However, in the shop windows and on Instagram, no reference to the fashion show is found and users are only invited to watch the show; in addition, the background is coloured in shades of grey without reference to the core themes of the collection.

Even Dolce & Gabbana, thanks to their flower and colourful textures, can be categorised in the *collection-led integration* group. Red and gold are present in the fashion show and the shop windows, but, even in this case, no idea or concept going beyond the stylistic code of the collection is identified.

In the case of Versace, the same outfits are presented both in the shop windows and in the advertising campaign, even though the background of the shop windows, made of columns and fluorescent lights, is not found in the advertising campaign. However, a sort of continuity is identifiable in the bright colours of some garments showcased during the fashion show and the background of the shop windows. In addition, a golden blow-up of the logo is well highlighted on the catwalk to recall the brand identity.

In some labels, the fashion tale may be based on several themes. This is the case for Michael Kors' collection. On the one hand, the core subject is the flower theme applied to the garments of the fashion show and the advertising campaign. On the other hand, the collection is also inspired by Studio 54. During the show, the brand decorated the location walls with a play of light; the catwalk was covered in golden confetti that recalled Studio 54, the famous New York club. However, while the first concept characterises the fashion show and the advertising campaign, the second is less synergic. In fact, the idea of Studio 54 is not found in the advertising campaigns and in the shop windows. The advertising campaign does not recall the location of the fashion show, which is only mentioned on Instagram when the brand invites its followers to watch the show live.

Interview with Francesco Freschi, General Manager at ETRO SPA

How has the luxury concept evolved and how do you think it will evolve in the future?
Luxury needs time to be conceived, created, and, most of all, appreciated. To return to its original nature, stylistic beauty must coincide with beauty in thoughts and companies' behaviours. It is an issue that involves both ethics and aesthetics, it is a promise of deceleration and sustainability that we will be able to keep only if we all follow the same track.

How is the competitive scenario of luxury evolving?
The crisis that has hit the world is an opportunity to think, to re-align everything, to define a more authentic and true framework. For the first time in history, all luxury brands are the same. We have to be synchronised with time, which, for Etro, is founded on some pivotal principles for our business model: the return to timeless beauty, sustainability in terms of rhythm and products, a more emphatic and honest communication.

How are you facing the challenge of new generations (Millennials, Generation Z)?
For years, new generations have focused only on streetwear, a category of merchandise that is not very similar to our brand. On our part, we have brought them closer to the brand, its products and values, mainly thanks to a more inclusive digital communication able to address a target that possibly encompasses a wider age range.

How do you comprise the topic of sustainability in luxury?
Can we really speak about sustainability in a system that produces the triple of what it needs? Real sustainability is not the advertised usage of organic or recycled fabrics, but it also implies certain productive processes. Not wasting does not mean not producing, but being willing to do less, yet better. Sustainability means thinking and acting local, which is the core of a conversation about the future.

How have brand communication levers changed?
Lately, communication has undergone a radical transformation. Digital platforms have allowed brands to reach a more and more extended audience and have given a voice to everyone. Journalists, newspapers and magazines now have a less relevant role which, despite the inferior coverage, preserve their prestige. The right communication strategy for a brand mixes both online and offline tools. Besides the techniques, we also need to consider the contents. Advertising campaigns, for instance, have to express more and more quality and common sense: fashion cannot and should not be superficial, it has to move people, to go in-depth their lives and entertain them without aiming simply at pushing sales.

How has communication changed with the invention of social media?
The invention of social media has made communication swifter and its messages more usable and direct, exposing brands to an intense and continuous content creation, as well as to potential critiques by a more involved audience. Even in this field, change is more necessary than ever: social media should not be a stage for ostentation and overexposure, but a meeting point where new stories are uncovered. Influencers will have to become the ambassadors of the talent and commitment behind the creative process.

Do you think that prices will change in the luxury sector?
The market evolution will not necessarily affect prices. I believe that consumers will be more informed and conscious and will reward those brands that best interpret the values they share.

How are distribution strategies changing in the sector?
The people-first-oriented omnichannel business is the only cornerstone for the future. Fashion must go further in its dialogue with the consumer to create an empathic and more democratic relationship.

How does Etro differentiate in an industry dominated by brands that are strongly ready-to-wear and accessories-driven?
We have always expressed our idea of timeless elegance by making accessories and garments enclosing an intrinsic meaning that represents the reason why they should be purchased: it is the value of durable items that go beyond time to be re-discovered and handed down to generations.

Student activities

Choose a brand and based on your choice:

- define the sustainability actions to be applied in the future;
- identify the combination product/price segment/target where to diversify;
- identify a social media and the content typology to be developed;
- define which of the following formats – brick-and-mortar mono-brand store, brick-and-mortar multi-brand store, shop-in-shop in department stores, online mono-brand shop and online multi-brand platform – need to be developed the most;
- verify the degree of synergy among the aesthetic elements of the latest collection: the fashion show, social networks, mono-brand store windows and advertising campaign.

Notes

1 This paragraph is based on the one described in the book *Fashion Business Model* (Golizia, 2016), chapter 3, paragraph 3.1.
2 This paragraph is based on the one described in the book *Fashion Business Model* (Golizia, 2016), chapter 3, paragraph 3.9.2.
3 This paragraph is based on the one described in the book *Fashion Business Model* (Golizia, 2016), chapter 3, paragraph 3.9.1.
4 For research purposes, Giorgio Armani and Dolce & Gabbana were considered.
5 The word refers to Instagram, whose name is the combination of *insta* – as instantaneous – and *gram* from Telegram. It means a quick posted image.
6 For Armani: Farfetch, Luisaviaroma, Yoox, Matches Fashion, Amazon (only fragrances), Ssense; for Ralph Lauren: Farfetch, Luisaviaroma, Yoox.

5

INDUSTRIAL FASHION BRANDS

Reading: the cool hunter

Cool hunters are young and curious people with an eye on current trends and able to antic-ipate future ones. Their role has become very important since marketing has transformed into *societing* (word resulting from the sum of marketing and sociology invented by Italian sociologist Giampaolo Fabris, 2009) and markets have become places of relation, symbolic exchange, experiences and consumption. Cool hunters wander around the city where each corner or person can represent a discovery and something innovative. Like detectives, they attentively observe streets, bars and clubs; they go to art galleries, theatres, concerts, all locations where creativity is expressed genuinely and spontaneously. They gather material of different typologies: photographs, leaflets, exhibitions and concerts programmes, as well as business cards and gadgets. The research encompasses fashion, design, communication, distribution, cosmetics, all industries characterised by a very high aesthetic content. Their work offers an interesting overview of what is happening in the world, phenomena con-nected to new distributive formats, successful products and cult personalities. Their task involves observing and documenting new trends emerging from the street and that will potentially spread and conquer the global market in the future. Thanks to cool hunters' work, companies can understand whether they are going in the right direction or they have to find new a strategic inspiration.

5.1 Who are they?

What connects such different companies like Liu Jo, Max&Co. and Guess? They are all per-ceived as designer brands even if they aren't. Three main characteristics may be pointed out: no designer, accessible luxury and the perceived quality being higher than the actual one.

The first, no designer, is the variable that differentiates them from historic and contem-porary brands: in fact, they were not founded by designers (e.g. Gianni Versace) or by a couturier (e.g. Christian Dior), but by entrepreneurs.

The second, accessible luxury, is a consequence of the first because, together with other variables, it compels them to be positioned between the second line of contemporary brands and fast fashion companies. However, despite this, thanks to accurate communication strategies, their perceived quality is superior to the actual one.

5.2 Style, by Antonio Patruno[1]

The heterogeneity of industrial brands is also found in their style. Pinko, Patrizia Pepe and Liu Jo are inspired by contemporary brands and address their collections to a target with an inferior spending power, interested in following the latest trends. Conversely, Guess is endowed with its own style obtained through the transformation of denim into a "noble" product; despite having a men's line, its imprint is always hyper-feminine, sensual and retro. Max&Co. is a female line, for a young dynamic target. Collections have a very creative fashion content linked to seasonal trends, with a very good price/quality ratio. Although experimental, clothing is never excessive in terms of volumes so as to always maximise the target audience's confidence and loyalty.

5.3 Supply chain and sustainability, in collaboration with Celeste Corso

The productive strategy changes according to brand.

Pinko, Patrizia Pepe, Liu Jo and Guess mostly produce by outsourcing. A medium-effective-quality product of medium-small size neither allows nor requires an in-house integration of production.

Conversely, for Max&Co., production is mostly direct and integrated; the brand owns manufacturing plants in Italy, even though a small part of apparel production is outsourced (in Italy and abroad). For all brands, fragrances and eyewear are produced and distributed by licensing.

By analysing the group of industrial brands, one notices something interesting. Their website is well-structured and appealing, and they organise events that embody professionalism and coherence, but what about sustainability?

Behind the scenes, brands are definitely discussing about it, but the impression is that these companies are not ready to act yet. Compared to the previous clusters, this one is moving at a different speed; it is surprising to notice how fast fashion brands, whose essence is in contrast with sustainability (as explained in Chapter 6), speak (and act) much more about it. The messages of sustainability communicated by these brands are diluted and whispered. Even though we do not doubt about their commitment, only sparse and sporadic information is provided. It is worth remembering the following initiatives.

Since 2015 Guess has published its sustainability report with the list of sustainable initiatives (Guess, 2020); MaxMara presented *CameLux*, a revolutionary and innovative padding obtained from the post-production waste of its most precious materials. Manufacturing boasts low energy and water consumption as well as low CO_2 emissions (Camera Moda, 2019).

5.4 Segmentation strategies

Segmentation strategies vary according to brand. The first to be analysed is Liu Jo, which has taken its first steps with a target and product-driven strategy: medium-quality knitwear designed for women. Later on, with the offer of new categories of merchandise, the strategy evolved into a target-driven (women) one. A further product, but mainly target, diversification extended to men and young girls and turned the strategy into an undifferentiated approach that still pivots around a feminine target. This proves what has been described, in paragraph 1.11, that is, for some companies it is difficult to build a strategic evolution embracing lifestyle if they haven't been founded by a designer; in fact, when they debut leveraging on a consolidated specialisation (in product and/or target), this aspect conditions the market and shapes their brand image.

Even Guess adopts an undifferentiated segmentation strategy addressed to a young market interested in the latest trends. Its consumers, characterised by medium spending power and aged between 16 and 35, look for a bold, eye-catching style and logo, rather than for product quality.

On the other hand, brands belonging to MaxMara Fashion Group implement a target-driven strategy, that is, they define and reach a target to whom they address a wide product offer; moreover, among these products, sometimes, there is one that particularly identifies the brand (MaxMara and its famous 101801 coat).

5.5 Brand

In this group, the majority of brands owe their success to a characterising product – jeans for Guess, knitwear for Liu Jo – on which they have built their identity and awareness. However, the product is relevant also for those which do not boast a well-defined product. These companies have become renowned thanks to the target of reference they identify with, generally young and trendy like Patrizia Pepe and Pinko's woman.

Over the years, these brands have followed a total-look strategy to be perceived as lifestyle brands; nevertheless, they have remained loyal to their DNA. They all applied a horizontal diversification by extending their product portfolio. Rare are the examples of vertical diversification: Max&Co. and Sport Max are second lines of the parent brand MaxMara. These second lines have achieved outstanding results thanks to the perfect blend of their parent brand reputation – MaxMara – and the new value proposition: inferior price and more informal use occasions. The merchandise range is expanding, even though it is not comparable to that of contemporary brands.

During an interview with the author, Riccardo Sciutto – former managing director at Hogan and currently CEO at Sergio Rossi – affirmed that the strict association with the original product or a specialisation in a target makes it difficult to reposition the company to a lifestyle one.

From some general considerations on the cluster, we move on to evaluate Pinko, Patriza Pepe and Liu Jo (the heterogeneity of the cluster makes it impossible to fully homogenise the topic under discussion).

These brands are characterised by products that are chiefly defined by intangible features (branding and perceived quality) rather than by tangible ones. Production is outsourced and raw materials aren't particularly good; hence, effective quality is medium-low. The choice of production delocalisation is almost mandatory to compete in a more and more crowded and less and less profitable segment. However, thanks to innovative communication campaigns, the perceived quality is higher than the effective, and the target of these brands perceives them as designer labels. These companies do not boast iconic products and consequently push the sales of seasonal items; however, being aware of their importance, they are investing many resources in representative products (e.g. jeans for Liu Jo)

Due to their recent establishment (in the 90s), it was impossible to build a strong bond with their country of origin. As a consequence, the latter is less relevant than for the brands discussed in the previous chapters. Despite the core business still being womenswear, they have added other categories of merchandise such as bags, glasses, watches, perfumes in order to acquire the status of lifestyle brands, as mentioned in the previous paragraph.

They were not named after their founders, but with pseudonyms: in fact, such a strategy would not add any value to the corporate or to the brands; the market doesn't perceive the name of an entrepreneur as valuable as that of a Creative Director to be worshipped.

5.6 Pricing, in collaboration with Benedetta Breschi

The brands that are the subject of this analysis have a clear positioning "between the mass market and the first and second lines of European designers" (Corbellini and Saviolo, 2009, p. 109).

A lower positioning as compared to second lines – as partially proven in Chapter 4 – depends on the intangible brand components and the tangible product characteristics. Speaking of the former, for a company established by an entrepreneur (rather than a creative

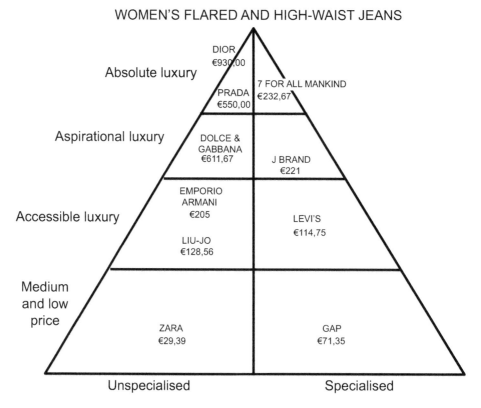

FIGURE 5.1 Golizia's pyramid of women's flared and high–waist jeans
Source: Prepared by Dario Golizia.

designer), the impossibility of relying on heritage, and not on iconic products, plays a crucial role. Among the latter, we find the usage of inferior-quality raw materials, mainly outsourced production and a creative content inspired by designer labels: a combination of these factors makes industrial brands to be perceived as inferior, as compared to second lines, and also lowers their prices.

Conversely, Liu Jo's price positioning is superior to that of fast fashion brands (for this cluster we consider Zara) in all product categories: plus 244.3% for the shopper, plus 157.2% for the blazer, plus 243% for sneakers, plus 337.4% for jeans, plus 415.8% for hoodies, plus 145.6% for formal men's suits and plus 341.4% for pumps. Nevertheless, these higher prices are not as much influenced by a better actual quality of the product as by a superior perceived value evoked. Industrial brands have invested in advertising campaigns and in prestigious fashion magazines (see paragraph 5.7.4.), and have connected their name to very famous top models; these actions allowed them to create a "superior" brand identity as compared to fast fashion brands. They are rethinking their identity, aiming at being seen as designer brands rather than as industrial brands (Golizia, 2016).

5.7 Communication

We now proceed with the definition of the image of the cluster; afterwards, we study how the marketing and communication function is organised and managed by a company from the same group. Finally, we outline the communication mix applied by some brands.

5.7.1 Cluster image

The most common words associated with these brands are accessible luxury, product specialisation, medium actual quality, medium/high perceived quality, entrepreneur-founder.

5.7.2 Marketing function and communication, in collaboration with Michele Leoni

Liu Jo, located in Carpi, the most important Italian knitwear district, was established by Marco Marchi, current Sole Administrator, 25 years ago. The marketing and communication office is coordinated by the Marketing and Communication Director who reports directly to the Sole Administrator. This department includes a team that is in charge of creating and communicating the brand identity (advertising campaigns, look-books, catalogues, etc.) and of coordinating external productions; moreover, they organise the presentation of collections to the retail network.

The marketing area also includes a digital and social media department as well as a public relations and CRM (customer relationship management) division. The former is in charge of all social media activities, with the support of specialised agencies, which include the editorial planning of the main social media (Instagram and Facebook), social media advertising, projects involving influencer marketing and the coordination of video contents production for social media (mainly Instagram). The Public Relations Department, with the support of eight external agencies, is responsible for the organisation of worldwide public relations activities: the main purpose is to gain editorial visibility with a focus on product and corporate. Finally, the CRM role is to implement and monitor customer relationship management systems, building activities that prioritise the customer.

The marketing office mainly works on the analysis and planning of advertising in different areas: print and online press, TV and Out of Home Advertising (OOH), retail marketing and in-store activities, from the concept to the actual creation, with the help of consultancy agencies and in accordance with the company guidelines. Events planning for the customers of the boutique is also considered.

5.7.3 Fashion shows and trade fairs, in collaboration with Andrea Doroldi

This cluster is divided into two. On the one hand, we find brands like MaxMara that present their collections organising fashion shows. On the other hand, we have Liu Jo, Pinko and Patrizia Pepe that do not employ this methodology and did not participate in Mipel and Pitti Immagine in 2019 and 2020.[2]

Concerning the second group, the brands' showrooms (initially Milan's), in collaboration with the PR offices, arrange those events aimed at presenting collections to the sales force, to buyers and to influencers; the budget and the resources are significantly inferior as compared to those of the previously examined brands.

Some brands design ad hoc pieces to participate in the Salone del Mobile, yet always in the *Fuori Salone*, even if they do not have an interior design line. In 2018, MaxMara, together with the Safilo Group, presented a limited edition of sunglasses made by German artist Kerstin Bratsch and by the duo United Brothers.

5.7.4 Advertising, editorial, advertorial, in collaboration with Benedetta Breschi

In the 2019 edition, Max&Co. was added to the brands examined in the previous research (2016) – Liu Jo, Patrizia Pepe and Pinko. Max&Co. replaced MaxMara whose strategic logics are more similar to those of luxury brands, rather than to the one of bridge brands. As for the three clusters examined in the previous chapters, we can highlight how the three brands studied in both research studies in 2019 decreased their investments in advertising pages by 57.5%, as compared to 2015. Speaking of the 2019 research, the group, on the whole, is third in ranking for purchased advertising pages (first in 2015), above contemporary brands. However, despite buying 63.6% more advertising pages compared to contemporary brands, the group is dedicated 70.3% less to fashion editorials. This proves its inferior influence when compared to other brands enjoying more brand awareness and a strong distinctive positioning.

TABLE 5.1 Advertising, fashion editorial and advertorials of industrial brands

Industrial Brands	L'Officiel			Vogue			Vanity Fair			Elle			Glamour			Total		
	A	FE	AD	A	FE	AD	A	FE	AD	A	FE	AD	A	FE	AD	A	FE	AD
Liu Jo	1	0	0	2	2	1	1	1	0	3	0	1	1	2	1	8	5	3
Patrizia Pepe	0	0	0	2	0	0	1	1	0	0	0	0	0	0	0	3	1	0
Pinko	0	0	0	2	1	0	0	0	0	0	0	1	1	1	1	3	2	2
Max&Co.	0	0	0	0	0	0	0	0	0	0	0	0	0	0	0	0	0	0
Total	**1**	**0**	**0**	**6**	**3**	**1**	**2**	**2**	**0**	**3**	**0**	**2**	**2**	**3**	**2**	**14**	**8**	**5**

Source: Authors' data processing on the basis of fashion magazines published in Italy in September 2019. A, FE and AD stand for advertising, fashion editorial and advertorial, respectively.

5.7.5 Influencers, gifting, endorsement, by Lavinia Biancalani

Driven by the desire to increase their awareness, industrial brands invested considerably in digital and influencer marketing. Aware of the impossibility of leveraging either on the same values as luxury brands or on fast fashion prices, social media are used to gain market shares among a young target with an inferior spending power. Often lacking in a solid communication structure, many brands rely on external agencies for the management of traditional, but most of all, digital communication.

MaxMara Fashion Group is a benchmark because it owns brands with different positioning and strategies.

The leader brand, MaxMara, aspiring to a high-end set of values, delayed its approach to influencer marketing like historic brands. The recent opening to this strategy relies on a long-term activity based on *friends-of-the-house* influencers, invites to fashion shows, gifting and sometimes tours in the headquarter and production plants in Reggio Emilia. Occasionally, for content creation a long-term collaboration leads to one-off collaborations. Consistent with its high-end brand positioning, fashion influencers and personalities like Bryan Grey Jambao and Olivia Palermo are usually invited to Milan fashion shows and to the cities where MaxMara presents its pre-collections.

In 2019, Max&Co. announced a strategy change, mainly in terms of product and retail concept. At the same time, during the September 2019 fashion week, the brand organised a party in its Milanese store inviting several influencers and models with many followers such as Olivia Palermo, *international style ambassador* for Max&Co. Even though Elia Maramotti, Max&Co. brand director, hadn't mentioned to the press the new digital communication strategies, since 2019, the brand has increased the presence of influencers and celebrities on its Instagram profile.

The strategy adopted by the other brands of MaxMara Fashion Group (Marella, iBlues and Pennyblack) is significantly different and responds to the cluster trend to more aggressively embrace projects of influencer marketing, in line with its positioning. The plan focuses on long-term projects where several influencers are chosen for different targets – simultaneously with the launch of the collection – and always as content creators. For example, #MarellaGirls – an ongoing project that gathers influencers associated to the brand – saw the collaboration of, among others, Taylor LaShae, Alessia Bossi and Lucia Serafini from Wearelovers.it.

The American brand Guess was definitely a pioneer of influencer marketing, applying the strategy in advance compared to other players of the cluster and using unusual methods. In 2012, before other brands, Guess Jeans had promoted on Pinterest a project named *Color Me Inspired* with the participation of influencers – at the time known as fashion bloggers – Kristina Bazan from Kayture, Michelle Koesnadi from Glisters and Blisters, Jennifer Rand from Belle De Couture and Samantha Hutchinson from Could I Have That. Through a call to action, users were asked to create their board inspired by some key colours of the seasonal denim collection; the prize was a $500 Guess coupon. In 2018, Guess announced a partnership with TikTok, a social network specialising in the creation of short and viral video clips. From 1 until 6 September, the Guess challenge (this is the name of the video routines proposed by TikTok users) known as #InMyDenim was sponsored and users were redirected to it when opening the social network. A group of very influential TikTokers were invited to participate in the challenge to increase the reach. By means of a constant indirect endorsement (which means without payment) known on Instagram through the hashtag #LoveGUESS, the brand promotes the cross-posting of contents created by influencers that wear its garments and repost them on their channel.

Moreover, Patrizia Pepe has recently boosted its influencer marketing strategy starting project *Patrizia Pepe 4P*, through which some of its global ambassadors were hired to create social network contents and to sign limited edition capsule collections. Among them, Evangeline Smyrniotaki, known as Styleheroine, created contents for social networks and a pair of earrings. The push on the collection is also supported by *adv* contents for which local ambassadors like Veronica Ferraro, Rocky Barnesare and others were hired. One-off collaborations with several influencers are gathered under the hashtag #PatriziaPepeGang and include single projects with Beatrice Valli, Chiara Nasti and others.

5.7.6 Social media

MaxMara is active on Instagram and Facebook, the main communication platforms, but it also reaches its audience through Twitter and YouTube. The typology of contents is adapted to the formats of each channel. Several actions such as collection presentations, launches of products or specific focuses on one category of merchandise (e.g. accessories, bags and the iconic coat) share the same goals: to communicate the brand identity and the product. Prominent visibility is provided to street style photos, which direct the attention to the fashion week, to the guests sitting in the front row and to the backstage of the fashion show, without forgetting the garments showcased on the catwalk. Not only the product but also the brand lifestyle, the communication of events and special projects with the participation of influencers and international celebrities are portrayed. Contents follow a very accurate editorial aesthetic. The Facebook page is fed through the contents posted on Instagram with which it shares the same editorial plan and the posting of ad hoc topics. However, Facebook is also dedicated to specific contents such as the live chat with a personal stylist who answers the users' questions and gives fashion advice. On Twitter, the company posts shared contents in accordance with its editorial plan, whereas on YouTube it gathers the videos of the campaign and those dedicated to specific projects, like *Max Mara World*, which witnesses the opening of new stores or events with the participation of celebrities and brand ambassadors.

Guess has been one of the first brands to start a marketing campaign on TikTok, well-aware of the appeal of the new platform among Generation Z. The brand is, in fact, trying to reposition itself on this target and in 2018 started a series of collaborations with niche streetwear brands like the London-based Places+Faces. The success on TikTok was confirmed by more than 38 million views for the *#inMyDenim* challenge, which has become a benchmark. Guess is also active on Facebook and Instagram with an accurate aesthetic, but closer to the concept of real life appreciated by a younger target. To dialogue with this audience, Guess has also chosen to communicate with simple and straightforward captions conceived for new generations who have the lowest attention threshold – they almost don't read texts – and that are constantly stimulated by advertising. The label has also signed several collaborations with talents and celebrities; generally speaking, the brand privileges photos to videos.

Patrizia Pepe has been among the first to use social networks. In the last few years, the brand has managed to build a good relationship with its community, bearing in mind a well-remembered crisis caused by a mistake of the Community Manager. In 2011, the latter aggressively reacted to the words of two fans who had criticised the excessive thinness of the model in the advertising campaign posted on Facebook. The controversy has become a *worst* case. However, the brand was able to gain from the experience and benefit from it and, after apologising, started to build a well-defined identity, based also on the relationship with influencers, celebrities and brand ambassadors. In 2013, Patrizia Pepe was among the first to design a capsule collection with blogger Chiara Biasi and, recently, to sign a collaboration with Evangelie Smyrniotaki. Instagram follows an editorial plan based on aesthetics, with a focus on the product – almost always worn – and on lifestyle; moreover, all its contents are produced specifically for the channel. Facebook is often used for the sharing of contents (links to interviews of the brand owners, collaborations etc.) and is characterised by a more exhaustive tone of voice, whereas Twitter is less employed. Moreover, in 2017, Patrizia Pepe was among the first to open a profile on Musical.ly, currently known as TikTok and to collaborate with TikTokers to reach Generation Z.

The purpose of analysing brands is to raise interest in the brand, not only to work on brand awareness and identity but also to generate traffic in online and brick-and-mortar stores.

MaxMara works on brand awareness stressing the history of the company, as well as its collections and iconic products. To do so, the label starts conversations on social media about events and specific activities. *Women empowerment* is one of the values promoted by the company by means of events like the *Art Prize for Women*, which rewards the work of young women artists. Moreover, MaxMara invests in scholarships for the education of new generations of professionals, specific roles that require an excellent training.

Guess' social media strategy is aimed at reaching Generation Z. To do so, the brand tells its story in lifestyle and product-focused contents. Positioning seems to be the first objective, besides the desire to increase online and offline sales. Moreover, the brand introduced *Guess Eco*, a sustainable jeans collection, to be aligned with the interests of new generations.

Among its communication goals, Patrizia Pepe includes the usage of new social media channels to intercept Millennials and the younger generation Z. If we consider this cluster, the brand has been a precursor of the web: it has been among the first to exploit the visibility of influencers and brand personalities and to invest in digital and social contents. Its innovative digital approach represents one of its main communication leverages.

5.7.7 Sponsorships and co-branding

Most of the brands of this cluster rely less on sponsorships and co-branding, as compared to the companies examined in the previous chapters. These labels organise events in partnership with local organisations and artists due to their inferior economic and financial resources and to their less widespread distribution network.

For instance, Liu Jo is the main sponsor of the Bologna football team, whereas, in 2017 Patrizia Pepe sponsored the event *Settembre Prato è Spettacolo* and Pinko endorsed *Football Leader 2017.*

MaxMara, instead, like the companies studied in the previous chapters, organises the *Max Mara Art Prize for Women* aimed at strengthening its image of a luxury brand. Hence the choice to support young UK artists and to stress once again its international status and the bond with the world of art and its exclusively feminine target.

Co-branding actions follow the same pattern. While Guess and Pinko collaborate with niche sportswear brands – Invicta and Burton, respectively – MaxMara chiefly cooperates with artists (Liu Wei, Shantell Martin) for the above-discussed reason. Liu Jo-Candiani Denim is an interesting case because it represents a first step towards the issue of sustainability, with a focus on denim, the core product.

5.7.8 Museums, foundations and leisure time activities, in collaboration with Andrea Pittana

The characterising element of the brands of this cluster is the lack of significant historic contents; this aspect oriented their strategy towards a more contemporary focus. On the one hand, we find Guess, which established a foundation to support projects in harmony with its values, on the other, we find the remaining brands, which did not develop any activity of this type and are still relying on traditional touch points like shops whose content is the product.

Guess opened the *Marciano Art Foundation*, a permanent exhibiting space located in Los Angeles. The place shares with an international audience the value and importance of contemporary art. However, the brand hasn't created any leisure time activity suitable only for companies endowed with a very extended product portfolio and that intend to transmit a lifestyle. In this case, the company, despite diversifying in many product categories, is still characterised by an original-product-based image, jeans, and is reluctant to distance itself from its strategic origin.

Conversely, Liu Jo and Patriza Pepe haven't developed any significant initiative in terms of foundations, museums and leisure time activities. The reason must be found in the considerable investments made in product diversification and direct distribution, whose profit will be collected only in the long term. At present, any investment in different strategies would be useless.

5.8 Distribution, in collaboration with Andrea Doroldi

Being a rather heterogeneous group, the distribution strategies of the cluster of industrial brands vary from company to company. A common characteristic is, instead, the stores' location, which is rather heterogeneous. For instance, in Milan, they all have a shop in a prestigious fashion district (Pinko in Via Montenapoleone) or in its proximity (Max&Co. in Corso Vittorio Emanuele, Guess in Piazza San Babila); but the mono-brand stores are also located in other areas of the city (never in the periphery): the aim is to reach a more extended target compared to that of designer labels.

Pinko has a total of 256 shops worldwide – either directly managed or in franchising. The number of mono-brand stores and the choice of their location differ from those of historic brands: in Milan, for instance, the company has its own shop-in-shop at La Rinascente, and six mono-brand stores, whose location is heterogeneous – located in Via Montenapolene – as if the label wanted to claim its place among the "big" of fashion – in the high street Corso Vittorio Emanuele, in the fashion street Corso Como, in the residential area of Via Belfiore, in the central Via Ponte Vetero and in Linate airport. Moreover, the company distributes in more than 1,000 multi-brand boutiques of medium level whose assortment consists of commercial brands for a target with medium spending power. They offer a renowned brand to a big audience for an accessible price.

The MaxMara Fashion Group, encompassing numerous brands, counts on more than 10,000 multi-brand and 2,668 points of sale comprising mono-brand shops and shops-in-shop in department stores; in Milan, some are positioned next to each other – MaxMara, Max&Co., Sport Max, Marella, Marina Rinaldi and Penny Black – in Corso Vittorio Emanuele, a few metres away from the famous fashion district; Max&Co., having six shops in Milan, sells, differently from Pinko, only in mono-brand stores or in shop-in-shops, as well as in its e-commerce (mono-brand and platforms/marketplaces).

The ex-jeanswear brand, Guess, boasts amazing figures: 1,169 direct mono-brand stores and 183 concessions. Moreover, with the help of some external partners, it has also opened 560 mono-brand stores and 211 concessions. In Milan, the flagship store is located in Piazza San Babila, a place where heritage and innovation flow into each other. The brand is also present in Corso Buenos Aires, the most "fast fashion street" in town, and in the popular Central Station, and Via Torino.

We now consider Pinko's and Patrizia Pepe's online strategy. These brands have their own e-commerce where the whole assortment is available. They are present on online platforms, but only on three of them, and they are both are available on Farfetch, Yoox and Amazon. The remaining platforms – being more specialised in high-end products – do not comprise industrial brands. The most available categories of product are ready-to-wear – the core business – and leather goods. If we compare the price of a product on their e-commerce to the one of Farfetch, we see that Pinko can impose the same price, whereas Patrizia Pepe's price on the platform is slightly inferior. They both allow for the purchase with mobile devices thanks to a responsive design.

5.9 Omnichannel, in collaboration with Sabrina Pomodoro and Benedetta Breschi

Among industrial brands, Max&Co. results as the only brand that adopts an integrated communication approach, even though the inspiration of the collection and the integrating factor of promotional activities is just a stylistic element and not an actual concept. For this reason, the integration can be defined as *collection-led integration*. In particular, the leitmotif element is red: it is found in the shop windows, in the collection and in the red tag applied to the cocktails served during the presentation event, as well as in the colour of the invite to the event, posted on the Instagram page.

Unlike Max&Co., Liu Jo, for its fall-winter 2019/2020 collection, demonstrated a total absence of integration: the advertising campaign was shot in a studio without a specific setting and the Instagram page presents a campaign that is different from those published in magazines.

The same strategy was followed by Patrizia Pepe and Pinko. The former, despite presenting a sensual and provocative woman set in natural scenarios in its advertising campaigns, does not portray the same character on its Instagram page. Moreover, the outfits shot in the campaign are not the same displayed in the shop windows. Also, in Pinko stores, maxi-led screens broadcast the images of the fall-winter 2019/2020 collection; however, no direct connections with either the Instagram page or the advertising campaign – which seems to have been shot in a studio – were identified.

Interview with Anna Baschirotto, global Marketing and Communication Director at Liu Jo spa

What are the essential characteristics of your product?
Liu Jo's collections are wide and diversified; they are designed to satisfy numerous daily needs and occasions of use of contemporary women. Our mantra is *body booster, ego booster*: empowering women by making them feel beautiful.

How is the competitive scenario in which Liu Jo competes evolving?
In the premium segment where we compete, only brands offering a clear product proposal, and an evolved quality and service, inclusive of brand experience, are keeping their positioning without being beaten by fast fashion.

How are you facing the challenge of new consumers (Millennials, Generation Z)?
The consideration of new consumers is at the base of all our ideas and strategies: the choice of endorsers, CRM, influencer marketing, and the pivotal role of social media.

How is Liu Jo facing the sustainability challenge?
The company is acquiring new competencies and has chosen its iconic product – denim – to launch campaigns and messages that can sensitise our consumers.

How have brand communication levers changed?
Investments have become fragmented because targets and niches of consumers are much differentiated and do not blend. Print press has inevitably decreased to the advantage of digital communication and social media where the overcrowded space compels to do better and better to gain visibility.

Do you think that prices in Liu Jo's competitive segment may vary in the close future?
At the moment, I have no evidence of future considerable variations of price.

How are distributive strategies evolving?
Omnichannel is a fact, a premise to be made when discussing consumers. A strong brand must start from customer relationship, independently from the logics of the channel. E-commerce will always be pivotal as well as in-store experience. The new luxury offers many opportunities to premium brands: we need ideas, contaminations and stories.

Is having a defined business model essential?
It is fundamental. We've just launched our new business model based on a structural change and on new collection timing: from a classic two-launch model, to one based on simple drops, and more aligned with the market needs. Our unique and distinctive identity is our strength, the feeling of belonging of our tribe of consumers and the central role of communication.

Student activities

Choose a brand and based on your choice:

- define the sustainability actions to be applied in the future;
- identify the combination product/price segment/target where to diversify;

- identify a social media and the content typology to be developed;
- define which of the following formats – brick-and-mortar mono-brand store, brick-and-mortar multi-brand store, shop-in-shop in department stores, online mono-brand shop and online multi-brand platform – need to be developed the most;
- verify the degree of synergy among the aesthetic elements of the latest collection: the fashion show, social networks, mono-brand store windows and advertising campaign.

Notes

1 This paragraph is based on the one described in the book *Fashion Business Model* (Golizia, 2016), chapter 4, paragraph 4.9.2.
2 Patrizia Pepe and Liu Jo participated in Pitti in January 2019, with the kidswear collection only.

6

FAST FASHION BRANDS

Reading: the patternmaker

The patternmaker is a fashion professional who is in charge of bringing the designer's sketches to life. They have the pivotal role of mediating between the ideas of the creative department and the techniques applied by the production department. Their main function is to create a pattern (subsequently used to make the prototype), which must satisfy and combine the creativity of the designer, the wearability of the garment and the economic restrictions (Zinola, 2011). The patternmaker is also in charge of creating the different sizes, that is, of replicating the basic pattern into several sizes without modifying its wearability and aesthetic. This professional is curious, creative and endowed with an extensive knowledge of collections: their role is pivotal, even though they are never in the limelight. They possess tailoring skills, artisanal skills and, with the arrival of new software, also computer competences. They are very meticulous, almost like surgeons, when it comes to measuring and creating all the different components of a garment. They rarely work as freelancers and are chiefly employed by fashion houses: in this case, team-work skills are necessary since they need to collaborate with the designer and the production department, for following the entire cycle.

6.1 Who are they?[1]

Fast fashion brands have redesigned the boundaries of the fashion industry in the past 20 years. Despite their deep roots, their success is not based on heritage, but on new millennium customers who love changing, playing multiple roles and showing their multifaceted self. Fast fashion brands have taken advantage of the needs of the new consumer and, thanks to the multiple economic crisis of the past 20 years, they have transformed their small anonymous companies into billion-euro leaders. Thanks to their supersonic rapidity in capturing trends and producing garments displayed in their stores, scattered all around the globe, they can satisfy, with accessible prices and up-to-date outfits, a transversal market. A short time to market allows them to deliver new products to stores (almost) weekly: hence the replacement of the two classic fashion collections a year by many micro-collections, distributed and sold according to the changing taste and needs of customers. By increasing the frequency of the issuing of new items and by reducing the variety of products in basic collections, Benetton can understand consumers' trends faster and better plan its offer (Camuffo, Romani and Vinelli, 2002). Zara and H&M are the undisputed leaders.

6.2 Style, by Diana Murek[2]

Even for fast fashion brands, style depends on the adopted strategies and in particular on the number of brands owned by the controlling group and the consequent need for differentiation. For instance, those brands belonging to the Inditex group have different creative strategies. Zara's style is strongly influenced by trends and changes considerably from season to season, whereas Massimo Dutti is relatively loyal to its Ralph Lauren-inspired fashion. The same style differentiation may be identified in Swedish groups: H&M offers seasonal trend-driven looks, whereas COS portrays a well-defined minimal style. Substantially, there are brands that vary their style according to seasonal trends, while others are bound to a defined style that is interpreted each year on the basis of trends, but that always preserve their basic features: for instance, Pull&Bear, bound to a young streetstyle expressed in collections composed by the same typologies of garments, is generally hyper-printed and trendy.

6.3 Supply chain and sustainability, in collaboration with Celeste Corso

The productive strategy of fast fashion brands is based on efficiency and decentralisation. Production doesn't take place in their own plants but is outsourced to suppliers in countries with a low labour cost. This, in turn, diminishes investments to the minimum and allows price reduction and sales increase. The need is to have a faster, more flexible and efficient supply chain.

Supply chain control is high even though the production is outsourced. However, it is not exercised through the (partial) ownership of production plants – as in the case of contemporary and some historic and industrial brands – but by means of a "strong persuasive power" that such big companies can impose on suppliers. The latter are compelled to accept their rules: fast fashion companies, in fact, state a price of the service to guarantee an adequate margin to sub-suppliers (Sabbadin, 1997).

In this context, logistics represents a crucial factor: it generates a virtual circle of connection between stores and productive plants and allows for the maximisation of companies' effectiveness and efficiency. Logistics is the core of fast fashion and is endowed with an information system that collects all the data of the stores to better plan production and deliveries. Since logistics is a pivotal function, it is not outsourced, but directly managed by the company.

Hyper-production and hyper-consumption have always been the mantra of fast fashion. Every week, new products are delivered to stores to enrich and update the offer and convince the customer to purchase more and more. What about sustainability then? How can we put together such opposite concepts? Hyper-recycling is a dream that does not contemplate the difficulty of requalifying garments made with blends of different fibres. It detaches form the idea of circular economy based on product recycling. In an industry where everything is *hyper*, consuming less and applying the principles of sustainability is complex. Despite this, the players of this segment are very active in this sense.

For instance, H&M dedicates to sustainability a section of its website where sustainable goals are stated and data and annual reports are supplied. In alignment with these principles, H&M, Mango, Zara and Uniqlo have already developed their conscious collections. Even the Inditex group informs customers on sustainability by listing the fields of action involved in its programme. Like H&M, Zara designs *Join Life*, a collection made with sustainable materials and collect, in some of their stores, second-hand garments to be recycled or donated to no-profit associations (Inditex, 2020). Likewise, Benetton incorporates, in its sustainability plan, goals, data and reports, as well as a series of actions to safeguard the planet (Benetton, 2020).

Gap, instead, created the Personal Advancement & Career Enhancement (PACE) programme, to support women workers in the fashion industry. The brand also collaborates with the *Ellen Mc Arthur Foundation* to produce materials with a low loss of micro-plastics, which are highly polluting for the sea and dangerous for the marine fauna (Gap, 2020).

6.4 Segmentation strategies

Unlike historic and contemporary brands – for which it doesn't make sense to talk about segmentation strategy in the classic sense of the word, as they apply a lifestyle approach – fast fashion brands implement a traditional undifferentiated segmentation plan. Concerning the product, its offer is wide: apparel – inclusive of several categories (formalwear, casualwear, streetwear and underwear) – shoes, bags, fragrances and other accessories. Zara and H&M also offer items, like home collection products, that don't belong to fashion. Their market is very extended and one of the most transversal in the fashion industry.

6.5 Brand

The fast fashion approach to branding is totally different. In fact, the main factors contributing to success are low price for a high fashion content, a regular assortment of new products in the shops, a wide product range and medium/low actual quality, a simple but winning marketing recipe, which has compensated for the lack of history, of a famous designer to "show off", and of iconic products to exhibit. Price is discussed in the following paragraph, while style content has already been analysed. We now focus on the constant turnover of new items on the shelves. According to Sabbadin (1997), in the 90s Benetton was among the first to radically change the structure of collections. One typology is the "traditional" collection, which constitutes the majority of garments, that encompasses carryovers and seasonal items. The remaining part includes the so-called flash products, a series of garments presented in the stores, in the middle of the season, to keep pace with new consumption trends. Inditex, which controls Zara, has perfected and speeded up Benetton's model: it can restock its shops with new mini-collections 1.5 times a week. This strategy generates a higher traffic in the stores: the customer is attracted by new trendy items and impulsively purchases them for accessible prices.

Another characteristic is the extended variety of the offer, mainly reached by the two leader labels, through the from-scratch creation of brands. The same goal is sometimes achieved through the acquisition of companies.

However, it is important to start by saying that from the beginning, most fast fashion brands – unlike designer labels, which debuted with a specialised product range – have offered a wide assortment. In the course of time, the same product range has expanded more and more. According to Badia (2011), the idea of opening new chains of stores to address specific targets, different from Zara's, is aligned with the main goal of the group: growth. Inditex is a significant case: Zara is the original brand and also first in terms of store number and sales; the group decided to add and create from scratch new brands such as Pull&Bear, Bershka, Oysho, Zara Home and Uterqüe. In contrast, Massimo Dutti and Stradivarius were acquired. Each brand has their own product-market combination. For instance, Oysho was launched to enter the underwear segment, and Massimo Dutti to diversify in medium-level formal menswear. A similar strategy was implemented by the other leader brand that launched COS to reach a more sophisticated target – compared to H&M – and acquired Cheap Monday to access the jeanswear segment.

Speaking about the naming strategy, we can observe how, as in the case of industrial brands, and for the same reasons, their names are pseudonyms rather than those of their founders. Moreover, in the case of Inditex, the name of the founder, the name of the corporate and the name of brands are totally detached. The founder's name, Ortega, does not correspond either to the corporate name, Inditex, or to the original brand, Zara. Even the subsequently established labels bear different names. The only brand extension is epitomised by Zara Home, justified by the need to swiftly acquire shares in the home decoration market. The name was chosen to benefit from the association with the parent brand and its high awareness (AAker, 1991).

In brief, the actual quality is generally medium or medium-low, depending on the brand. This factor is irrelevant for the consumer who is prevalently looking for a high stylistic content for a medium-low price. However, in order to improve their perceived quality, these brands are investing many resources in communication (see following paragraphs).

None of them boasts a famous Creative Director, recognised by the market and able to add value to the company. Many designers are employed to draw thousands and thousands of styles, which embody the latest trends, every year. On the contrary, H&M with its capsule collections, has associated its name with the most famous personalities and brands of the fashion system: from Karl Lagerfeld to Maison Margiela. For these companies, the country of origin is irrelevant. Zara is among the few to offer a customisation service in some selected stores and for few items.

6.6 Pricing, in collaboration with Benedetta Breschi

Until the end of the 90s, the medium-low apparel segment was chiefly occupied by unbranded companies that offered a basic-styled product. Consumers were compelled to spend considerable amounts of money to buy trendy garments. In the last 20 years, the scenario has changed. Fast fashion brands have identified this gap in the mass market segment and have bridged it by proposing a product system whose competitive advantage leverages on high brand awareness, up-to-date style and accessible price.

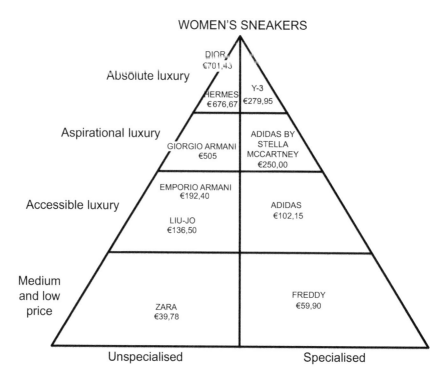

FIGURE 6.1 Golizia's pyramid of women's sneakers
Source: Prepared by Dario Golizia.

For (almost) every company, discussing pricing without considering the variable of communication is very hard. But the fast fashion brands make this bond strong and explicit. For instance, H&M, in the first two pages of its 2013 annual report, before the table of contents, made its low price strategy explicit showing two products and their respective prices (Golizia, 2016).

It has already been demonstrated and argued, in Chapter 5, that Zara's price positioning compared to the industrial brand Liu Jo is lower for all product categories.

Among the companies of this cluster, the Swedish group is an interesting case for this topic. It has applied a two-pronged strategy: on the one hand, it has increased the maximum price of H&M with capsule collections designed by renowned designers; on the other hand, it has launched a new brand, COS, inspired by Jil Sander, and having a higher positioning than H&M's capsule collections. For instance, the maximum price of an H&M T-shirt, that of an H&M T-shirt from the 2020 capsule collection by Gianbattista Valli and that of COS are, respectively, €12.99, €29.99 and €35. So, the group manages, albeit in the medium–low segment, to reach different targets by means of different prices.

6.7 Communication

We now proceed with the definition of the image of the cluster; afterwards, we study how the marketing and communication function is organised and managed by a company from the same group. Finally, we outline the communication mix applied by some brands.

6.7.1 Cluster image

Speed, medium/low price, trendy products, numerous mono-brand stores, many new products, periodical deliveries all define fast fashion brands.

6.7.2 Marketing function and communication, in collaboration with Michele Leoni

The headquarters of H&M's marketing and communication is located in Stockholm, and in every region it is supported by a press office reporting to the central department.

In Italy, H&M owns both a Press/Communication and a Marketing Office. The first is managed by the Director of the Italian Press Office who, with their team, is in charge of corporate brand communication and of the projects promoted by the Swedish Headquarters (e.g. collaborations with fashion brands and store openings). The Editorial Manager reports to the Director of the Press Office who, with their team, is responsible for the samples supplied to the shootings to be published on magazines. In Italy, H&M has opened its Marketing Office, which reports to the Swedish one.

The marketing department deals with the management of the numerous campaigns organised for the crucial commercial events of the brand and/or for the collaboration with interesting personalities of the fashion system. The acquisition of advertising spaces is coordinated by an external media centre. The H&M marketing department also encompasses the internal communication office – in charge of promoting the main projects and of communicating eventual news among employees – and the events office which, in collaboration with external agencies, works on the planning of international and local events.

6.7.3 Fashion shows and trade fairs, in collaboration with Andrea Doroldi

Fast fashion brands do not participate in traditional fashion weeks since, as already stressed, the latter are the source of inspiration for the design of their collections. Some events of this type were organised in the past: for instance, Top Shop presented its spring-summer 2017 collection during the London fashion week, whereas the following year H&M took part in the Paris fashion week.

The analysed brands – H&M, Zara, Mango, Benetton, Gap – did not take part in the Mipel and Pitti Immagine 2019 and 2020 editions.

Since all these brands exclusively use mono-brand stores (direct and indirect), they do not need trade fairs to present their collections to the buyers of multi-brand stores. In fact, they apply different digital tools (without samples and show rooms) quite significantly to showcase their product assortments to franchising partners, whereas for Directly Operated Store (DOS), they simply decide the assortments in their headquarters. Sometimes they organise in-store events: on the occasion of the launch of its *Conscious Collection*, H&M organised an event in its stores of Milan and Los Angeles with the participation of numerous journalists and influencers (Scafati, 2019).

Another interesting experience is Zara's participation in Milan's Salone del Mobile in 2019 (always in the *Fuori Salone*). In order to launch its sustainable *Join Life* collection, the brand displayed in its flagship store an installation that celebrated the concept of infinite multiplication of recycled material/waste produced by man.

6.7.4 Advertising, editorial, advertorial, in collaboration with Benedetta Breschi

In order to examine the same number of brands for each cluster, Gap and Top Shop – included with H&M, Zara, Benetton and Mango in the previous research (Golizia, 2016) – have been excluded from the analysis. As in the case of previous groups, in 2019, even fast fashion brands bought fewer advertising pages compared to 2015 – 50% less – thus being sixth in ranking. It is worth highlighting how, among the four brands, only Benetton and Mango made this type of investment, while Zara and H&M did not purchase a single advertising page, the former being naturally unwilling to invest in advertising, the latter preferring billboards.

6.7.5 Influencers, gifting, endorsement, by Lavinia Biancalani

At first, fast fashion brands did not resort to structured advertising campaigns for their online communication. The change in the competitive scenario, where both online and mono-brand stores are not enough anymore, persuaded them to modify their strategy. Instagram feeds have become a quick and simple shopping experience to purchase items worn by celebrities and influencers for accessible prices.

H&M has always used social networks with its institutional profiles (Instagram, Facebook, YouTube, etc.), but only lately has it organised more structured influencer marketing campaigns with long-term projects prevailing over one-time actions. High-profile celebrities and influencers like Irina Shayk and Dakota Fanning, who generally collaborate with luxury brands, have been involved in specific projects like the launch of the *H&M Conscious Collection*. Even H&M has begun to recognise the value of influencers and content creators in the planning of well-organised social media projects. In 2019, H&M created an international team of 22 content creators – the #HMLeague – to work on social media contents for the promotion of its collections.

Benetton and its ethical advertising campaigns of the 80s and 90s, for an entire age, influenced our ethics emphasising the brand values rather than the product. On the web, the company relies on social networks to showcase its collections and applies an editorial plan that goes at the same pace as the more structured digital projects. In 2019, web personalities like Valentina Ferragni and Alessandra Airò documented, through their social media, the spring-summer 2020 fashion show.

TABLE 6.1 Advertising, fashion editorial and advertorials of fast fashion brands

Fast Fashion Brands	L'Officiel			Vogue			Vanity Fair			Elle			Glamour			Total		
	A	FE	AD	A	FE	AD	A	FE	AD	A	FE	AD	A	FE	AD	A	FE	AD
Zara	0	0	0	0	0	0	0	0	0	0	0	0	0	0	0	0	0	0
H&M	0	0	0	0	0	0	0	1	0	0	0	0	0	1	0	0	2	0
Benetton	0	0	0	2	4	0	0	0	0	0	2	1	0	1	0	2	4	0
Mango	0	0	0	2	0	0	0	0	0	0	0	1	0	0	1	2	0	0
Total	**0**	**0**	**0**	**4**	**4**	**0**	**0**	**1**	**0**	**0**	**2**	**2**	**0**	**2**	**1**	**4**	**6**	**0**

Source: Authors' data processing on the basis of fashion magazines published in Italy in September 2019. A, FE and AD stand for advertising, fashion editorial and advertorial, respectively.

Mango employs all social networks with extreme accuracy: contents are clearly written and conceived for the web and stand out for their plain and effective social media language. Its strategy became evident when, in 2015 and 2016, the digital public relation activities included a fortunate collaboration with Kendall Jenner and invented a new way to communicate on social media. In fact, the brand chose to promote its collections through many micro launches entrusted to several ambassadors, and by posting on its channels new contents every second week: an innovative social media strategy for that time. With some of them, Mango has built an ongoing relationship: Leandra Medine, founder of website Man Repeller, who, in 2019, signed a limited edition capsule collection.

Zara is the only brand of this cluster that does not consider social media as indispensable for the company. The brand owns social media channels as well as one of the most successful online stores, but, traditionally, a low percentage of revenues are invested in communication. In Italy, except for some events, the brand does not employ influencers to work on structured projects. In fact, it is influencers who voluntarily buy the company's garments.

6.7.6 Social media

Even though these brands employ the same social media – in particular Instagram and Facebook – Zara and H&M, the subject of the following analysis, apply different strategies.

Zara's feed is so professional that it may be confused with that of a high-end brand. Posts mainly display ad hoc contents for social media. The brands of this cluster publish numerous contents daily to offer suggestions on future trends and to inform on the latest offers. Very-high-quality videos make the profile fascinating and attract the attention of consumers also from an artistic point of view.

Even H&M posts advice on new products and recent trends; however, the attitude is less distant compared to Zara's and more typical of mass market companies. In fact, sometimes H&M reposts users' contents (in jargon known as #regram).

All the players share the same purposes: usability, clarity and the possibility to easily recognise and buy the product. However, every brand pursues different and specific objectives.

Zara leverages on users' brand experience, which is "nourished" as if followers were its own influencers; the company also encourages followers to promote word of mouth. Professor Kohan, teaching at the Fashion Institute of Technology, states that consumers visit Zara's stores more frequently as compared to other labels, and this is a sign of brand loyalty. Its customers, who share the positive in-store experience with their network of acquaintances, become the main communication tool. Zara has created two-way communication with its consumers, through constant improvements in products and services (Danziger, 2018). The Spanish brand has been the first to understand the importance of an online community. Zara had started investing in its fan base and good-quality contents even before other brands began to use social media to generate engagement and increase sales. This method has allowed the company to invest only in social media, while other brands, following the illusion of creating fast and profitable online contents with a low budget, insisted on allocating most of their money to print press and TV advertising (Nazir, 2019).

On the contrary, H&M understood the potential of social media only later and, for years, it has invested – and is still putting money – in traditional communication, mainly in billboards. In order to compensate for this deficit, the company increased the digital budget, closed some brick-and-mortar stores and implemented initiatives to improve the customer experience.

Under the pressure of the media, due to the negative impact of their environmental policies, fast fashion brands put a lot of energy in current and very debated issues like in-clusivity and sustainability. For instance, H&M's Instagram profile has chosen to promote its collections employing imperfect models, without photo retouch, showing cellulite and stretch marks. This strategy brought numerous positive comments, confirming the success-ful choice (Tecchiato, 2019).

6.7.7 Sponsorships and co-branding

Fast fashion brands are currently implementing few sponsorships, yet two are worth mentioning.

The first was signed in 1983 by Benetton, which endorsed the Formula 1 team Tyrrel; three years later, the brand acquired Toleman, which, with the new name Benetton Formula Limited, won two world championships thanks to the then unknown pilot, Michael Schumacher. This strategy made Benetton renowned in markets where it wasn't distributed.

The second example is H&M. The company created the platform H&M We Love Horses to offer digital contents about horses. Why would a mass market company implement a strategy so similar to that of luxury brands? The reason is not to be found in the little num-ber of people who go horse-riding, but in the very high percentage of the population who loves horses, a target consistent with the transversal one of H&M. As in the case of capsule collections signed with important designers, even in this case, H&M adopted an innovative strategy (Elevent, 2020).

Co-branding projects are more frequent and are conceived for the following goals: to improve and strengthen the brand image, to raise brand awareness or to reach new targets.

Once again, in 2004, H&M was a pioneer in this field by launching collaborations with famous artists, which has definitely improved its brand image. Instead, Oysho – the un-derwear, homewear and beachwear brand belonging to the Inditex group – reinforced its identity and launched a new sports line through the creation of three lines with Adidas.

Partnerships with universally recognised mega-brands have increased brand visibility; for instance, Benetton with Renault first and Barbie later; Zara with Coca-Cola and Pull&Bear with Vespa. Similar reasons justify the partnership with online companies and TV channels, having no direct connection with fashion, but being part of people's everyday life. We can mention H&M, Topshop and Pull&Bear with Netflix; or Bershka for Spotify and Topshop for Facebook.

Aimed at appealing to extremely young targets, collaborations with cartoons are also signed: among them Zara for Disney and The Simpsons and Bershka with Hello Kitty and Pokémon.

6.7.8 Museums, foundations and leisure time activities, in collaboration with Andrea Pittana

For fast fashion brands, foundations play a crucial role because they allow them to enhance the corporate reputation and to align it with the values of sustainability. The important pa-tronage activities give them the opportunity to "wash" their image, thus building a positive relation with their target, based on sensitive contents and topics.

H&M Foundation, by means of partnerships with world-renowned institutions, supports the United Nations in their plan for sustainable development. The mission of H&M Foundation is to bring about durable and positive changes to improve life conditions by investing in people, communities and innovative ideas (H&M, 2019).

Fondazione Benetton Studi Ricerche (Benetton Foundation for Studies and Research) is committed to safeguarding world landscapes with particular attention to the most widespread environmental issues (Benetton 2019a). The brand also collaborated with Fondazione Unhate, an institution established to contain hate and to promote tolerance, which is consistent with the values of the Benetton Group (Benetton, 2019b).

Gap Foundation has always preserved the values of its founders: to donate and to give back to the community the value and the fortune generated by the company. In 2016, Gap's employees volunteered for more than 450,000 hours to help the local population and participated in donation and tutoring initiatives for children as well as in other projects (Mooney, 2017).

6.8 Distribution, in collaboration with Andrea Doroldi

The distribution strategy of fast fashion brands is characterised by homogeneity, a factor that we don't find in any other cluster. Almost all companies distribute exclusively by means of a very high number of mono-brand, directly operated (representing 80–90% of the distribution network of big groups like Inditex and H&M) and/or franchising shops (representing more than 50% for Italian brands), located in numerous countries. On 10 September 2019, the Inditex group was present in 96 countries with a network of 7,412 stores, while its competitor H&M "controlled" the markets with 5,058 shops (of which only 277 are in franchising).

The 2015 annual report of the Swedish group stated that the points of sale are managed by H&M, except for some markets where they collaborate with franchising partners; however, the report specified that this last methodology does not belong to their general strategy of expansion (Golizia, 2016). Franchising agreements often depend on the specific local legislation (e.g. Middle East).

Other brands apply direct control only over those stores that are located in strategic areas, while they rely on franchising for the remaining ones. In this way, the parent company takes care of "supervising" the shops – from sales monitoring to stocks management, from visual merchandising, to customer care – while the affiliate focuses on sales. Capillarity is not the only strategy.

Even the location plays a crucial role. In fact, the points of sale are positioned in the most important high streets of cities with a high foot-fall, in order to guarantee an (almost) total coverage of the territory and reach the widest possible market. In Milan, for instance, in Corso Buenos Aires we find H&M, Zara, Mango and Benetton.

H&M on its website reported that its stores must always occupy the best commercial position. The group also adds that renting rather than buying the shops allows the company to be more flexible in the constantly evolving retail scenario, and it also guarantees its constant presence in the crucial streets and shopping malls of the market (Golizia, 2016). Some brands, in order to increase their perceived quality, have also chosen locations in more prestigious streets to be positioned close to luxury boutiques; for example, COS is situated in Corso Venezia in Milan, a few steps away from the Dolce & Gabbana store.

Another channel employed by fast fashion brands are shopping malls which include labels belonging to diverse price segments, from luxury to fast fashion.

A further characteristic of these shops is the huge surface, suitable to display the whole extensive merchandise offer.

For all brands, but in particular for fast fashion companies, mono-brand stores, to increase their awareness and convey their identity, are pivotal to gather information on sales figures and to plan the future offer and adapt it to the actual market trend.

We now consider the online distribution strategy of Zara, H&M, Uniqlo and Mango. They can rely on their own e-commerce where it is possible to purchase the whole assortment, but they do not contemplate distributing in multi-brand stores: the entire product range is available only on their official websites and brick-and-mortar stores. Websites are frequently updated, even more than once a week, and products are uploaded and/or substituted according to their sale performance. Moreover, the four brands distribute their collections on official websites that are easily accessible from any device: they are the precursors of the *buy online – collect in store* logic.

6.9 Omnichannel, in collaboration with Sabrina Pomodoro and Benedetta Breschi

Among fast fashion brands, the most committed company to a synergic and consistent communication, according to the modalities of *creative-idea-led integration*, is Benetton. The fashion tale presents a cross-media leitmotif: from the fashion show to the store, from advertising to Instagram. The union "colour and industrial tradition" – chosen as a tribute to Benetton's DNA stylistic codes – is the inspiration for the fall–winter 2019/2020 collection and becomes the subject of the entire fashion tale. The collection is characterised by pop colours, oversize silhouettes, Peanuts and Mickey Mouse prints. On the Instagram page, Luciano Benetton, in order to promote the collection, is portrayed in front of many cans of primary colours such as red, yellow and blue; the same are found on the clothes worn by the models on the catwalk. This theme also inspired the advertising campaign and the shop windows.

No degree of integration is identified in H&M, Mango and Zara communication. In their Instagram pages, these brands attempt to promote a lifestyle the consumer may identify with; their time to market is too swift to allow a coordination among the advertising campaign, the shop window and the Instagram page. Moreover, the campaign generally aims at conveying the product price rather than a specific concept.

Interview with Gaetano Sallorenzo, former CEO MIROGLIO SPA

How will the competitive scenario of fast fashion evolve?
It is undeniable that the issue of sustainability is affecting fast fashion. Movements that encourage to consume less and more ethically were born. Nevertheless, the role of fast fashion won't change: it will still continuously supply new items. For sure, companies will do it more consciously, but they cannot radically change their system. Sustainability will be incorporated by companies in their new business models also because new generations and Millennials are strongly asking for it.

What about e-commerce?
A further change involves e-commerce. Online stores are much easier to access and allow for a faster purchasing process that cannot be compared to traditional shops. However, what is missing is the store atmosphere and the "warm" physical contact. For this reason, it is necessary to rethink the layout of the points of sales in order to offer something different and involving.

How are you facing the challenge of new consumers like Generation Z and Millennials?
Among new generations, it's difficult to identify targets and consumption models. "Old" generations always followed the same pattern: one person had a classic style, another a sporty one, etc. Today, the consumer doesn't choose a total look from one brand, but is disloyal and easily moves from label to label, matching a Zara t-shirt with Balenciaga shoes. Consequently, the challenge for the fashion industry is to identify behavioural schemes. To tackle this new issue, there is no recipe, but we shouldn't impose the same models. The brand doesn't dictate a look – as it used to do – but it offers products that can be mixed with other brands.

How have communication levers changed for fast fashion?
The world has changed due to the evolution of its rhythms: technology and the online allow companies to specifically reach different clusters of consumers that cannot be addressed with traditional media. The real challenge for every business is language: youth speaks a different language, and this must be understood; managers still communicate "vertically", while what we need is a horizontal dialogue which says: "the brand is by your side" not "the brand is above you".

Consequently, have print press investments experienced a slump in the last few years?
Yes, but not because – as everyone is saying – people do not read anymore, but because print press hasn't updated its business model. The current rhythm doesn't allow for the concept of "monthly". I don't think it is correct to frantically run after the online, as I don't believe that there is one successful idea. It is necessary to reset the offline and online communication mix: a marketing manager needs to understand what messages to convey and how. The brand authority should still be transmitted through offline tools like print media, billboards, and TV. While other messages, aimed for instance at attracting customers to both online and offline stores, must employ online solutions.

What about social media and influencers?
They are the new heroes who speak a new language; however, we must be cautious. The most important concept that emerges from social media is that of community. New generations want to be part of a community where an influencer tells them what to wear, so influencers have a very high capacity to do direct consumption. However, every target has its social medium: so I believe that companies should rely on the support of professionals who know the rules of this world and can select the right media.

Do you think that fast fashion prices will change?
I believe they won't because the product portfolio can satisfy a wide range of needs. Price is important, but young consumers are conscious of the quality-price ratio and also of sustainability, and they are more willing to spend for them than past generations.

How are the Fast Fashion brands' distribution strategies changing?
Even in the world of fast fashion, I believe the future isn't just online. They need an increasingly omnichannel, more integrated solution that reconciles the two requirements: a physical format capable of delivering a higher experience but at a higher cost; a cheaper online channel that does not, however, allow the same experience to be provided. However, many fashion businesses lack the expertise to tackle this path, and they need to improve the speed at which they need to integrate digital skills. It is easier to rely on specialised partners at the beginning, and these skills can only be internalised later.

Is it important to have a business model that's defined?
Yeah, but it is equally critical that the business model has the potential to evolve. The companies that will be successful will be the efficient businesses able to redefine their strategies.

Student activities

Choose a brand and based on your choice:

- define the sustainability actions to be applied in the future;
- identify the combination product/price segment/target where to diversify;
- identify a social media and the content typology to be developed;
- define which of the following formats – brick-and-mortar mono-brand store, brick-and-mortar multi-brand store, shop-in-shop in department stores, online mono-brand shop and online multi-brand platform – need to be developed the most;
- verify the degree of synergy among the aesthetic elements of the latest collection: the fashion show, social networks, mono-brand store windows and advertising campaign.

Notes

1 This paragraph is based on the one described in the book *Fashion Business Model* (Golizia, 2016), chapter 5, paragraph 5.1.
2 This paragraph is based on the one described in the book *Fashion Business Model* (Golizia, 2016), chapter 5, paragraph 5.9.2.

7

EMERGING BRANDS SPECIALISING IN READY-TO-WEAR

Reading: the fashion merchandiser[1]

In the current retail scenario, the role of merchandiser has become of vital importance. Their task is to analyse the market, to set the collection and to manage the distribution, the seasonal re-orders and eventual markdowns, in order to maximise profitability. For this purpose, he or she defines the guidelines and the contents of the collection plan, which is then shared with other departments (style, production, sales). "The plan outlines desired level of complexity defined in terms of number of Stock Keeping Unit (SKU), product range, price positioning, target, gross margin, product cost structure, choice of carryovers ... that will be presented again from the past collection" (Corbellini and Saviolo, 2009, p. 182). In order to draw the collection plan, the merchandiser analyses the sales figures from the past seasons and collects information from the store's network and studies competitors. During the season, to increase sales and reduce unsold items, he or she promotes and applies a set of initiatives such as marking down merchandise, the reallocation of items from different points of sale and their re-assortment. The recent phenomena of omnichannel and globalisation have increased the complexity of this profession. In fact, it is necessary to satisfy the specific needs of every distribution channel, all having different features, as well as those of the numerous geographical markets, often characterised by events that require ad hoc collections (e.g. Ramadan and Chinese New Year). The necessary competences to be a fashion merchandiser are a knowledge of the market and of the product, analytic skills and the ability to interact with the other company's departments.

7.1 Who are they?

This cluster comprises companies founded by extremely talented and visionary creative designers – often distant from the business context – who propose a distinctly avant-garde and experimental style. Frequently labelled as niche brands, they address a sophisticated and well-informed-about fashion target, who prefers an original nonconformist aesthetic that doesn't comply with the standards in force. The group is rather heterogeneous; the only possible classification is based on the distinction between those brands belonging to or being partially controlled by the two luxury groups (LVMH and Kering), which include Alexander McQueen, Stella McCartney and Marc Jacobs – the first two already examined in the second chapter – and "other brands". Among the latter, some are partially controlled by small groups or investment funds too: for instance, Maison Margiela and MSGM, respectively, controlled by Only the Brave and Style Capital; in addition, in the chapter, Alexander Wang, Rick Owens and Antonio Marras are also discussed.

7.2 Style, in collaboration with Daniela Guariento

In ready-to-wear, we find a niche of designers that interprets their own vision of fashion in a new way. The Japanese influences of Miyake, Yamamoto and Rei Kawakubo are reflected in the unstructured and unconventional garments of Maison Margiela, or Alexander Wang. Creativity is founded on the experimentation of patterns, graphics and/or tailoring techniques, thus giving birth to collections rich in innovative details and not-easy-to-wear.

In the course of time, Margiela, thanks to its experimentation, has designed iconic garments recognisable by fashion victims, such as the hand-sewn labels whose stitches are visible on the outer side of clothes, or the *TABI* boots. The brand has worked considerably on the finishing (raw cut and overlock stitches that for years had been considered, by traditional brands, only for the inner side of garments), as well as on graphics (applied to finished garments) or on the unusual match of different materials. In terms of patternmaking, the brand studies new shapes that make its products timeless and unique.

Alexander Wang's collections are conceptual but with an evident vintage inspiration; their harmony of colours makes experimental silhouettes easier to wear. Accessories are more basic: bags, in particular, are "mainstream" in their shapes, but experimental in the use of metals.

7.3 Supply chain and sustainability, in collaboration with Celeste Corso

Ready-to-wear-specialised brands do not have the resources for an in-house production, that is, through their own productive plants: their turnover, economic results and cash do not allow for such investments. As a consequence, apparel production is outsourced, while the manufacturing and distribution of fragrances and eyewear is licensed to specialised companies.

For instance, Staff International, controlled by Only the Brave, works on research, development and production for several brands, including Margiela. On its website, the group explains that it directly manages the prototyping phase, while production is outsourced to local partners located in the northeast of Italy and over which rigorous control is exercised (Otb, 2019).

The ready-to-wear segment is characterised by eccentric, experimental and avant-garde brands. Their wonderful productions epitomise the research on silhouettes, a very high degree of innovation and iconic and well-identified aesthetics. While this aspect is also evident for non-fashion professionals, sustainability is not as explicit and is struggling to find its own defined space. Compared to the clusters analysed before, the "behaviour" of these brands in the field of sustainability is atypical and peculiar: their green communication is "encrypted", probably because of the power of their own image. This does not mean that they do not implement sustainable strategies, but that they tend not to stress it in favour of a more consistent focus on creativity. In general, signs of commitment to environmental issues are few and weak.

7.4 Segmentation strategies

The segmentation strategy of this cluster is absolutely the most complex to classify. Besides Alexander McQueen and Stella McCartney that adopt a clear and defined segmentation strategy, already defined in Chapter 2, the other brands belonging to this cluster don't seem to adopt a scheme of reference in this sense. As written at the beginning of the chapter, these companies were established by very talented creatives, often unprepared in terms of business management. Their distinguishing factor is not their strategic structure, but, again, their "experimental" stylistic values. For this reason, we believe it is unnecessary to attempt to classify something that cannot be schematised.

7.5 Brand

Avant-garde and experimental style is the main characteristic of the branding policy of these companies. They debuted in ready-to-wear and later extended their offer to different categories of products such as shoes, bags and accessories. However, their diversification is inferior to that of the previously examined clusters. Maison Margiela also designs high fashion, and Rick Owens furniture. Concerning the brand extension line, they stand in between historic brands, which do not apply this strategy, and the leaders of contemporary brands, which strongly implement it. This choice is due to the desire to preserve and strengthen their status of niche brands. Mainly established from the second half of the 80s, they cannot boast any heritage, a very important factor for other typologies of brands.

They stand out, not so much for their iconic products, but for the stylistic experimentation discussed in paragraph 7.2. Fashion experts associate some representative products to these labels: leather jackets for Rick Owens, the TABI boots for Margiela, the Rockie bag for Alexander Wang. On the other hand, stylistic codes are pivotal: the absence of logo and the prevalence of black for Owens; elements taken from many cultures, ethnic patterns, recycled and reused materials for Margiela (Vergani, 2010); the red thread and the hand-made decorations for Marras.

The effective quality is extremely high and is based on artisanal techniques, applied by the hands of mostly Italian skilled craftsmen, on excellent raw materials and on small-scale production.

Marras is the only brand that seems to leverage on the *Made in*, with a particular focus on Sardinia, his land of origin.

In most of the cases, the founder designer is also the Creative Director of the homonymous brand: Rick Owens, Antonio Marras and Alexander Wang. An important exception is Maison Margiela, whose Creative Director is John Galliano. Many of them in the past used to work in the creative direction of renewed brands (Marras-Kenzo, Galliano-Dior, Margiela-Hermès) and this has made them acquire considerable visibility.

Only some of them offer a customisation service (e.g. Maison Margiela and Alexander Wang) for few selected garments.

7.6 Pricing, in collaboration with Benedetta Breschi

In the previous chapters, we focused on unspecialised companies for which we analysed the prices of eight different products in order to have an overall vision. For specialised brands – subject of this and of the following seven chapters – we considered only one product, among the above-mentioned eight, that best represents the cluster.[2]

For the examined group, the representative product is women's blazer. As in the previous chapters, we compare the positioning to other clusters: to the historic brand belonging to Louis Vuitton Moët Hennessy (LVMH), Dior (see Chapter 2); to the historic "independent" brand Prada (Chapter 3); to the first and second lines of contemporary brands, Giorgio Armani and Emporio Armani (Chapter 4); and finally to two "particular" industrial brands, Max Mara and Max&Co.

Concerning the comparison with Dior and Prada, what was stated in the previous chapters is still valid: these brands have a higher price as compared to Margiela because they are perceived differently, rather than for the actual product quality, which is very high for all the three companies.

Margiela, like all the brands of this cluster, has neither the same degree of awareness nor the same brand identity, which is stronger for the more famous and "older" fashion houses. Even Giorgio Armani boasts a higher price positioning: partially for similar reasons as

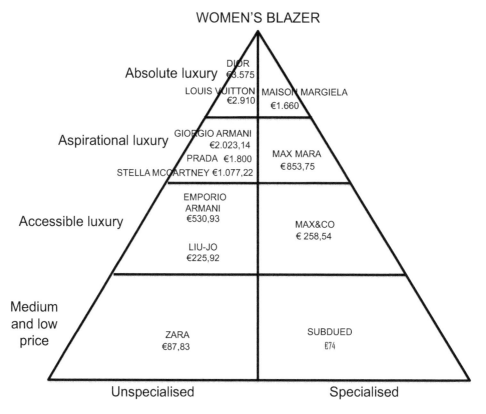

FIGURE 7.1 Golizia's pyramid of women's blazer
Source: Prepared by Dario Golizia.

historic brands – higher degree of recognition and clear and distinctive price positioning – and mainly because its women's blazer is an iconic garment that has made the history of fashion and dress: this confirms the fact that a specific product can have a crucial role on the brand perception and its consequent positioning. On the other hand, Emporio Armani, Max&Co. and Max Mara are at a lower level as compared to Maison Margiela. The first two are second lines and target a more transversal market; furthermore, they are characterised by an inferior actual quality and industrial production (often outsourced abroad), whereas Margiela, which addresses a more niche target, boasts an excellent actual quality, resulting from artisanal production. Max Mara has an interesting positioning in the pyramid: horizontally, it stands in the middle because it offers a very extended product range, yet very specialised in ready-to-wear; vertically, its price is the perfect example of those few "premium brands, very creative and exclusive, that are perceived as fashion houses even if they do not have a designer" (Corbellini and Saviolo, 2009, p. 107). However, despite being perceived as fashion houses, they cannot aspire to reaching the same positioning; nevertheless, they have been able to identify a price gap between the first and second lines (in our example Armani), where they have settled.

7.7 Communication

We now proceed with the definition of the image of the cluster; afterwards, we study how the marketing and communication function is organised and managed by a company from the same group. Finally, we outline the communication mix applied by some brands.

7.7.1 Cluster image

"Emerging" conceptual designers, destructured looks and unseen cuts, excess, avant-garde, unusual materials are the concepts that define the cluster image.

7.7.2 Marketing function and communication, in collaboration with Michele Leoni

MSGM, established in 2009 by Massimo Giorgetti, current Creative Director, is controlled by the investment fund Style Capital. The Communication Office is entrusted to a consultancy agency that takes care of international and local press relations, corporate and editorial/ product communication, negotiation and the buying of advertising pages in international and local magazines, organisation of fashion shows and events involving the press. Conversely, digital communication, social networks and celebrities' management are taken care of by an internal team. The team is in charge of organising ad hoc seeding (delivery to influencers and celebrities of the most representative garments) and of content creation for social networks.

7.7.3 Fashion shows and trade fairs, in collaboration with Andrea Doroldi

For these brands, the fashion show is the most important communication tool as it allows them to show off their creativity and enhance the otherwise low visibility. They participate in the same fashion weeks mentioned in the previous chapters, and the PR office – sometimes internal, sometimes external – is the department in charge of their organisation.

Even in this case, the guests of the fashion shows are buyers, journalists, influencers and international celebrities.

These brands were established in relatively recently, and they are small in terms of turnover, with the exception of Alexander McQueen and Stella McCartney, which belong to, or are controlled by, the groups examined in Chapter 2 and, for this reason, can take advantage of more financial resources.

By applying the usual classification of fashion shows, Ironico's analysis states that most of them belong to the conceptual category, characterised by the aim to launch a message, to encourage thinking and to challenge the conventional codes of language as in the case of Martin Margiela (Ironico, 2014).

Even these "young" brands produce cruise collections. However, the majority of them, since they have inferior budgets, do not organise ad hoc fashion shows for their promotion, but only present them to the sales force during internal events and in their showrooms.

Among the examined fairs, Antonio Marras participated in the 2019 edition of Pitti Immagine. Speaking of Salone del Mobile, he participated in the event in collaboration with Kiasmo (designer Vincenzo D'Alba) to create a collection of ceramics, vases, plates and candles, showcased in the *Nonostantemarras* space (Maggiore, 2019).

7.7.4 Advertising, editorial, advertorial, in collaboration with Benedetta Breschi

This group had not been studied in the previous book (Golizia, 2016) and research; consequently, only the 2019 ranking is examined. Concerning the ranking for the number of advertising pages purchased in 2019, the group is in the seventh position. Moreover, it is worth noticing how all the pages were bought by one brand, MSGM, which, among the four, is the least unconventional. The remaining two are, in fact, very active on social media.

7.7.5 Influencers, gifting, endorsement, by Lavinia Biancalani

The fashion industry pivots on two actions: to dictate trends and to create a strong sense of belonging to the brand, two crucial themes for the usage of Instagram, whose communities have been a factor of success for both emerging and well-known brands. The former, which cannot count on high investments, have applied seeding and gifting strategies with the

TABLE 7.1 Advertising, fashion editorial and advertorials of emerging ready-to-wear-specialised brands

Emerging (ready to wear) RTW Specialised Brands	L'Officiel			Vogue			Vanity Fair			Elle			Glamour			Total		
	A	FE	AD	A	FE	AD	A	FE	AD	A	FE	AD	A	FE	AD	A	FE	AD
Alexander Wang	0	0	0	0	0	0	0	0	0	0	0	1	0	0	0	0	0	1
MSGM	1	1	0	2	0	0	0	0	0	0	0	0	0	0	0	3	1	0
Maison Margiela	0	2	0	0	0	0	0	0	0	0	0	0	0	0	0	0	2	0
Rick Ownes	0	0	0	0	0	0	0	0	0	0	0	0	0	0	0	0	0	0
Total	**1**	**3**	**0**	**2**	**0**	**0**	**0**	**0**	**0**	**0**	**0**	**1**	**0**	**0**	**0**	**3**	**3**	**1**

Source: Authors' data processing on the basis of fashion magazines published in Italy in September 2019. A, FE and AD stand for advertising, fashion editorial and advertorial, respectively.

intent of engaging influencers and increasing their online visibility. Some of them employ structured social media and influencer marketing strategies, which, however, due to the niche positioning and the limited product diversification, consist of only a small number of collaborations. Margiela and Alexander Wang were analysed; Stella McCartney, endowed with similar characteristics, was discussed in Chapter 2, because it is controlled by LVMH.

After years of silence, Martin Margiela, a discrete fashion icon, made a statement in which he distanced himself from social networks, declaring that he had left fashion ten years before to detach from the growing pressure of the market. He also added that the glut of information through social media had undermined the thrill of waiting (Diciotto, 2018). No influencer marketing campaigns are planned for fashion collections; however, an interesting project was designed for the launch of the fragrance Maison Margiela, a confirmation that often social media communication strategies for this type of product are made ad hoc. Moreover, in 2019, five international influencers/artists interpreted the nonconformist manifesto *Mutiny* by Maison Margiela that had been revealed by John Galliano in a podcast. The designer had declared that mutiny was in the air and that when rules were broken by an organisation, the community became a family. He had also added that creativity had no gender or nationality.

Alexander Wang counts on more that 5 million followers on Instagram where it preserves its authentic, ironic and irreverent personality. The brand is always on the front line on social networks to promote its values; it works very accurately on the storytelling of events and shows and adapts its social media communication according to the audience, to make sure to include an inclusive story. An interesting case history is the collaboration Adidas for Alexander Wang signed in 2017 and announced during the after-show party. With more than 1,200 guests (editors, bloggers, retailers, stylists and celebrities like Madonna and Kylie Jenner), the initiative was very appreciated by the digital press.

7.7.6 Social media

Many brands have been compelled to rethink their communication because of the influence of social media and youth culture. In the following analysis, we prove how the brands of this cluster have become addicted to Instagram, Facebook and Twitter because of their intense use.

The studied labels express themselves differently by means of diverse contents; however, to survive in the overcrowded fashion system, they all need the approval of the target they address.

Margiela's social media editorial plan is cross-platform and based on the substantial replication of the same contents on Instagram and Facebook. The approach is only partially product-focused and the centre of attention is mainly the aesthetic of the brand conveyed during fashion shows and events. Contents are conceived to generate a discordant effect obtained with unconventional cuts and framings. To do so, the brand manipulates the photos of the campaigns and of the fashion shows to create unusual photographic compositions. Still life pictures are rarely used, and chiefly for accessories; they are generally conceived specifically for social media and designed according to the aesthetic of fashion editorials. The majority of contents are photos; videos are occasionally posted to give a preview of fashion shows. Even Spotify is sometimes employed as an accessory social media: in 2018, the brand launched a series of podcasts, called *The Memory of… with John Galliano*. In this series, the designer described the creative process of every collection and opened to everyone a special moment that had always been a privilege of journalists.

Alexander Wang is active on Instagram, where it posts engaging images, but also on Twitter and Facebook. In an interview with Maloy (2018), Brooke Bunce, Social Media Manager of the brand, outlined the social media strategy. He says that he likes to imagine Twitter as a conversation, Facebook as information and Instagram as a visual narrative. Brooke Bunce continues by saying that contents are adapted to each platform because it is crucial to study their specific audience and their expectations. The focus on narration is a key aspect and a priority that originates in the vision of the founder, who is very active on his personal account, and that increases the interest in the company. Bunce continues by saying that while a significant part of the efforts made by the brand is aimed at selling, an even more important part is dedicated to telling the story of products. When discussing social media, the team focuses on how to convert engagement into sales, but the most important thing are the communities of followers that keep your accounts healthy. Bunce concludes by af[...] on, independent of the content, [...]

The primary [...] ive stylistic content, for the abi[...] reative Directors who can comm[...]

The brand s[...] e of the models, the iconic fashi[...] embraced inclusivity in his fas[...] were chosen to showcase the c[...] season in which fashion shows [...] his models were black. Fashion [...]

Handwritten notes:
1. 1ST EXAMPLE. 'NICHE' BRAND X BIG BRAND EX; H&M X ALEX. WANG.
= 2 IMPORTANT RESULTS —
1. INCREASE VISIBILITY
2. INCREASE ECONOMIC RESULTS
2. 2ND EXAMPLE. COLLABS AIMED TO STRENGTHEN IDENTITY + AESTHETIC VISION.
Ex ANTONIO MARRAS (FASHION) X 'FURNITURE INDUSTRY'

7.7.7 Sponso[...]

In this cluster, [...] MSGM sponsoring the exhibit[...] *Floyd.*

Co-brandin[...] nto two typologies: the first in[...] and the other is specific for this [...]

In the first category, we include those carried out with sportswear brands (mainly for shoes): Rick Owens x Adidas, Maison Margiela x Converse, Alexander Wang x Adidas as well as with fast fashion brands: Maison Martin Margiela x H&M, Alexander Wang x H&M, Alexander Wang x Uniqlo. Both allow these "small-sized" niche brands to achieve two important results: to increase their visibility and their economic results.

The second category encompasses collaborations aimed at strengthening the characterising element of the identity of these brands: the aesthetic vision of the Creative Director. For instance, Antonio Marras implemented some collaborations (mostly in the design and furniture industry) inspired by the cultural, social and historic context of his land of origin, Sardinia.

7.7.8 Museums, foundations and leisure time activities, in collaboration with Andrea Pittana

This cluster comprises very young brands, which, for the reasons explained in Chapter 2, neither have grown a significant heritage nor feel the need to promote lifestyle projects.

Their resources are invested in more effective and straightforward communication channels like social media and influencers. However, brands with similar characteristics but controlled by the big luxury groups discussed in Chapter 2 – Alexander McQueen and Stella McCartney – are an exception.

7.8 Distribution, in collaboration with Andrea Doroldi

The distribution strategies of this cluster are very similar to those studied in Chapter 2 for Stella McCartney and Alexander McQueen: few mono-brand and many multi-brand stores. For the former, the numbers are as follows: Maison Margiela, Rick Owens and Alexander Wang own, respectively, 62, 10 and 32 mono-brand stores. In Milan, the first has three stores of which two are in the fashion district; the second has one in Via Monte di Pietà, a sort of destination point for the brand's addicts; the last has no store.

While the number of multi-brand shops is far superior, Owens is present in about 800 of them worldwide and Wang in 483 inclusive of multi-brand and department stores (no concessions); the data for Margiela is not available. As a consequence, we hypothesise that the percentage on the total turnover represented by direct retail is rather inferior than that of wholesale; the main causes can be found in the fact that these are "emerging" brands having a less extended product assortment, addressing a niche target and having economic and financial resources that are not comparable to those of the most famous fashion labels. It would be unnecessary to underline that the multi-brand stores where these brands are distributed are the most avant-garde and luxurious in the territory.

We now consider the online distribution strategy of Maison Margiela, Rick Owens and Alexander Wang. They own their e-commerce where the whole assortment is purchasable. The first brand is also available on nine online platforms, Rick Owens on eight (not available on Amazon) and Alexander Wang on seven (absent on Matches Fashion and Ssense). The most displayed categories are ready-to-wear for the three of them but also shoes for Margiela and bags for Wang. By comparing the prices on their e-commerce with Farfetch we see that they impose the same price. All websites allow for mobile purchases thanks to an adequate design.

7.9 Omnichannel, in collaboration with Sabrina Pomodoro and Benedetta Breschi

Speaking about brands specialising in ready-to-wear, MSGM belongs to the *collection-led integration* category. On all its communication tools, the brand presents the core garment of the collection, which is given visibility on the catwalk, in an advertising campaign – shot in what looks like a wheat field – as well as on Instagram where the same campaign is posted. However, no idea or concept going beyond the style of the collection is identified.

With regard to Maison Margiela and Rick Ownes, which are less conventional than MSGM and address a more avant-garde target, no consistency in the fashion show, the advertising campaign, the shops and the Instagram page is observed; for this reason, they are classified as *absence-of-integration* brands. Nevertheless, this strategy is, paradoxically, consistent with their brand identity. Below are the reasons. These brands are led by avant-garde and nonconformist designers recognisable for an abstract and unconventional style; they do not feel the need to find and communicate a common thread among their means of communication in order to advertise their own collections, which are in turn, noncon-formist. Because they are not conventional brands, the communication of a single message across their media would not be effective.

Concerning Alexander Wang, no advertising campaign was found for the fall–winter 2019/2020 womenswear collection in the sources examined for the previous brands. None-theless, the degree of integration of the collection can be studied analysing only two means of communication: the fashion show and the Instagram page. A common thread between the two was observed. On the Instagram page, the user is invited to watch the show: "A MUST WATCH", "Relieve our #Collection2 runway" (official Instagram page of alexan-derwang). Moreover, on the same page, an image of the location of the show was posted as well as an "invite" to watch it in live streaming. In short, the degree of integration of Alexander Wang belongs to the category of *visual and iconic integration*. Although an inte-gration with a clear message is absent, a connection between the outfits showcased in the fashion show and the Instagram page is observed.

Interview with Filippo Cavalli, board member at MSGM

What are the essential characteristics of your product?
MSGM's product is the quintessence of freshness and colour, it expresses the joy of life and the positivity that are essential constituents of our DNA. The brand doesn't take itself too seriously and downplays the sometimes-excessive holiness of the fashion world.

How is the competitive scenario in which MSGM competes evolving?
The scenario is becoming more and more complex; the ability to create a strong bond with the consumer – who is becoming more and more informed and exposed to multiple stimuli – is essential.

How are you facing the challenge of new consumers (Millennials, Generation Z)?
The challenge of new consumers is faced by interacting with new generations by means of communication channels and codes that are suitable for digital natives. It is useless to believe that we can reach them by applying past schemes; today, everything passes through the digital world; consider, for instance, the role of WeChat which, in China, dominates all daily activities.

What's MSGM's productive strategy and how is it facing the sustainability challenge?
MSGM is proudly 100% Made in Italy and has turned this characteristic into a merit and a fundamental qualitative distinctive element. Sustainability is a hot and dear topic, and we are comprehensively working on it at a product and at a more general company level. The awareness that we have only one planet and that we must protect and respect it is very clear.

How have brand communication levers changed? Have investments in print press lost importance com-pared to the past?
As I mentioned earlier, the levers have changed because we need to speak to consumers through the channels they use every day in their real life. If the brand cannot do it, it is not perceived as cool as customers expect and want it to be. Print press investments have a less central role, and it is evident. Other media allow for a more straightforward and, most of all, two-way interaction with customers.

Do you think that prices in MSGM's competitive segment may vary in the close future?
MSGM's price segment is not dominated by a price-based competition; the most important factors are intangible elements like product appeal and brand coolness. An adequate price-quality ratio is a key to success; however, it is neither the only nor the fundamental driver.

How important is e-commerce for MSGM?
It is very important; consider that it gives the possibility to reach consumers in every corner of the world, even those who cannot go to a brick-and-mortar shop or to traditional wholesale distributors.

How important is the shopping experience?
The possibility to welcome a consumer in a mono-brand store is unique because the shop is the theatre where the brand can fully express its storytelling. For this reason, we have decided to establish – in two fundamental cities for the brand, Milan and London – two flagship stores, places where we can tell our world and values.

In an industry dominated by big groups, is there still space for niche brands? If yes, what are the strategic levers to differentiate and be successful?
Being unique and having a distinctive product proposition characterised by a strong personality. If you homologate, you become one of the many and you cannot compete with those who have more resources and power than you. For this reason, it is essential to reinvent oneself all the time and, simultaneously, to remain consistent.

How has the COVID pandemic impacted the fashion system?
The COVID-19 emergency has radically changed the world and its habits. Even fashion has undergone this tempest: consider, for instance, the deliveries of spring-summer 2020 that had started but have never been completed; the sales campaign for fall-winter 2020 collections that has been compromised; shops and showrooms have remained closed for months. Concerning distribution, we will reconsider our business partners and prefer the most reliable and resilient ones. Sales campaigns will employ more and more digital tools to compensate for the impossibility to travel, and the same methodology will be applied to the presentation of collections that will have to comply with social distancing regulations.

Student activities

Choose a brand and based on your choice:

- define the sustainability actions to be applied in the future;
- identify the combination product/price segment/target where to diversify;
- identify a social media and the content typology to be developed;
- define which of the following formats – brick-and-mortar mono-brand store, brick-and-mortar multi-brand store, shop-in-shop in department stores, online mono-brand shop and online multi-brand platform – need to be developed the most;
- verify the degree of synergy among the aesthetic elements of the latest collection: the fashion show, social networks, mono-brand store windows and the advertising campaign.

Notes

1 Thank you Claudia Astolfi – Merchandising & Buying Professional – for collaborating in the writing of this reading.
2 The women's blazer for ready-to-wear-specialised companies, the suit for brands specialised in men's formalwear, jeans for casualwear companies, the nightgown for underwear-specialised brands, sneakers for activewear brands, the hoodie for streetwear labels and the shopper for those specialised in leather goods and pumps for companies specialised in footwear.

8

BRANDS SPECIALISING IN FORMAL MENSWEAR

Reading: the fashion buyer

The fashion buyer is the person in charge of selecting and buying the collections for the different distributive channels: department stores, concept stores, multi-brand and mono-brand stores. They select what consumers will see in the shop windows and will buy in the close future. They are endowed with creativity as well as with a good degree of intuition and passion that allow them to find and test new brands, new styles and new trends that will satisfy the needs of the target. Nevertheless, fashion buyers also have an economic soul able to negotiate prices and guarantee good margins of profitability. For this reason, they rely on a very comprehensive background including economic skills such as budget management and margins calculation; creative skills like a good knowledge of fabrics and materials, and of future trends; organisational skills that allow them to travel the world to visit trade fairs and show rooms and attend fashion shows; a knowledge of the productive processes and their timing. The highest risk for a buyer is to purchase items that will not meet customers' taste and that will increase stocks and decrease the profitability of the store (Zinola, 2011).

8.1 Who are they?

The world of formalwear stands out for its excellent manufacturing quality and tradition. Bound to menswear, this sector was born to satisfy men's past and present necessity for elegance and formal style in their daily and professional life. The protagonist garments of this style have always been few and specific: the shirt, the trousers, the jacket and some accessories, which have led first to the opening of tailors' workshops, and then to the setting up of semi-artisanal production techniques. Traditionally bound to Italy and England, these companies are still universally recognised as symbols of quality and exclusivity. This sector has undergone a drastic reshaping due to the new purchasing habits of men who prefer casualwear to formalwear, used only for a few formal/professional occasions. This is a very concentrated industry where the leader company, Ermenegildo Zegna, lives side by side with very few other players. The former, despite starting a process of (almost) total product diversification, has been included in this cluster because it is still very much associated to the menswear market. Besides Zegna, in this chapter, we have also analysed Kiton and Canali.

8.2 Style, in collaboration with Daniela Guariento

The historic brand Ermenegildo Zegna plays a fundamental role in international luxury menswear. Its identity is defined by a top-quality product characterised by Italian taste, tailoring and technical skills that make garments both timeless and contemporary in their silhouette. The made-to-measure and couture lines respond to the demanding needs of the market through meticulous attention to detail and hand-made manufacturing. The brand doesn't accept any compromise in terms of fabrics: they choose the best in the world, guaranteeing specific performances and epitomising a contemporary classic style.

Even Kiton, another Italian historic brand, leverages on craftsmanship and takes care of each single detail of its products. The identifying features of the brand – hardly imitable – are refined knitwear, unstructured comfortable jackets, seven-pleated ties, a hand-made, Neapolitan manufacturing tradition. The company also boasts the usage of excellent fabrics: cashmere, silk, linen, vicuna wool and noble fibres renewed by design.

8.3 Supply chain and sustainability, in collaboration with Celeste Corso

In the book *Ermenegildo Zegna* (various authors, 2010), the authors state that in the plant of Trivero, Zegna transforms wool into fabric, while in the artisanal plant of Stabio, the fabric turns into a suit. This statement shows how this leader company boasts a high control of the supply chain: in fact, monitoring the whole process is essential to safeguard the perfection of manufacturing. In general, we can say that the companies of this cluster produce in directly owned plants located in Italy. Two distinct models can be identified. On the one hand, we find Zegna, which owns the whole productive process: from the raw material to the suit. In the above-mentioned book, we read that a Zegna's suit, before being displayed in a shop, is touched by 275 hands. Hands that have sheared sheep, woven the fabric, dyed it, knitted it, ironed it, cut it, sewn it and ironed it again. After all these steps, you have only the fabric, not the suit. Afterwards, the fabric is cut into pieces that would compose the suit and they are sewn together. On the other hand, we find the majority of companies which purchase raw materials from suppliers – but still pursuing excellence – and produce in-house the formal items of their collections, but delocalise and outsource the informal ones. Camuffo and Cappellari (1997) state that, even though the progressive extension of accessories, sportswear and informalwear product range implied a gradual and partial outsourcing of production, the degree of in-house manufacturing has not decreased. For instance, Kiton owns five productive plants in Italy and hires about 800 employees, half of whom are craftsmen (Forbes, 2019).

When we think of formal menswear, we associate it with words like rigour, quality and tailoring. This sector is rather atypical as compared to the previously analysed ones, representing almost a peculiar reality. The impression is that this industry is still frozen into the principle of "perfectly-made" and struggles to totally embrace the changes required by sustainability.

While the effective specialisation of productive models has allowed these brands to reach an excellent product standard, it has turned out to be penalising in terms of flexibility.

However, by embracing the values of craftsmanship and territoriality, these companies, above all Zegna, have indirectly acquired the "status" of sustainable labels (at least presumably). In fact, part of the resources generated by the business have been given back to the local community. The founder of Ermenegildo Zegna, an *ante litteram* environmentalist, used to say that his workers had helped him, and he had to give them back as much as he could. He donated to them the Zegna hospital, the Zegna swimming pool and the Zegna kindergarten (various authors, 2010). His heirs followed his heritage and founded the Zegna Oasis, a more-than-100-km^2 natural park whose purpose is to teach the community the respect for the environment (Zegna, 2019). The revenues of the collection *#WHATMAKESAMAN* supported a charity association aimed at constructing a better future.

8.4 Segmentation strategies

Also, for this topic, it is necessary to refer to two different strategic choices.

Except for Zegna, other players adopt a segmentation strategy combining two different strategies, product-focused and target-focused: in fact, they address an adult man, with a traditional style and very high income, who is offered several items with a specific focus on suits. On the contrary, Zegna has implemented a repositioning process aimed at being perceived not just as a formal menswear company, but as a lifestyle brand. Its symbols are the suit, wool, classic and elegant style, the territory of Trivero in Piedmont and ethical and environmental values. In this context, the main product, the suit, not only does not lose its appeal, but it is emphasised by the set of symbolic and emotional values of the parent company.

8.5 Brand

Among the analysed groups, this is the one with the most characterising product, the formal men's suit. While historic and contemporary brands regularly launch new trends, menswear labels seem to be living out of time. While Zegna established its business on fabric production to supply superior quality menswear (Vergani, 2010) and only later integrated downstream by producing the actual garment, the other brands debuted in apparel production, with Canali producing men's suits, characterised by simple lines, and Kiton with artisanal coats and jackets.

Even diversification has followed two paths.

On the one hand, we find Zegna that started its diversification process in a proactive way, predicting the crisis that involved luxury menswear at the end of the last decade. The first approach to menswear is traced back to 1968; later on, at the beginning of the 90s, came the sports line Zegna Sport. Subsequently, the company added Z Zegna, the most modern and trendy line (various authors, 2010). Finally, the brand also diversified into other categories such as footwear and accessories (e.g. trolleys, bags, backpacks, wallets and glasses). The aim of this deep transformation was to leave behind the old image of formal-menswear-specialised brand and to acquire a new one focused on lifestyle. The final goal was to improve economic results and to reduce the risks of basing the business on one single product.

On the other hand, we find other players whose diversification has had a more recent and less defined development. This is often limited to informal lines and the eventual design of other categories of merchandise hasn't had the necessary boost to rejuvenate the brand image and improve the economic results. This hesitant change was induced by the crisis in luxury formal menswear, which is undergoing a historic transition due to the new attitudes of global consumers. In this way, Canali introduced sneakers, T-shirts jersey tracksuits in its *Black Edition* collection, comprising sporty accessories and garments, standing out for their technical finishing, and defining the expressive code of a young man (Canali, 2019).

Furthermore, Kiton has also chosen to address a feminine target; however, this line only represents 10% of the company's total revenues. On the whole, excluding Zegna, this type of diversification is still poles apart from the comprehensive and impressive one applied by contemporary and historic brands.

The concept of made-in – of vital importance for historic brands and irrelevant for streetwear companies – is essential for this cluster as it characterises its tangible product (Kotler et al., 2008), the suit, which also represents their essence. The idea of Made in Italy is, in fact, associated with luxury menswear and it encompasses two factors: the place of origin and the production location. Moreover, these brands are also stressing the concept of local, meaning the specific area in which they were founded and grew their business: consider Zegna, which epitomises the district of Biella, one of the most important worldwide areas for wool production, while Kiton the Napolitan tailoring tradition.

While the iconic products of historic brands are diverse and play a crucial role in the spreading of heritage, in this cluster, we find one garment: the "professional uniform" composed of trousers, jacket, shirt and tie (various authors, 2010). The naming strategy is similar for the entire cluster: most of the brands bear the name of their founder, who is still alive in the superlative product and production quality. Kiton is an exception: its name, in fact, derives from *chitone*, the tunic worn by ancient Greeks when they prayed to their Gods. Unlike the companies established by couturiers or designers, the role of the founder in the consolidation of the brand image is marginal; yet, it is essential for the creation and development of their business formula. Finally, the standard of customisation services is excellent for all brands; even in this case, Zegna stands out for launching its made-to-measure service in 1972.

8.6 Pricing, in collaboration with Benedetta Breschi

For the present cluster, the reference product is the formal men's suit. In this case, two companies are considered since Ermenegildo Zegna and Canali, despite both competing in luxury, are positioned in different, yet adjoining, price segments. As in the previous chapters, we compare the positioning to other clusters: to the historic brand belonging to LVMH, Dior (Chapter 2); to the historic "independent" brand Prada (Chapter 3); to the first and second lines of contemporary brands, Giorgio Armani and Emporio Armani (Chapter 4).

Concerning the comparison with Dior and Prada, we confirm that they have a substantially similar price to Ermenegildo Zegna's; in fact, the latter is associated with specific characteristics – the status of a historic brand specialised in formal menswear, sustainability, excellent quality of raw materials, integrated control of the value chain, the status of leader of the industry – which have allowed for a construction and a communication of a brand image perceived as equal to that of any other brand (both specialised and unspecialised)

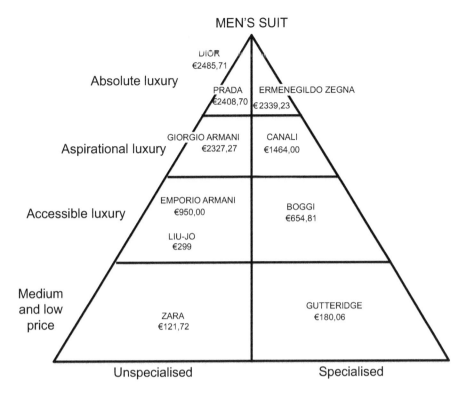

FIGURE 8.1 Golizia's pyramid of men's suit
Source: Prepared by Dario Golizia.

competing in the menswear segment. Even Giorgio Armani has a similar price positioning for the reason explained in the previous chapters: the formal men's suit of the Milanese brand has made the history of fashion.

Conversely, Canali is in a lower position as compared to the above-mentioned brands, yet above Emporio Armani: the latter is a second line and is not specialised either in the suit or in menswear; furthermore, its real quality is inferior. For Canali, we can reiterate the same consideration made for MaxMara because, likewise, it is positioned between Armani's first and second lines.

8.7 Communication

We now proceed with the definition of the image of the cluster; afterwards, we study how the marketing and communication function is organised and managed by a company from the same group. Finally, we outline the communication mix applied by some brands.

8.7.1 Cluster image

Suit, jacket, trousers, tie, formal menswear, Made in Italy, luxury, elegance, excellent raw materials and wearability are the key words of these brands.

8.7.2 Marketing function and communication, in collaboration with Michele Leoni

Established in 1934, Canali embodies excellence in the field of formal menswear and of Made in Italy. Its name is synonymous with Italian elegance and mastery. The marketing and communication function, whose head is the Group Marketing Director, reporting to the CEO, is divided into three macro areas. The first is the Creative Studio, that is, the graphic design and creative office managed by the Art Director who is responsible for the brand image. The second is the Digital Marketing and Media Area, in charge of social media management and of their content creation; the person responsible for this sector also deals with the planning and purchase of advertising spaces (advertising campaigns) both off- and online. The third division is the Press and Public Relations Office that manages external agencies subdivided according to geographical areas and in charge of corporate communication and samples management (for editorials) in close collaboration with Milan's headquarters. While for the planning and organisation of events, Canali collaborates with external consultants.

8.7.3 Fashion shows and trade fairs, in collaboration with Andrea Doroldi

Also, for this topic, it is fundamental to subdivide the cluster into two sub-groups: the first, which includes Ermenegildo Zegna, presents the collection during fashion shows, events, in its flagship showroom and in some trade fairs (only for the Z Zegna line). The second, which encompasses other brands like Canali and Kiton, showcases its collections during trade fairs.

The spectacular fashion shows of Zegna belong to the theatrical category; for instance, for the fall-winter 2018/2019 collection, whose theme was nature, models were walking on snow. This set led guests to easily associate the brand to its natural reserve project, Oasi Zegna, a property of the family. Both sub-groups usually do not design a cruise collection.

Concerning trade fairs, besides Salone del Mobile, which we will shortly discuss, we must highlight how these brands generally participate in Pitti Immagine Uomo, the most important international fair for this segment. Among the observed brands – Zegna and Canali – both participated in 2019 Pitti Uomo, but not in its 2020 digital edition. The former introduced its young line *Z Zegna* with a collection inspired by urban cycling, a perfect mix of tailoring and activewear. They did not take part in Mipel.

Despite not being specialised in interior design, they participate in Milan's Salone del Mobile, specifically with *Fuori Salone* events, enjoying important artistic collaborations; in 2019, Zegna presented the *Toyz* collection made in *Woven Leather* and including accessories and homewear products.

8.7.4 Advertising, editorial, advertorial, in collaboration with Benedetta Breschi

The group of menswear brands had not been studied in the previous book (Golizia, 2016) and research; consequently, only the 2019 ranking is examined. It is not a surprise that the above-mentioned brands did not buy any advertising page and are the last in ranking; in fact, they prefer to promote the product during fairs and in particular at Pitti Immagine Uomo.

TABLE 8.1 Advertising, fashion editorial and advertorials of formal menswear-specialised brands

Formal- Menswear-Specialised Brands	L'Officiel			Vogue			Vanity Fair			Elle			Glamour			Total		
	A	FE	AD	A	FE	AD	A	FE	AD	A	FE	AD	A	FE	AD	A	FE	AD
Zegna	0	0	0	0	0	0	0	0	0	0	0	0	0	0	0	0	0	0
Canali	0	0	0	0	0	0	0	0	0	0	0	0	0	0	0	0	0	0
Kiton	0	0	0	0	0	0	0	0	0	0	0	0	0	0	0	0	0	0
Total	**0**	**0**	**0**	**0**	**0**	**0**	**0**	**0**	**0**	**0**	**0**	**0**	**0**	**0**	**0**	**0**	**0**	**0**

Source: Authors' data processing on the basis of fashion magazines published in Italy in September 2019. A, FE and AD stand for advertising, fashion editorial, and advertorial, respectively.

8.7.5 Influencers, gifting, endorsement, by Lavinia Biancalani

For a long time, brands belonging to the formal menswear segment were reluctant to embrace online communication. On the one hand, sales have decreased in the last few years, hit by the "casualisation" of global trends and by the spreading of streetwear. On the other hand, the web is mainly used by Millennials and Generation Z that are not interested in their product.

In 2016, Ermenegildo Zegna was able to find an effective balance, between new and historic consumers, since the arrival of the Creative Director Alessandro Sartori who considerably renewed its image. Digital marketing strategies are aligned with this philosophy. In 2018, for the launch of *Tiziano* sneakers, Zegna worked on two categories of endorsement: *Shot by Zegna* and *Seeded by Zegna*. For the first category the brand took care directly of the contents (photos) shared on its Instagram profile and on those of the involved talents: among them, musician and social media personality Kojey Radical and Isaac Carew, having, respectively, 90,600 and 499,000 followers on Instagram. Conversely, the talents for Seeded by Zegna were asked to produce their own contents. In 2019, for the *What Makes a Man* campaign, focused on a modern concept of masculinity, Zegna hired, besides its CEO Gildo Zegna, also Oscar-awarded actor Mahershala Ali and Nicholas Tse.

Kiton is more "immature" than the former brand in terms of digital and influencer marketing; in fact, it only relies on seeding activities.

Traditional endorsement activities based purely on influencers is the pivot of Canali's developing strategy. Through the production of editorial shots and product seeding with social media talents, the brand aims to grow its visibility. Rocco Fasano and Ryan Clark are among the faces that posed for the launch of a coat for the fall-winter 2019/2020 collection. Other faces like Ivano Marino and Simon Nygard were the protagonists of the launch of Canali Black Edition sportswear collection, addressed to a younger target.

8.7.6 Social media

Alexa Tonner, co-founder of influencer network *Collectively*, states that social media have allowed consumers to differently discover luxury garments. Instagram, in particular, shows infinite perspectives as compared to traditional magazines. Men who would have never bought GQ or Esquire are now at ease in following social media accounts, most of all from the luxury segment (Biron, 2017). This is the reason why the brands of this cluster own their social media official profiles, even though their management is entrusted to external agencies.

Digital Transformation Factory Triboo is the agency supporting Kiton in the implementation of its digital strategy and in the creation of specific contents for the launch of campaigns and for social advertising. Contents are in a way similar to those posted by historic brands: the main topics are exclusivity, the accuracy of the productive process, made-to-measure services, with a frequent use of the words *tailored* and *custom*. Videos of campaigns are few and are mainly substituted by product and product detail images; another recurrent topic are events that show the participation of famous personalities. However, while in the groups analysed in Chapters 2 and 3 important guests are both men and women, in this specific case, they are mainly men. Conversely, the usage of colour is less intense: these brands produce elegant or professional garments for special occasions, featuring classic colours such as beige, blue, grey and black; the same shades are found in their images, videos and settings.

As mentioned in the previous paragraph, these brands have approached online communication with a conscious delay, and their product, the suit, is still the core of the strategy.

An exception is represented by Zegna, which opened a new way in the field of social communication. Edoardo Zegna explained the ongoing change and the purpose of social media by emphasising that today companies must accept the fact that consumers dictate what path to follow. Digital technology must be the focus of every division of the company and brands must be able to adapt their messages to the constant evolution of consumers. He concluded by saying that companies would be more and more marketing rather than product-led (FashionUnited, 2018).

As a consequence, the purpose is to comply with the requests of the consumer who is increasingly interested in social media images rather than in magazines. Consequently, other brands are following along. Triboo, the agency in charge of Kiton's digital communication, aims at strengthening brand awareness and engagement. The latter has become indispensable to keep the target active and to make it grow by posting images of events where celebrities wear the garments of the brand.

On social media, these companies tend to communicate their point of strength, the suit, and in particular, their made-to-measure service. However, they overlook crucial topics like sustainability and inclusivity. Zegna is once again an exception, being very active in this sense. The brand calls to action with #UseTheExisting a collection whose quilted coats are made of recycled polyester and whose jumpers are created with recyclable cashmere. Alessandro Sartori, Zegna's Art Director, affirms that to do traditional things in a different way, you need to first change your mentality. It is not possible to be 100% sustainable yet; however, the brand is working hard to reach this objective (Chodha, 2019).

8.7.7 Sponsorships and co-branding

Menswear brands are characterised by a limited usage of sponsorships and co-branding; in fact, they focus their marketing strategies on the functional characteristics of products and on the extremely high quality of raw materials, craftsmanship and on the participation in trade fairs. Therefore, they generally organise events that stress their peculiarity rather than invest in sponsorships. Zegna, instead, traditionally sponsors the China Soccer Association to raise brand awareness in the Chinese market.

Unlike the groups analysed in the previous chapters, co-branding actions with other companies or fashion retailers are rarely found; among the few, we may highlight Ermenegildo

Zegna x Barneys. More frequent are those with partners that share the same refined lifestyle Ermenegildo Zegna x Maserati, a super-expensive sports car, and Kiton x Benetti, a luxury yacht producer.

8.7.8 Museums, foundations and leisure time activities, in collaboration with Andrea Pittana

In this group, different approaches may be identified, each one due to the diverse strategies applied by brands and their financial resources.

On one side stands Ermenegildo Zegna, established as a textile company and transformed into a lifestyle brand whose values are rooted in its territory of origin. On the other hand, we find "other brands" that have not developed any meaningful project in this field.

In its historic headquarters in Trivero, Ermenegildo Zegna established Fondazione Zegna (Zegna Foundation), Casa Zegna (Zegna Home) and Oasi Zegna (Zegna Oasis). The philanthropic foundation is devoted to the valorisation of environmental resources, to the promotion of sustainable development in local communities as well as education, health and wellbeing (Zegna, 2019). Casa Zegna preserves the company's historic archive and, since 2013, its digital version. Oasi Zegna is an outdoor space aimed at enhancing the relationship between man, the mountains and nature and in which Bucaneve hotel is located, a luxury accommodation perfectly integrated in the surrounding territory.

Among other brands, Kiton may be examined. For 2019 Milan Design Week, the brand organised an exhibition, *The elegant man, da Van Dyck a Boldini* (Kiton, 2018) – hosted in its Milanese offices – where the brand displayed ten works that illustrated the evolution of menswear from the eighteenth to the twentieth century.

8.8 Distribution, in collaboration with Andrea Doroldi

In Milan, the points of sale of these brands are located in the fashion district; but also for this topic, we need to differentiate the choices made by Zegna from those by other companies.

The figures of the former are similar to those of historic brands: in fact, until 2018, it counted on 480 mono-brand stores, of which 267 (56%) are directly owned. However, it is necessary to underline that the number of direct and indirect mono-brand stores has slightly decreased in the last few years: at the end of 2015, they were 523 (of which 287 are directly owned). We reckon that the offline channel has been partially integrated/substituted by the online one (besides the fact that, in the last few years, formal menswear has been undergoing a crisis). In Milan, the brand has one mono-brand shop in Via Montenapoleone and one shop-in-shop at La Rinascente. The multi-brand distribution network is rather selective: Zegna's products are found in classic-style, mainly historic, points of sale boasting a cross-generational tradition, as well as in very few young multi-brand and avant-garde stores. Consequently, the percentage made by direct retail is presumably much higher than that of wholesale.

The follower brand, Canali, is characterised by totally different figures: at the end of 2018, it counted on 160 mono-brand stores, of which 40 (25%) are directly owned; in Milan, it has one single mono-brand store in Via Verri, a cross street of Via Montenapoleone. Conversely, the multi-brand distribution network is extended and comprises 900 historic and classic stores; even though there is no official data, we hypothesise that the percentage made by direct retail is considerably inferior than the wholesale one.

The figures are even lower for Kiton, which has 47 mono-brand stores, of which 15 are in franchising and five in concessions/shop-in-shops; in Milan the company has only one store in Via del Gesù (next to Via Montenapoleone): no data concerning the number of multi-brand stores is available, but we presume that the multi-brand distribution is rather selective. In this case, the percentages of turnover deriving from both direct retail and wholesale are presumably balanced.

We now consider the online distribution strategy of Ermenegildo Zegna, Canali and Kiton. The first two have their e-commerce where the whole assortment is available; the last brand owns a website where the collections are displayed but not directly purchasable; in fact, the company still prefers a traditional, physical distribution that welcomes the customer to the store and offers them a comprehensive and extremely customised shopping experience. The three brands are available in a limited number of online platforms: Zegna in four, Kiton in three, Canali in two (Farfetch and Yoox for all[1]). We presume that the merchandise offered by these brands is not particularly appealing for the most modern and fashion-oriented online platforms/players. This is due to the market composition and the taste and age of its target. The most offered product categories are formal menswear – their core business – and small leather goods, whose inferior average price makes it more accessible. If we compare the price on the companies' website and on Farfetch, we see that Kiton's prices coincide; Zegna's is imperceptibly superior on Farfetch, while Canali's is far higher. Zegna and Canali also allow purchases with mobile device thanks to a responsive website.

8.9 Omnichannel, in collaboration with Sabrina Pomodoro and Benedetta Breschi

Unlike casualwear and activewear, brands specialised in formal menswear use their means of communication with an integrated approach, even though, often, the synergy does not pivot on an actual communication theme and is only based on stylistic and aesthetic elements.

Among the four studied brands, Zegna is the only one in which for the fall-winter 2019/2020 collection, a second degree of integration, *creative-idea-led integration*, is observed. The collection is inspired by the theme of how, today, men are changing habits and lifestyle and is elaborated across the whole communication process. The hashtag *#whatmakesaman* is displayed on the windows of the boutiques of the brand together with several answers such as *#lovemakesaman* or *#freedommakesaman*. Next to these writings, the silhouette of a man constructed with various images of the advertising campaign is placed. The integration among communication tools was achieved through an idea that inspired both the style of the collection and the entire communication. Even on the Instagram page, images of men wearing a T-shirt saying *Change makes a man* are published.

The remaining two brands, Canali and Kiton, despite showing continuity and integration among its advertising campaign, Instagram page and shops, do not express an actual communication concept. For this reason, they belong to the *collection-led integration* category. In the case of these brands, we may say that the shop is the least integrated medium since neither the iconic garment of the collection nor the most promoted in advertising campaigns and on Instagram are displayed.

Interview with Andrea Lardini, President at Lardini

How has the menswear scenario changed in the last 40 years?
The change has been radical. Unfortunately, classic style is now out of fashion because it recalls something old. However, I hope this trend will pass and people will want to wear a well-made jacket and suit again.

What's the main characteristic of a menswear product?
Our product is tailored but industrialised, and wearability is its core factor. We are currently facing a generational transition which, in two years, has led us to hire 170 apprentices on a total of 480 employees. We are recreating the Made in Italy for a new generation, rethinking the company for our sons. Today, due to the different cultural models, much more patience is necessary to train new employees and transfer them the know-how: in the past, there were no Instagram, Facebook or social networks.

How are you tackling the challenge of new generations?
New generations don't just want a product, but a brand able to generate emotions. Our challenge is to conceive a new message whose DNA is still the jacket.

Is control over production still a factor of success for menswear?
Absolutely yes. Without naming anybody, some years ago, we assisted to production de-localisation in foreign countries; it is something that I've never understood. Lardini is a made-in-Italy product as well as a supplier for other brands. So far, our choice has been a factor of success, yet we must pursue this strategic vision based on specialization. Lardini has always manufactured jackets, if we did something else, we would lose the game.

Is there still room for specialised companies?
Yes, but to be competitive – considering that profitability has decreased in the last few years – many investments in human resources, technology, retail and communication are necessary.

What about sustainability?
Lardini has always paid great attention to this topic, we are pioneers in this sense. It is a cultural matter of respect for society, people and the workplace.

How has communication changed?
The speed and the channels have changed. Nowadays, everything is faster, maybe too fast. We would need more balance. We are investing less in print press and more in social media.

Do you think prices will change in the future?
If we start a price rush, we lose the battle. The strength of Made in Italy has always been the focus on the product, the idea of offering something different.

How have distributive strategies changed in the last few years?
They have considerably changed. In the past, distribution was simpler, characterised by wholesalers and chiefly multi-brand stores; today, it is paramount to be present in many channels, mono-brand and department stores, as well as online. We've been working on e-commerce for two seasons and the brand is growing; however, you need the right employees, modern and smart people.

Student activities

Choose a brand and based on your choice:

- define the sustainability actions to be applied in the future;
- identify the combination product/price segment/target where to diversify;
- identify a social media and the content typology to be developed;
- define which of the following formats – brick-and-mortar mono-brand store, brick-and-mortar multi-brand store, shop-in-shop in department stores, online mono-brand shop and online multi-brand platform – need to be developed the most;
- verify the degree of synergy among the aesthetic elements of the latest collection: the fashion show, social networks, mono-brand store windows and advertising campaign.

Note

1 Zegna is also available on SSense and Amazon (only fragrances) while Kiton is also on Amazon.

9

BRANDS SPECIALISING IN CASUALWEAR

Reading: the product manager

The product manager is the supervisor of the productive cycle of a fashion collection. This role was born about 30 years ago and is the connection among the different protagonists of a fashion company. In fact, their role embraces the whole supply chain that begins with the design and manufacturing of a collection up to its distribution. Nevertheless, their main task is to coordinate the making/production of a collection. After considering the feasibility of the ideas elaborated by the style office (Zinola, 2011), suggesting eventual modifications/ integrations to be made, the product manager takes care of the production of samples, calculating and checking the costs, the qualitative standards and the delivery time. Product managers are mostly hired directly by companies, but there are also cases of freelance collaborations with one or more firms. In addition to specific technical skills, from fabric knowledge to productive methodology, this figure needs to possess management competences in order to supervise the economic aspects as well as a leadership talent to discuss and interact with all the other figures of the company involved in the productive process.

9.1 Who are they?

In this chapter, we examine casualwear-specialised companies suitable for those customers looking for simple, practical, comfortable and informal outfits for (almost) every occasion. Due to the considerable variety of products offered by this segment, it is simpler to define what the word *casual* does not comprise: ceremony garments, outfits with a very high fashion content and avant-garde apparel. Casualwear, whose production is delocalised in low-product-cost countries, is a very complex sector where different groups of companies compete; for instance, jeanswear-specialised brands like Levi's proposing an urban style for an extended target or technical-casualwear-specialised labels like Patagonia whose innovative materials are addressed to a more specific target. In this chapter, we study the following companies: Moncler, Diesel, Levi's, Patagonia, North Face, Timberland, Stone Island, Paul & Shark and Herno.

9.2 Style[1]

In the last 20 years, casualwear, but also the entire apparel sector, has undergone a process of hybridisation. On the one hand, luxury ready to wear brands have introduced both sports and casual styles to their collections; on the other hand – and probably as a consequence – casualwear doesn't just comprise products that satisfy specific needs (e.g. weekend, free time) anymore. The result of this evolution is called athleisure: a style whose athletic/active elements are used in a new, daily, urban and non-sports context. However, hybridisation is not just a matter of styling, that is, the matching of casual and sports items with formal ones, but it has acquired a more extended nature involving technical aspects, technology and materials. A classic example is the new use of nylon proposed by Prada: the company transferred a typical sportswear material to an urban and elegant context. The casualwear segment, characterised by a variegated presence of thousands of companies, presents very different styles discussed in this paragraph. The first sub-group encompasses "historic denim" brands whose undisputed leader is Levi's. Historically, denim had always been a resistant workwear material until Levi Strauss patented his innovative and classic-style jeans that would become iconic. Another sub-category is that of "contemporary denim" whose most representative example is Diesel; besides its communication, it has always stood out for its innovative style characterised by new baggy silhouettes, original washes and a modern streetwear spirit. Moving on to the third sub-group, we find the "mountaineers" like Patagonia, North Face and Timberland. These brands are characterised by two main factors: the first is the importance of sustainability, which has always been a relevant topic, even before it became a trend; the second is the product evolution that has transformed a mountaineering brand into an urban one. Another casualwear sub-group is "outerwear", where Moncler and Aspesi are two opposite, yet significant, examples. The managerial skills of Ruffini, Moncler's leader, have turned a functional, versatile, protective, light and comfortable product into a luxury desirable object. On the contrary, Aspesi has always been loyal to itself and its philosophy, which has remained unchanged in the course of time, and recognisable for its well-made, functional and timeless products. To conclude, the last group is called "general sportswear" and is epitomised by Lacoste. Lacoste's iconic product is the polo shirt: a combination of T-shirt, a functional garment and an elegant shirt.

9.3 Supply chain and sustainability, in collaboration with Celeste Corso

Casualwear-specialised brands are characterised by products with a high technical component, multiple functions and chiefly made by outsourcing. Camuffo and Cappellari (1997) in his description of Diesel's productive strategy stated that the usage of outsourcing is necessary in a preliminary phase to compensate for the shortage of financial resources and to flexibly face a variable demand. When the company can self-finance its production, the same choice is required.

Conversely, Moncler applies a semi-integrated business model: the most relevant productive steps, such as design, raw material purchase and prototype production, are made in-house. However, the cutting and sewing are generally outsourced to Eastern European factories that are supervised by the brand.

The technical aspect and the performance of materials, as well as technological innovation, are peculiar characteristics of these labels. For instance, Stone Island uses futuristic, reflecting, photoluminescent and thermochromic materials, while the items used by North Face or Patagonia have to guarantee water repellence and breathability in extreme weather conditions. Since most of these features are obtained with a chemical finish, it is obvious to wonder whether these products can be considered as sustainable. The answer is yes.

Well aware of the impact of their products on the environment, the examined brands have found a way to reduce the consequences of the productive cycle and have become activists of sustainability.

An exemplary case is the Worn Wear project by Patagonia: worn-out products are reconditioned and delivered as new to their owners, thus extending their life cycle. With this project, the brand, besides communicating that repairing is better than discarding, won the *Circular Economy Multinational Award*, received at the World Economic Forum (Patagonia, 2020).

Timberland thinks green: with the launch of *Plant the Change*, the brand has helped the planting of 50 million trees in five years. *Reducing, recycling* and *re-thinking* are the keywords of the brand's sustainable manifesto whose ambitious objectives include the production of PVC-free shoes and a waste-recycling rate of 95% (Timberland, 2020).

In the outerwear sub-group, we find Stone Island that signed the *ZDHC, Roadmap to Zero Programme* for the reduction of chemical usage. The initiative promotes the best practices in the textile industries such as the application of "green" chemistry (Stone Island, 2020).

9.4 Segmentation strategies

Considering the high number and the heterogeneity of the companies of this cluster, segmentation strategies vary considerably according to brand. All labels share a strong focus on category – casualwear – and, in some cases on a specific product (e.g. Diesel and jeans) the market identifies them with. In the course of time, some of them have managed to build and communicate a lifestyle image, associating values, symbols and a territory to a specific product. We now consider the cases of Levi's and Patagonia.

The former initially adopted a product- and target-driven segmentation strategy: jeans for workers; afterwards, due to the product being used by different targets, the strategy evolved to become only product-focused. In fact, in the 50s and 60s, jeans became an iconic item among youth movements; moreover, in the course of time, this garment has allowed for the overcoming of any generational, cultural and social barrier. As a result, based on this strong jeans-bound identity, the company shaped an image of lifestyle founded on the following values: heritage, 150 years of history, an iconic garment – Levi's 501 – a territory – the US – and freedom.

Also, Patagonia debuted with a product- and target-driven strategy, leveraging on climbing equipment. Later on, after extending its offer, the brand defined its territory whose main values are sustainability, respect for nature and life.

In both cases, the product (jeans) and the use occasion (high-performance outdoor activities and the necessary equipment) not only do not lose their importance, but they are empowered by the values of the respective corporates positively influencing their brands.

9.5 Brand

In order to explore the branding policy, we examine brands belonging to different sub-clusters: Levis' for the group of "historic denim", Paul & Shark for the "yachting" sub-category, Timberland for "mountaineering" and finally Moncler. The latter is an extremely interesting case of a casualwear brand which has become a luxury company thanks to a new business model.

They are all characterised by the product that has made them famous and recognisable: the blue jeans for Levi's, the "yellow boots" for Timberland, the famous *COP918* woollen and hydro repellent pullover for Paul & Shark, the feather jacket for Moncler.

Despite being specialised in casualwear, these companies have diversified too, yet in a less decisive way as compared to the first five analysed clusters. Some of them have chosen this strategy to gain the status of lifestyle labels, while others mainly to enhance their brand image, or, as in the case of others, to modify it.

Levi's, which has made an extensive diversification, inclusive of new casual products such as T-shirts, sweaters, skirts, jackets and accessories for women, men and kids, belongs to the first group. Conversely, Paul & Shark hasn't applied a product diversification in the strict sense of the term, but it has added new lines, offering its most representative items also to women and kids and still leveraging on the brand essence, its practicality and technical features. Timberland diversified (less than Levi's and Paul & Shark) with the main aim to rejuvenate its brand image.

Moncler is worth a specific mention: its diversification was extended to embrace the whole apparel field, accessories and footwear, and to satisfy the needs of men, women and kids. This process has radically transformed the company that is now considered one of the main players of the luxury industry.

For these companies, the concept of made-in is pivotal to define the brand territory; nevertheless, its relevance is inferior as compared to contemporary and historic brands. In fact, we identify different "geographical origins": Made in Italy for Paul & Shark, Made in the USA for Timberland and Levi's and a hybrid between Made in France and Made in Italy for Moncler.

Concerning the naming strategy, only Levi's – whose founder is considered the quintessence of jeans – chose a patronymic. Moncler is a peculiar case whose brilliant president and CEO, Remo Ruffini, despite not being a designer, is considered a star in the fashion system for having led an excellent turnaround.

In the field of casualwear, there is not much difference between perceived and actual quality and the two vary according to the brand positioning. Perceived and actual quality are similar is because of the lack of assets that we identified for the brands observed in the first chapters – being established by couturiers or designers and having a specific heritage – allowing them to increase perceived quality. Nevertheless, the actual quality of the studied brands is, on average, high because their merchandise needs to be performing, durable and practical.

Some of these brands have their own iconic products representing their identity. Some of them have made history for being an expression of youth cultural movements: Levi's blue jeans were worn by James Dean in the famous film Rebel without a Cause and became a symbol of rebellion and anti-conformism; Timberland's *Yellow Boots* together with Moncler's down jacket were symbols of the 80s Italian youth movement called *Paninari*. In the last few years, the latter has become one of the icons of luxury, thanks to the activities promoted by Ruffini and explained in the following paragraphs. Unlike historic, contemporary and ready-to-wear-specialised brands, the creative designer, except for Moncler (see paragraph 9.7.5), which has radically changed their function, doesn't play such an important role for the brand image. Also, customisation is not a fundamental characteristic for such basic garments The permanent stylistic code of these brands is represented by a traditional style suitable for daily life; yet, even in this case, Moncler stands out for overturning the canons of its collections.

9.6 Pricing, in collaboration with Benedetta Breschi

For the examined cluster, we have studied the price of high-waist and flared jeans.

What comes to light from the comparison is that the highest price segment is, once again, occupied by unspecialised companies; historic brands like Dior and Prada, as well as Dolce & Gabbana, a contemporary brand, can impose a higher price than the specialised company 7 for all mankind. The reasons were exhaustively explained in the previous chapters.

The latter (7 for all mankind), together with J BRAND, is positioned at a superior level compared to the industrial brand Liu Jo, thanks to the superior quality of materials and to some manufacturing phases, in particular, specific washing.

The price difference between Liu Jo and Levi's, instead, is irrelevant (in absolute terms about €14): Denim, as understood in the interview reported in Chapter 5, represents the core product of the Italian company, which, in turn, aims at communicating this strategy even by positioning itself slightly higher than the American brand. In the medium-low

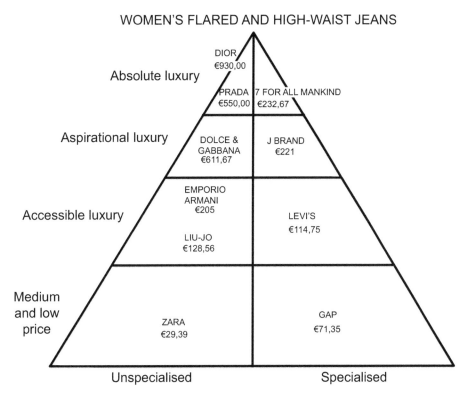

FIGURE 9.1 Golizia's pyramid of women's flared and high-waist jeans
Source: Prepared by Dario Golizia.

segment, Gap has an interesting positioning with a 142.7% higher price than Zara's: the former, in fact, horizontally, is positioned in the middle of the pyramid because, despite being a company with an extensive range of products, it is very specialised in jeans. This aspect has endowed the brand with a better reputation, as compared to Zara, and justifies a higher price difference.

9.7 Communication

We now proceed with the definition of the image of the cluster; afterwards, we study how the marketing and communication function is organised and managed by a company from the same group. Finally, we outline the communication mix applied by some brands.

9.7.1 Cluster image

Sportswear, comfort and made-in (in some rare cases) are the keywords associated with these brands. The brand image of casual brands is strongly connected to a specific product which is not general like bags for historic brands and ready-to-wear for contemporary ones; it varies from label to label. For instance, Timberland is specialised in high-quality outdoor apparel, and identified with yellow boots; Levi's iconic item are 501 jeans and the brand boasts a bond with the Made in USA; Moncler's image is associated to its iconic product, the dawn jacket, and has evolved into a luxury metropolitan style.

9.7.2 Marketing function and communication, in collaboration with Michele Leoni

Diesel's marketing and communication headquarters is in Italy, specifically in Breganze (province of Vicenza). Each region of the world, where Diesel distributes directly, has their own marketing division reporting to the central one and to the regional CEO. Concerning Italy, the department is located in Milan and directly supported by the corporate team, thanks to its convenient geographical position. All brand and communication strategies – press office included – are managed by the corporate team with the support of local resources.

The Italian press/communication office is coordinated by the local Press Office Director who acts according to the guidelines and the projects defined by the corporate office. Public relations specialists – in charge of the contacts with the local press, of samples for celebrities, influencers and for editorial shootings – report to the director of the Italian Press Office.

The Italian Marketing Division works on the actualisation of campaigns and brand projects for commercial purposes, for collaborations and capsule collections developed with brands and personalities of fashion and other industries. The acquisition of offline and online advertising spaces is entrusted to an external media centre or to an internal corporate team, depending on the type of project. The CRM office, responsible for all retailers' omnichannel strategies and implementation, and the events office, in charge of local and international events in collaboration with external agencies, both belong to the Marketing Division of Diesel.

9.7.3 Fashion shows and trade fairs, in collaboration with Andrea Doroldi

In this cluster, only one brand organises fashion shows, Moncler; most companies, in fact, showcase their new collections during trade fairs. Moncler, however, has radically transformed the concept of fashion show with its *Moncler Genius Building* project (see para-graph 9.7.5) and Vilaseca's (2010) scheme cannot be adopted.

Nonetheless, they generally participate in trade fairs, in particular in Pitti. At the 2019 Pitti Uomo, we saw the participation of Woolrich, North & Sails, Timberland, Belstaff and Paul & Shark; the latter was the only one to also participate in its digital edition in 2020. For the majority of sportswear brands, Pitti Uomo is still a fundamental and unique showcase to start their sales campaigns.

Moreover, some of them take part in Milan's Salone del Mobile: in 2019, Diesel par-ticipated in *Design Pride* signing a new Tempo handkerchief box that became a collector's object. In the same year, Timberland introduced *RoBOTL* with the intent of transforming polluting items into artistic objects: a majestic installation was made with recycled plastic bottles and production waste from the design industry (Fuorisalone, 2019).

9.7.4 Advertising, editorial, advertorial, in collaboration with Benedetta Breschi

This group had not been examined in the previous book (Golizia, 2016) and research. In terms of advertising investments, based on a sample of magazines in September 2019, the group is eighth in ranking, together with brands specialised in bags. It is worth noticing how only Herno purchased an advertising page on *Elle* and how Levi's – the historic denim brand – despite purchasing none, was dedicated, on the same magazine, five fashion edito-rials; such a result is achieved thanks to its extremely high brand awareness.

9.7.5 Influencers, gifting, endorsement, by Lavinia Biancalani

Casualwear brands, all characterised by the lack of beauty products, rely on seeding and gifting activities and mostly organise structured influencer marketing campaigns. However, they all apply different strategies. Some of them organise in-store events to meet their fan base. Others are working on the transformation of the relationship with their followers into experiences that propose new services and products to generate value.

Moncler is an example of best practice: in 2003, Remo Ruffini, president and CEO, purchased the brand while on the verge of bankruptcy and saved it thanks to a philosophy hinging on digital culture. Moncler conceives digital marketing as a crucial omnichannel tool for global growth. Very innovative and courageous decisions were made; among them

TABLE 9.1 Advertising, fashion editorial and advertorials of casualwear-specialised brands

Casualwear-Specialised Brands	*L'Officiel*			*Vogue*			*Vanity Fair*			*Elle*			*Glamour*			*Total*		
	A	FE	AD	A	FE	AD	A	FE	AD	A	FE	AD	A	FE	AD	A	FE	AD
Herno	0	0	0	0	0	0	0	0	0	1	0	0	0	0	0	1	0	0
Timberland	0	0	0	0	0	0	0	0	0	0	0	0	0	0	0	0	0	0
Paul & Shark	0	0	0	0	0	0	0	0	0	0	0	0	0	0	0	0	0	0
Levi's	0	0	0	0	1	0	0	0	0	0	5	0	0	0	1	0	6	1
Total	**0**	**0**	**0**	**0**	**1**	**0**	**0**	**0**	**0**	**1**	**5**	**0**	**0**	**0**	**1**	**1**	**6**	**1**

Source: Authors' data processing on the basis of fashion magazines published in Italy in September 2019. A, FE and AD stand for advertising, fashion editorial and advertorials, respectively.

we find the launch of *Moncler Genius – One House Different Voices*, a creative and communicative project of the brand to strengthen its presence on social media (Moncler, 2020). With *Moncler Genius*, Ruffini began the most ambitious revision substituting seasonal collections with monthly collaborations entrusted to a team of guest designers. The goal is to keep pace with the market that now longs for a quick innovation, as swift as Instagram. *Genius* is thus a project comprising eight collections, each one designed by a designer with the objective of conveying unicity and preserving the brand identity. The interaction with consumers is daily, weekly and monthly and it's to attract customers – mainly Millennials – with interesting contents and a series of public events that are told on social networks. In the first phase, on social media, the company posted contents to promote the concept epitomised by the image of *Moncler Genius Building*, generating much curiosity on the web. The building represents the brand as a house with eight windows and eight voices that embody the collections. Later on, Moncler started to create contents in collaboration with influencers, both physical and digital, connected to one another by the image of the building represented by an evocative sweater of the brand. Each personality was associated with a city (e.g. Milano, New York) to spread the message worldwide.

Levi's has chosen a winning but not revolutionary strategy. In 2017, A. Van Eynde, VP of EU brand marketing, declared that the company believed in the power of personalised experiences to capture the attention of the customer – lasting for only three seconds – and to build a relationship (FashionNetwork, 2017a). In the last few years, the strategy was based on three objectives: to become the most appreciated jeans brand, to transform products into a white canvas where the consumer can express themselves and, finally, to be a mainstream brand. Live in Levi's is the platform built around these three goals and allows the brand to be part of its customers' daily life as well as to become one of the most famous brands among Millennials. Since its debut on social media in 2009, Levi's has been successful because it doesn't simply sell a product, but it talks to its target. This strategy has proven to be effective; Millennials, in fact, yearn for experience and Levi's offers contents inclusive of music and fashion. Levi's collaborates with more than 30 festivals in Europe, from Glastonbury to Eurock, with a special *Levi's Tailor Shop*, a tour that encourages participants to customise their Levi's garment with prints, patches and pins and to share the experience on social networks. This strategy creates millions of impressions. It is also worth mentioning collaborations with celebrities and influencers (from Justin Timberlake to Snoop Dogg), hired to reinterpret the Trucker Jacket that has inspired many denim jackets in the last 50 years.

Diesel is known for its surprising communication strategies, also on social networks. *The be Stupid, Global Warming Ready* and *Live Fast campaigns* were conceived to generate buzz offline and, most of all, in online communities. With the *Go with the Flaw* strategy, the brand encouraged its fan base to accept flaws, imperfections and differences through an offline, digital and social media campaign, also supported by guerrilla marketing tactics. To do so, the brand deleted all the contents from its Instagram profile and restarted the account with the promotion of the new campaign. Most online campaigns are supported by seeding, gifting and endorsement activities involving both national and international bloggers and influencers. An interesting example is the capsule collection designed in collaboration with several artists and personalities. From the cooperation with Beyoncè, for whom the brand designed the outfits for the 2014 world tour, to the one with rapper Fedez for his concerts.

NORTH SAILS is famous for its innovative sailing technologies. Today, the motto of the brand is *Go Beyond* and it supports initiatives for ocean preservation: 1% of its revenues are donated to the cause. On social networks, the brand is characterised by a niche fan base; despite this, in 2014, it organised initiatives like the *Free the sea campaign* with selected influencers and involving personalities like Ocean Ramsey, a marine biologist and environmentalist boasting a high number of followers on social media. In 2018, the *To the Ocean* campaign was organised offline, but it was supported by three videos designed specifically for the web and social media. Three chapters for three stories, each one interpreted by a different character telling about their love for the sea and the consequences of pollution. The project saw the participation of influencers like environmentalist Sam Potter, model Simon Nessman and champion of bodyboarding Johana Schenker.

9.7.6 Social media

The brands belonging to this cluster utilise the usual social networks, Instagram, Facebook, Twitter and LinkedIn. However, Moncler goes beyond ordinary platforms and also employs WeChat in China, APAC LINE in Japan and Kakao Talk in Korea.

The first thing that can be noticed is that brands tend to post images and videos of the most recognisable and renowned product, the one that has contributed to their success: jeans for Levi's, boots for Timberland, the iconic tartan fabric for Woolrich and feather coats for Moncler. Nevertheless, some differences must be highlighted.

Some brands like Timberland are bashfully trying – through a slow, risky and long path – to change their positioning in order to "free themselves" from their iconic product. Frank Hwang, Timberland's Senior Media Manager, affirmed that the strategy must encompass several lines of products, as well as channels and regions in order to convey a clear message (Aull, 2019).

On the other hand, some companies have definitively liberated themselves from the "burden" of iconic products. It is the case with Moncler, exhaustively discussed in the previous paragraph, where plenipotential Mr. Ruffini was able to understand that the internet would modify consumers' behaviour forever and that a synchronised strategy among Facebook, Instagram and Twitter would be effective for the creation of a constructive and revolutionary dialogue.

The main, yet not only, purpose is to increase visibility and provide information on new products. Social media, to prevent companies from remaining "stuck" in their iconic items, must show their world, the so-called "behind the brand".

For instance, Woolrich describes the creative phase; as stated by Andrea Cané, its Creative Director, it is necessary to implement a communication strategy from the beginning of the creative process. Social networks ask for the truth about this procedure, and storytelling is essential (Bolelli, 2019).

Moncler aims at guaranteeing a multi-channel and unique experience for the consumer.

Brand commitment to sustainability is a key objective for Patagonia, as already discussed in a dedicated paragraph. Concerning other labels, the approach is different. Those specialising in denim, a fabric whose production requires a high amount of water and energy, have adopted a defensive approach, while those in the field of yachting and mountaineering, with a focus on sport and nature, show a proactive attitude and communicate the impact of production-generated waste (Morgan, 2019).

9.7.7 Sponsorships and co-branding

Casualwear brands have promoted outstanding sponsorships with the world of sports. On the one hand, they share with it the values of free time and a young target and, on the other hand, the functional characteristics of the product. Diesel's example refers to the first case: the company in the past had been the sponsor of the Milan football team, with which it also shared the Italian essence. The second case can be exemplified by the collaboration between Paul & Shark – whose logo is a shark – and the famous regatta *International Italian Dragon Cup*. Because, in this cluster, we find one of the best examples of co-branding in the fashion system, only a few sponsoring cases have been described.

The above-mentioned best practice is regarding Moncler, a company that has changed its business model and rooted it ion collaborations. This methodology allowed an ordinary sports brand to become a "luxury" company. Thanks to the *Moncler Genius Project*, discussed in the previous paragraph, the company radically changed a totem that had always characterised the fashion system: the fact that a luxury brand is to be "driven" by one Creative Director. The talented company CEO, Remo Ruffini, has presented an innovative approach based on the cooperation of multiple Creative Directors: one fashion house and eight different voices.

The purpose of this method is to reach an extended range of consumers, overturning and making it impossible to apply every marketing strategy that leverages on market segmentation. This model blends the idea of fashion collaborations (unique products available for a limited time) and the *drop* culture (regularly issued limited editions that are promoted online).

The other brands of this group have frequently launched capsule collections with streetwear brands with the goal of capturing a trendier segment; for instance, Levi's x Vetements, the North Face x Supreme, Timberland x Off-White.

Out of the box is Diesel's case, which by promoting causes in favour of society (see the collaboration with the *Stonewall Inn Gives Back Initiative* for the support of the LGBTQ+ [lesbian, gay, bisexual, transgender, and questioning] community) aims at strengthening the corporate reputation.

9.7.8 Museums, foundations and leisure time activities, in collaboration with Andrea Pittana

In this cluster, two strategies may be observed: the first is applied by Patagonia, whose business model is rooted in sustainability; the second characterises other brands that simply established their foundations.

Since its debut, Patagonia has put respect for nature before profit, paying great attention to both productive and selling processes and donating 1% of its revenues to environmental institutions. Its actions, also highlighted in annual reports as best practices to be shared in the fashion industry, have been and still are an example for several organisations, not exclusively in the fashion business.

To the second group belongs Levi's Foundation committed to underpinning and promoting social change and workers' rights (Levi's, 2019).

9.8 Distribution, in collaboration with Andrea Doroldi

Due to their extent and heterogeneity, the distributive choices of this cluster cannot be described as uniform. For this reason, we describe two companies that adopt opposite strategies: Moncler and Diesel.

The former, as we have already observed, adopts a methodology that can be defined as more similar to that of historic designer labels. At the end of 2019, it counted on 273 mono-brand stores, of which 209 (76.5%) are directly owned and 64 are in franchising (23.5%). The composition of its distribution is consequently very similar to that of historic brands. In Milan, the brand has two mono-brand stores of which one in Via Montenapoleone and one in Via della Spiga (for kidswear), as well as two shops-in-shop at La Rinascente. The multi-brand distribution network is rather selective; the stores are historic, elegant and include excellent brands, such as Biffi in Milan. As a consequence, the percentage of turnover represented by direct retail is far higher than that of wholesale: 77% of total sales in 2019.

Diesel has adopted an opposite strategy; it sells through 400 mono-brand stores (the number of Directly Operated Store (DOS) is unknown) and 5,000 multi-brand points of sale. In Milan, the network comprises three mono-brand stores one of which (the flagship store of the group) is in Piazza San Babila. For this reason, we assume that the percentage of turnover generated by direct retail is considerably inferior than wholesale's.

We now consider the online distribution strategy of the same brands. They have their own e-commerce where the entire assortment is available. Moncler is available on all nine platforms; while Diesel only on four (Farfetch, Luisaviaroma, Yoox and Amazon). This data confirms the diminishing interest – by top players – in the denim industry (always subjected to cycles), compared to sportswear. Ready-to-wear is definitely the most displayed category. If we compare the price of a product on their e-commerce with that of Farfetch, we see that they are the same. Moreover, the website is also available for mobile devices thanks to a responsive design and graphic.

9.9 Omnichannel, in collaboration with Sabrina Pomodoro and Benedetta Breschi

The brands studied – except for Herno – did not apply an integrated communication model for their fall-winter 2019/2020 collection.

Levi's, Timberland and Paul & Shark express their brand identity by means of advertising campaigns, but because they design versatile and rather carryover garments from season to season, they do not coordinate their communicative actions across stores, social networks and advertising. On their Instagram pages, the concept of consumers' active and casual lifestyle is stressed; nevertheless, neither the advertising campaign nor the collection is explicitly mentioned.

For Herno, a *visual and iconic integration* is observed: the same product, the feather jacket being the core business of the brand, is, in fact, proposed in the advertising campaign as well as on social media and in the shop windows.

Interview with Massimo Piombini, CEO at Diesel

What are the characteristics of casual products and how are they evolving?
A few years ago, the so-called streetwear phenomenon was born, a neologism defining a cooler concept of casual, which made some habits transversal. For instance, the comfort of wearing tracksuits and sweaters has become trendier and has spread across the different segments; nowadays, less and less people see formalwear as a model of reference, and they look to casualwear as a synonym of comfort.

How is the casualwear competitive scenario evolving?
COVID-19, and the consequent lockdown, forced 3 billion people to work from home and facilitated this trend. People, independently from their profession, worked for 8 hours a day without needing to follow a specific dress code: important entrepreneurs made 20 participant online calls wearing jeans and a sweater. This new style has been an important discovery, and employees and professionals don't want to give it up. Consequently, sportswear and casualwear − that are currently blending − will benefit from this and will become an important opportunity for the industry.

What are the needs of casualwear consumers? How will they change after COVID-19?
Coronavirus reduced consumers' needs because, being home, they did not have any particular necessity except for an Internet connection and a computer. I've understood that some behaviours imposed by the lockdown may become virtuous at the end of the emergency, and one of them involves style: managers have understood that they can achieve results and be efficient even when they don't wear a suit. At Diesel's, when we restarted, we adopted a new manifesto: "from forced to virtuous behaviours".

How do you tackle sustainability in casualwear?
Diesel has invested much and we have a green line − *Diesel for Responsible Living* − responding to specific sustainability requirements in terms of product and labour. We employ sustainable materials and productive methodologies, and we make sure that all the conditions that make a product sustainable are respected. We have made a partnership with Eco Age, Livia Firth's company, which advises us on sustainability, and we have signed the Fashion Pact.

Is diversity a strong topic nowadays?
For me and for the company, diversity means equal opportunities: a chance is given to everyone. When we decide if a person is talented, we do not consider the colour of their skin, but only their skills. However, diversity becomes a mistake when it is used as a protection for the lack of talent; I believe that a company should find a balance between offering opportunities to everyone and recognising someone's talent.

How are brand communication levers changing, in general, and also in particular at Diesel's?
Communication is one of the most important aspects of the *Sunshine* project; an approach that needs to leave behind old patterns that "interrupted" the consumer's life, whereas, now we aim to become part of it. Diesel should undergo a change: from lifestyle brand to "style of living brand".

Have the investments in print media lost their importance? How have print media been integrated/ substituted with/by social media and influencers?
Investments in print press are over. The project of digital communication can be integrated; the social media campaign becomes shoppable and merges with e-commerce, generating a virtuous circle of sales opportunities where the consumer is engaged.

Do you think that casualwear prices will change in the near future?
In casualwear, price is very flexible: you can buy jeans for €30 or €300. In this industry, price changes according to brand perception: some sell a pair of jeans for €700 and are very successful, others struggle to sell them for €100.

How are distribution strategies evolving?

For the next spring-summer 2021 campaign, brands will employ virtual showrooms: this is a typical example of how the whole value chain may change. We may just make digital collections and virtual samples; people wouldn't need to travel, and sales campaigns would become more sustainable and companies would even save a lot of money. Moreover, clients can order whenever and whatever they want; there will be no need to touch the product, but rather to understand it without physical contact, a classic example of a forced behaviour turning into a virtuous one. Brick-and-mortar stores have a future only if integrated with the digital experience. If virtual showrooms are successful, it will be a historic change and we will both produce and sell differently. We will design garments working on 3D models, we won't need the physical garment anymore. Do you understand the impact on production and on samples creation?

In a system dominated by big luxury groups and fast fashion, is there room for specialised brands like Diesel?

Yes, because we reach very good sales results, but we also need to grow as a brand and as Only the Brave group: having a critical mass is essential because it allows for negotiation.

Since you have worked for both luxury and casualwear companies, what do you think are the differences between the two?

Luxury and casual are very diverse: in luxury, the sense of urgency is higher and the market reacts with an impressive speed. If you are not smart, you are out; you need to understand trends and act swiftly. More attentive care for details is another differentiating aspect, mainly in retail.

Student activities

Choose a brand and based on your choice:

- define the sustainability actions to be applied in the future;
- identify the combination product/price segment/target where to diversify;
- identify a social media and the content typology to be developed;
- define which of the following formats – brick-and-mortar mono-brand store, brick-and-mortar multi-brand store, shop-in-shop in department stores, online mono-brand shop and online multi-brand platform – need to be developed the most;
- verify the degree of synergy among the aesthetic elements of the latest collection: the fashion show, social networks, mono-brand store windows and the advertising campaign.

Note

1 Thank you, Alberto Costabello, for collaborating in the writing of this paragraph.

10

BRANDS SPECIALISING IN UNDERWEAR

Reading: the public relation director

The fashion industry is the one where PR is paramount. The PR Director is a communication professional in charge of spreading news about brands and companies in order to make them more known and recognisable. For this purpose, they create, manage and entertain a network of relationships with different target audiences: from press offices to institutions, from influencers to celebrities, up to the final consumer: their task is to spread the news about an event, an exhibition, a sponsoring and a collaboration with an artist. According to the size of the company, the PR Director may work directly on the creation and organisation of the event. The main activity involves both preparing and sending the press kit to journalists, before an event and in organising the sending of the sample garments chosen by fashion editors for their shootings. In the last few years, the role of PR has evolved: the technological development that has extended the target audience, including among others, celebrities and influencers, has shifted the focus and modified communication tools and strategies towards new realities more fluid than print press (Zinola, 2011). In some cases, the PR Director can also be asked to manage a crisis where they have to prove to be endowed with two important skills: transparency and promptness. The PR Director can be either internal or external and can work for agencies that offer a consultancy service. The background to be a good PR Director includes a very in-depth knowledge of communication, a remarkable talent in managing public relations and the essential skill of empathy.

10.1 Who are they?

The group encompasses underwear-specialised brands manufacturing products such as pants, boxer shorts, bras, nightgowns, pyjamas, suspender belts and tights. It is a very fragmented segment including very different firms: from La Perla and Agent Provocateur, offering luxury underwear made with excellent materials and only for women, to Intimissimi and Yamamay whose assortment and medium-low price is addressed to a more extended market. Besides the above-mentioned brands, in this chapter, we observe the following labels: Parah, Chantelle, Victoria's Secret, Triumph, Rosamosario and Eres.

10.2 Style, in collaboration with Daniela Guariento

In the underwear scenario, Parah, a prestigious Italian brand, creatively develops trendy prints and graphics for jersey and satin fabrics. These are enriched with embroideries and applications which make the product recognisable and more appealing.

La Perla's product is also very well-finished and marked by a sober and sophisticated style, a less daring material matching and a more refined taste for colour. Items are chic and sober with a less aggressive sensuality also thanks to their very good manufacturing. Collections, despite being influenced by seasonal trends, always boast a vintage touch and timeless taste.

Chantelle proposes a more classic product – apparently more minimal – but with more contemporary and conceptual finishing and with attention to sculpting wearabilities, as compared to sexier and more provocative brands. In this last typology, we find Agent Provocateur whose collections, as suggested by the name, aim at communicating a strong and provocative sensuality. Even though materials are traditional – lace, jersey, satin – the wearability and the style, characterised by transparency and laces, make the product very audacious.

Victoria's Secret, a very renowned brand for its Angels – strictly selected top models – and stenographic fashion shows, presents very mainstream collections whose femininity and sensuality are not excessive.

Triumph has made very good wearability, the quality of materials and the finishing its forte. Traditionally classic, the brand produces collections recognisable for their balanced and reassuring style for an average target.

Intimissimi proposes a very comprehensive collection with five types of cups and several wearabilities, to satisfy any need of its target, and with several typologies of products: underwear, fully fashioned knitwear and nightwear. The colour range encompasses trendy and classic shades; products are never too aggressive in their style and always functional with a good fashion content.

10.3 Supply chain and sustainability, in collaboration with Celeste Corso

Concerning supply chain management, underwear brands show substantial differences according to their positioning.

In the luxury segment, Parah, as stated in the company website, obtains a high product quality thanks to its artisanal Made in Italy production that encompasses the entire supply chain, from design to avant-garde production techniques (Parah, 2019).

In the medium segment, Triumph produces both through directly owned plants and by outsourcing, monitoring and supporting the whole process to homologate the qualitative standards (Triumph, 2019).

In the medium-low segment, Intimissimi shows characteristics similar to fast fashion leaders. In an interview, Sandro Veronesi, president of the group, stated that the peculiarity of Calzedonia is its vertical structure: design, production and distribution – both direct and through affiliates – of all products are taken care of (Business People, 2018). Nevertheless, unlike the rigorous 100% Made in Italy boasted by Parah, Intimissimi also outsources its production to Sri Lanka, Croatia, Romania, Bulgaria and Serbia.

In order to discuss sustainability in the underwear cluster, a premise is necessary. These brands, like those specialised in activewear, are strongly focused on the actual and ergonomic performance of the product. As a consequence, their manufacturing must be perfect. In order to manufacture these items, excellent technical competences in material choice, patternmaking and sewing are required. This premise makes us understand the reasons behind their moderate sustainability initiatives. The use of resources and the research of materials and new technologies have always had the comfort of the product as their final objective: sustainability is still a "young" topic, although it is growing very rapidly and is now starting to become a priority for the players of this sector. Despite this, something is happening.

Parah Green is a programme created by the luxury brand to reduce emissions through the usage of solar panels. Triumph is more dedicated to social sustainability and safeguards the environment by promoting *Together We Recycle*, a programme of collection, sorting and recycling of used items (Crivelli, 2019).

Also, Intimissimi is active in the field of sustainability: for many years the brand has collected and recycled disused items, optimised the usage of paper and cardboard in packaging and reduced the use of plastic materials by substituting PVC with PET (Calzedoniagroup, 2019a).

10.4 Segmentation strategies

None of the brands in this cluster can define a lifestyle strategy. In the past, La Perla, by diversifying in ready-to-wear, had attempted to achieve this goal; yet the long-lasting negative results persuaded managers to focus only on underwear. Even Victoria's Secret had approached this type of strategy whose main characteristics were the cult of beauty, sexy merchandise and a comprehensive product portfolio; the applied communication tools, first among everything, the flamboyant fashion show, had been able to convey the message. However, the new inclusivity trend – as explained in the following paragraphs – has overturned the strategic structure of the company identity, causing an unprecedented crisis. Consequently, the description of the segmentation policy for these companies is rather easy and based on three variables: the product they are specialised in, lingerie and the chosen target and price segment. Some of them like La Perla address women with high spending power; others like Intimissimi have an average price and target both genders having a lower spending power.

10.5 Brand

For the analysis of this cluster, four companies were considered: Intimissimi, Victoria's Secret, La Perla and Rosamosario. These brands, despite sharing the same sector – underwear – satisfy different needs of the target.

Rosamosario has always inspired and been inspired by high fashion, being characterised as a haute couture lingerie brand. Since its debut, La Perla has stood out for a very high style content, the use of precious materials and the attention to detail; these factors turned the brand into the protagonist of women's luxury segment. When established, Victoria's Secret had launched a lingerie line for both genders[1] (Il Post, 2013) and, later on, decided to focus on only women's segment. Intimissimi has specialised in the feminine target[2] and, thanks to its medium-low price and basic style, has become a leader of this segment.

These brands diverge for the diversification process applied. They are mainly vertical (or line-based) for Intimissimi, which has added men's underwear, knitwear and nightwear lines for both genders: a choice consistent with its distinctive positioning. They are chiefly horizontal for Victoria's Secret, whose new product categories – fragrances, cosmetics and beachwear – until a few years ago had had a relevant role in the transformation of the brand into a status symbol of this segment. La Perla has applied both vertical and horizontal diversification, to implement a very strong strategy. At first, the company launched nightwear and beachwear collections, in line with the original product, and loyal to the brand values recognised by the market: underwear, luxury, specialisation in the feminine target. Subsequently, the brand (riskily) ventured into different categories of product – inconsistent with its original values – such as fragrances, bags, footwear and, most of all, ready-to-wear, which caused its decline. The awkward attempt to "imitate" the extensive successful diversification of some historic and contemporary brands established by designers and couturiers proved to be disastrous. Not only didn't this methodology improve the economic results, but it also destroyed the most important brand asset: the values associated with the brand by the market, which guaranteed a distinctive positioning. While Rosamosario initially competed in a niche dedicated to high-end lingerie and nightwear, in the course of time, it has consistently and slightly extended its field of action through mini ready-to-wear and bridal collections, whose style evokes the world of lingerie and guarantees brand consistency.

The *made-in* is definitely important for underwear brands, yet not as much as for historic and contemporary brands (note that the concept refers to the country of origin and not the place of production). La Perla, Intimissimi and Rosamosario leverage much on their Italian "genes", the first and the third stressing a typical Italian value like the accurate artisanal production, the second emphasising the value of a good life quality typical of the *Bel Paese*.

For high-end products by La Perla, the perceived and effective quality correspond and are both excellent. Conversely, for entry-price merchandise, the former is higher than the latter thanks to brand awareness and to the prestige values of the parent brand that are spread to cheaper products. Rosamosario boasts both an excellent perceived and an actual quality: its products are characterised by high fashion production techniques that are also correctly communicated and recognised by the customer. Intimissimi's perceived quality is superior to the effective one: the considerable investments in communication and the collaborations with famous endorsers (e.g. Sarah Jessica Parker and Chiara Ferragni) have allowed the company to reach outstanding results in terms of image. Until a few years ago, the same outcome had been achieved by Victoria's Secret – whose perceived quality was higher than the actual one – thanks to its legendary fashion shows. By involving famous top models and celebrities wearing scenographic Angel's wings, the American brand attracted the attention of the media. After some serious statements in which the top manager, Ed Razek, declared that the company's standards could not include curvy models, Victoria's Secret lost its appeal and will have to totally rethink its image.

Also, for these brands we cannot identify any iconic item, according to the definition given in Chapter 2, but we rather find representative products. For Intimissimi, we can mention the black bra, a basic women's underwear item; for Victoria's Secret, the push up; for Rosamosario the nightgown dress; while for La Perla, the refined macramé decoration. Customisation and made-to-measure services are not offered by lower-price brands like Intimissimi and Victoria's Secret, even if, in some stores of the latter, we find the bra specialist who advices the customer in the choice of the most suitable underwear. On the contrary, these services are pivotal for luxury brands like La Perla and Rosamosario because they supply a high added value.

10.6 Pricing, in collaboration with Benedetta Breschi

For this cluster, the analysed product is the silk nightgown. As in the previous chapters, we compare the positioning with other clusters.

The research shows that the historic brands[3] studied in the previous chapters do not offer lingerie; Dior proposes a limited assortment of underwear which does not encompass nightgowns. As a consequence, the highest price, among both unspecialised and specialised companies, is occupied by the contemporary brand Dolce & Gabbana.[4] Amid the latter, La Perla stands in the highest position, yet with a considerably lower price (−57.6%) than the Sicilian brand. The latter was able to build a "superior" image in this segment thanks to a very sexy and provocative style and also because it was one of the first brands to design the so-called "exhibited underwear", which allowed for a superior positioning as compared to the historic leader, La Perla. Under La Perla, we find Eres, a brand controlled by Hermès, whose price is 80.7% higher than Emporio Armani: the former is a refined specialised brand characterised by a supreme actual quality and boasting a superior brand image than the latter, in the lingerie sector. A step below, we find Victoria's Secret whose average price is almost half of Emporio Armani's and Liu Jo's: being a designer label or being perceived as such offers the latter the chance to boast this positioning. Vice versa, in the medium/low segment, Yamamay has a more-than-double price compared to H&M[5]: its underwear specialisations allow it, apart from other reasons, to enjoy a premium price.

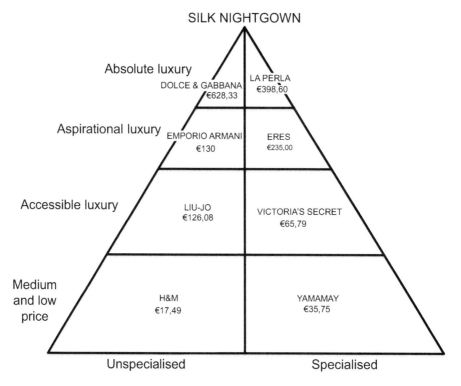

FIGURE 10.1 Golizia's pyramid of silk nightgown
Source: Prepared by Dario Golizia.

10.7 Communication

We now proceed with the definition of the image of the cluster; afterwards, we study how the marketing and communication function is organised and managed by a company from the same group. Finally, we outline the communication mix applied by some brands.

10.7.1 Cluster image

Underwear is the word associated with every brand from this cluster. It may sound banal, but there is no other cluster whose image is so bound to the product. Each brand stands out for other variables that define their brand identity and, consequently, positioning; for instance, Agent Provocateur is associated with the word sexy, while Intimissimi with a basic style offered for a medium price to a vast market.

10.7.2 Marketing function and communication, in collaboration with Michele Leoni

Intimissimi is an Italian underwear brand established in the 90s and belonging to the Calzedonia Group, which relies on the collaboration of external agencies to elaborate its communication in strategic countries.

Concerning brand communication in Italy, the Brand Manager, who develops and implements marketing projects, is the link between the corporate and the external agency. The latter deals with the corporate brand communication (not for Calzedonia Group which has its own structure) and announces all the information and news about the company, including special collaborations with talents involved in print and TV advertising campaigns. Moreover, it takes care of editorials by supplying items from the collection for the shootings that will be published on magazines.

The purchase and the planning of printed, online and TV advertising spaces is entirely managed by the brand as well as digital communication (content development and publication). The brand also plans and organises events based on trunk shows and short fashion shows dedicated to its sales force.

10.7.3 Fashion shows and trade fairs, in collaboration with Andrea Doroldi

Lingerie brands apply different strategies. La Perla and Victoria's Secret (the latter until a couple of seasons ago) showcase their collections through fashion shows; Intimissimi organises ad hoc events, while Chantelle participates in fairs.

By applying the usual classification (Vilaseca, 2010) to those companies that organise fashion shows, we can say that Victoria's Secret used to organise theatrical fashion shows; nevertheless, as explained in paragraph 10.7.5. in the last seasons, the brand hasn't organised any fashion show. La Perla gives more importance to the product and, consequently, the catwalk and the scenography are neutral, generally of dark colours. For instance, La Perla's show in Macaco for the spring-summer 2018 collection presented models walking on a totally black catwalk that naturally encouraged the audience to focus on the lace, satin, chiffon and silk items of the collection.

Speaking of Intimissimi, the company organises internal fashion shows/events that do not follow the official calendar.

Concerning the aforementioned fairs – Mipel and Pitti Immagine cannot be considered because these brands refer to other specific trade fairs such as:

- the Salon International de la lingérie in Paris;
- the Bride Show in Abu Dhabi;
- Pure London in London.

Therefore, considering the 2019 and 2021 editions, amidst the analysed brands – La Perla, Parah, Agent Provocateur, Rosamosario, Triumph, Princesse Tam Tam, Victoria's Secret, Chantelle – only the latter participated in the Salon International de la lingérie in 2019, where it will also participate in 2021.

These brands rarely take part in the Salone del Mobile in Milan (in the *Fuori Salone* events): an exception is represented by La Perla which, in 2016, in collaboration with designer Walter Terruso, had created a "custom vanity table", exhibited in its mono-brand store in Milan.

10.7.4 Advertising, editorial, advertorial, in collaboration with Benedetta Breschi

In the previous book (Golizia, 2016), underwear brands had not been examined; consequently, only 2019 advertising investments ranking is observed. As for menswear brands, it is not surprising that they didn't purchase a single advertising page, thus being last in ranking. Nevertheless, La Perla, Intimissimi and Victoria's Secret were mentioned in some of the magazines studied, in line with their price positioning. On *L'Officiel* we find La Perla, whose target is adult and with a higher spending power, whereas the remaining two, whose consumer is younger and with a lower spending power, were mentioned on *Glamour*.

10.7.5 Influencers, gifting, endorsement, by Lavinia Biancalani

This cluster is very active in the field of influencer and digital marketing because it proposes a transversal product for a very wide target. Brands competing in the medium and medium-low price segment have managed to achieve very good results thanks to effective and structured digital marketing in the long and medium term, which included seeding,

TABLE 10.1 Advertising, fashion editorial and advertorials of underwear-specialised brands

Underwear-Specialised Brands	L'Officiel			Vogue			Vanity Fair			Elle			Glamour			Total		
	A	FE	AD	A	FE	AD	A	FE	AD	A	FE	AD	A	FE	AD	A	FE	AD
La Perla	0	1	0	0	0	0	0	0	0	0	0	0	0	0	0	0	1	0
Victoria's Secret	0	0	0	0	0	0	0	0	0	0	0	0	0	1	0	0	1	0
Intimissimi	0	0	0	0	0	0	0	0	0	0	0	0	0	1	1	0	1	1
Triumph	0	0	0	0	0	0	0	0	0	0	0	0	0	0	0	0	0	0
Total	**0**	**1**	**0**	**0**	**0**	**0**	**0**	**0**	**0**	**0**	**0**	**0**	**0**	**2**	**1**	**0**	**3**	**1**

Source: Authors' data processing on the basis of fashion magazines published in Italy in September 2019. A, FE and AD stand for advertising, fashion editorial and advertorial, respectively.

gifting and endorsement activities. The brands positioned in the highest price segment were not able to effectively adopt similar initiatives.

Intimissimi is an exemplary case that shows the amount of investments allocated to this strategy. For instance, Chiara Ferragni was chosen to participate in several events like the famous *Intimissimi on Ice* for which she designed the 2017 edition costumes. Chiara Ferragni declared that this partnership was an occasion to challenge herself and to live a new experience as a designer (Fashion Network, 2017b). This collaboration gave birth to other activities with Chiara Ferragni who is also the digital ambassador of the company. Ferragni is a constant presence on the brand's Instagram page together with models like Irina Shayk and Gisele Bündchen. Moreover, Intimissimi works on less structured endorsement initiatives all gathered under the hashtag #intimissimigirls, having an international and cross-generational resonance. In 2019, for its men's line, Intimissimi Uomo, the brand chose Fedez, Ferragni's husband, as the digital ambassador.

Yamamay, manifesting its intention to exploit all the possibilities to generate social network engagement, planned a very extensive strategy which includes diversified endorsements for product launch, brand values storytelling and the opening of flagship stores; another initiative are the collaborations for capsule collections. In 2017, the company teamed up with Chiara Ferragni's *The Blonde Salad* for the launch of co-branded corsets; recently, in 2019, on the occasion of the opening of a flagship store in Milan, the brand hired ten Italian influencers and invited them to the event and to share it on their Instagram stories. The employing of web influencers for the launch of new products is spread all year long as a witnessing of a long-term, well-structured strategy. An unusual partnership was signed in 2018 and confirmed in 2019 with Cristiano Ronaldo (boasting 200 million followers on Instagram), whose CR7 Underwear line is distributed by Yamamay in the Italian market.

Victoria's Secret has been a benchmark for the segment thanks to its effective online and offline marketing and communication strategies. Unlike the above-mentioned brands, its influencer marketing is characterised by a unique peculiarity. The majority of its offline promotion relies on the fashion shows that the company organised every year from 1995 until 2018. The success of the show was due to its extravagance, guests and the endorsement of celebrity top models, known as Victoria's Secret's Angels, who contributed to enhance the company image. In 1999, for the first time, the show was broadcast online and followed by 1.5 million spectators; since 2001, it had been regularly broadcast on American television. Among the brand Angels we find models such as Naomi Campbell, Claudia Schiffer, Gisele Bunchen, Laetitia Casta, Adriana Lima and many others also boasting numerous followers online.

Given that this strategy is strongly rooted in the target's imaginary, it's not a surprise that, in spring 2019, when the brand posted on its Instagram feed photos with influencers like Jenny Cipoletti and Cara Santana (459,000 and 780,000 followers, respectively), which were not appreciated by followers, the company decided to delete them. We can conclude that, despite the brand being a precursor of digital marketing strategies and cross-pollination between online and offline contents, its target audience preferred those personalities that had become famous offline (models), rather than influencers who had gained their status online. The future scenario is uncertain. Due to a slump in sales since 2017, Stuart B. Burgdoerfer, Chief Financial Officer and Executive Vice President of L Brands, had declared that no show would be organised in 2019. He had also reassured that the brand would continue to communicate through other channels, social networks included.

The least active segment in the field of social media marketing is the premium-luxury one, whose sales are currently suffering. Agent Provocateur is an exception in this sub-cluster for the promotion of structured traditional influencer marketing campaigns. Through the hashtag #unApologetic, expressing the theme of the fall-winter 2019/2020 collection, the company employed some social talents to create *adv* contents. Among them, we find Ali Tate and Alexandrina Turcan (216,000 and 60,100 followers, respectively, on Instagram). Singer Charlie XCX (3.7 million followers) is the face of the 2019 holiday campaign, while a group of personalities with a strong online presence including Caroline Vreeland (395,000 followers on Instagram) were chosen for #APTalks: there were video sessions about body confidence for social networks and for the company's UK website.

10.7.6 Social media

In this section, we study the approaches to social media applied by Victoria's Secret, La Perla and Intimissimi. The social media platform most used is Instagram; however, unlike other clusters where Facebook and Twitter play a secondary role, in this case, they are essential for total coverage of the communication strategy.

By observing Victoria's Secret's, we can identify various typologies of social media contents. The brand exploits the visual appeal of Instagram, where the majority of images portray products, the company's name is well-displayed and both colours and locations are beautiful. Concerning Facebook, visual elements are once again the main characteristic; subjects are usually backstage pictures, promotions and launches of new products, all described by short captions. The brand also employs video teasers about upcoming shows aimed at increasing followers' engagement. Twitter is used to communicate flash news about product launches and new arrivals, while YouTube presents the catalogues of new collections (Ramakrishnan, 2019).

La Perla's platforms display captivating images of products and lines, as well as unpublished contents. Instagram doesn't just consist of a beautiful photo album, but it also offers a service to customers who can order and check the product availability and delivery; consumers can also write reviews and share opinions (Lettly, 2016).

Intimissimi stands out for its different and still product-driven approach. The brand chiefly utilises Instagram where it boasts 3 million users and transfers exactly the same posts to Facebook, whereas the usage of other social media is not significant. The company conveys its product range in a linear way without involving the audience and applying a vertical brand-user communication. To do so, it publishes highly engaging product images and dedicates a considerable number of posts to its collaborations with influencers and digital talents. However, it is worth considering how the brand exploits the platform to generate traffic on the online shop, resulting in conversion. This intention is evident in the implementation of the Instagram Shopping function on the majority of posts, but also in the writing of the item code in the caption to facilitate purchases. As mentioned above, much attention is paid to the posting of contents related to the numerous collaborations with influencers and digital talents with the aim of making the storytelling more engaging.

Underwear had always been considered a functional item until the arrival of social media, which have changed its perception and created engagement and inclusivity.

Speaking of this topic, we hereby describe two examples, a negative and a positive one, both involving Victoria's Secret. On the one hand, the American company has always taken care of its followers by involving them through questions, surveys and content sharing. For instance, the initiative #pinktruck, based on the usage of Twitter, informed users about the university campus where the brand would organise a game that would involve founding Victoria's Secret mascot (Lettly, 2016). On the other hand, the label, which has always leveraged on provocative beauty, hasn't proven to be ready to respond to the need of inclusivity. People magazine tweeted that Victoria's Secret would prefer to cancel its world annual event rather than include women with ordinary bodies (Forrester, 2019).

Green issues are another hot topic as witnessed by Intimissimi that promoted an initiative to recycle used garments – by any brand – which were collected in its shops (Zanzi, 2019).

10.7.7 Sponsorships and co-branding

Underwear brands rarely implement sponsorships. Lingerie, in fact, is still considered by consumers as an ordinary purchase with a functional purpose. Hence, the lack of need to enhance the perceived value of the product by organising sponsorships. A rare example is the partnership between *Intimissimi Uomo* and the important cycling event *Giro d'Italia*: it represents an evident attempt of a women-underwear-specialised brand to enhance its diversification into menswear.

For the above-explained reasons, these companies put less effort in co-branding, as compared to the previous clusters. The most common initiatives are collaborations with beautiful, sensual and fascinating influencers: see, for example, *Agent Provocateur x Penelope and Monica Cruz* and *Intimissimi x Chiara Ferragni*.

10.7.8 Museums, foundations and leisure time activities, in collaboration with Andrea Pittana

The business models of this cluster do not express the necessity to develop contents and relations based on heritage and lifestyle. Strategies are mainly focused on product development and on digital marketing. Among the few experiences in this sector, we may point out the one by the Calzedonia Group. In 1999, its president, Sandro Veronesi, created Fondazione San Zeno (San Zeno Foundation) aimed at encouraging change in the labour world by organising training and courses for the development of solid skills.

10.8 Distribution, in collaboration with Andrea Doroldi

Also, for lingerie-specialised companies, it is hard to make a homogeneous description of their distribution choices.

On the one hand, we have La Perla, a brand with a luxury positioning, having 150 mono-brand stores of which 44 (29.3%) are directly owned. In Milan, the label has two mono-brand stores, of which one is in Via Montenapoleone, and a shop-in-shop is at La Rinascente. The multi-brand network is smaller: it mainly comprises points of sales specialising in the segment of underwear and having a small selection of products (the brand is also available in some unspecialised multi-brand stores). Consequently, the percentage made by direct retail is allegedly lower than that of wholesale.

On the other hand stands Victoria's Secret, which in March 2019, counted on more than 1,600 shops worldwide inclusive of Directly Operated Store (DOS), shop-in-shops, multi-brand stores and outlets. The lingerie giant was forced to reduce its retail channel by closing 53 stores in 2019. In Milan, the company has three mono brand stores all in franchising. As a consequence, the percentage of turnover made by direct retail is allegedly lower than the one generated by wholesale channels.

Intimissimi's strategy with 1,738 stores at the end of 2019, of which about 1,400 are in franchising, is exclusively mono-brand. Compared to Victoria's Secret, in the same year, Intimissimi assisted to an increase of 71 shops (of which 46 are for men). In Milan, the brand has 11 points of sale located in the high streets and central areas of the city. Due to the high impact of franchising, we presume that the percentage generated by direct retail is considerably inferior than by wholesale.

We hereby consider the online distribution strategy of the same brands. They can rely on their e-commerce where the whole assortment is available. La Perla is also sold on eight platforms; Victoria's Secret on only one (Amazon) and Intimissimi on none. The most present product category is of course lingerie for the first brand, whereas for Victoria's Secret we find fragrances, accessories and beauty. By comparing the price on La Perla e-commerce and that of Farfetch, we see that they coincide. All three brands also allow purchases using mobile devices thanks to a responsive website.

10.9 Omnichannel, in collaboration with Sabrina Pomodoro and Benedetta Breschi

Brands specialising in lingerie do not promote new collections on the basis of a core theme that extends to all their communication tools. Since all the studied brands, La Perla, Victoria's Secret, Triumph and Intimissimi, propose carryover garments from season to season, they do not convey an actual seasonal theme that goes beyond the simple promotion of their offer. For this reason, they belong to the *visual and iconic integration* group; they apply a strategic continuity among the outfits worn in the advertising campaign, those displayed in the shop windows and those posted on Instagram. With regard to the latter, the advertising campaign is promoted by posting its images, sometimes with sponsored posts.

Interview with Francesco Sama, Managing Director at Pianoforte Holding[6]

How has the underwear product evolved and how will it evolve in the future?
The paths are different and partially accelerated by the global context we're experiencing: the first path is about comfort, that is, products that guarantee both performance and comfort, as well as being user-friendly. The second path is sustainability, which implies using low-impact textiles materials and production processes. The third path is innovation, which is nothing but the execution of the first two. Finally, seduction is individual valorisation and a means to be self-confident.

How is the underwear scenario evolving?
The degree of loyalty is increasing, and the boundaries between the concepts of everyday and special occasions are more and more liquid for products that, even in daily life, are still seductive, yet comfortable. Socialisation opportunities are being restricted, and this is impacting the consumption habits of the apparel and underwear industries.

How are the needs of consumers changing?
The new habits generated by the COVID context, by the increase of smart working, and by the decrease of socialisation opportunities, impose new attention for versatile and multi-functional products, characterised by comfortable wearability, but at the same time seduction and fashion content.

How are you dealing with new generations (Millennials, Generation Z)?
The new generations are most sensitive to three important aspects: price, immediate and easy accessibility, and sustainability.

How do you include sustainability in fashion?
It's a crucial topic that should not be considered as greenwashing anymore, but as a structural attitude in the design process, in products and in contents. Price remains an important value, but it should leave room for more conscious and focused consumption. I believe that we could accelerate this change by specific incentives aimed at rewarding virtuous companies, at obliging all brands to publish their sustainability reports.

How have communication levers changed? Have investments in print press lost their importance compared to the past?
The advertising market, which was already moving to the digital, has undergone an acceleration, thanks to COVID-19, developing new skills and methods. Digital engagement, mobile-led, social commerce, live streaming, Artificial Intelligence are all activities that will evolve even more and that will contribute to shifting the focus on digital tools. However, we should pay attention to the topics of competition and monopoly, which require a more in-depth study.

How has communication evolved with the arrival of social media and influencers?
The fundamentals are the same in terms of credibility, content, impact and emotion, yet the tools, the frequency, the need for renewal and surprise, are experiencing the impact of new interpreters and protagonists. I believe that we will evolve up to the point that we will all become influencers and the opinion of a friend will be as valuable as that of an influencer who is paid to advertise a product. Web reputation will be built by customers rather than by digital actors.

Do you think that the price of underwear will change in the future?
We're living in a period of deflation rather than inflation. However, the new abovementioned contents are pushing in the opposite direction for substantial stability or slight increase: we're learning that exasperate consumption leads nowhere. I think that higher care for quality, sustainability and durability could re-balance the easy-opium of sales, called price.

How are distributive strategies changing in your sector?
Many balances are breaking, there is no limit between digital and physical anymore, we will have to reconsider the value and the costs of brick-and-mortar stores since their location and role are evolving. Experts say that in ten years, at least 70% of fashion consumption will start online to then move to offline stores. Consumers will first consult the web to understand more about the product and the brand. Shops will then become brand ambassadors and representatives of the brand experience, thing not always easy to achieve.

Is it essential to have a defined business model? How can a specialised brand win the challenge in a scenario dominated by big groups?

I believe that the most important things are brand relevance and brand trajectory on which to shape and renew the business model by adapting it to the commercial and technological evolutions. Niches are growing, most of all thanks to the digital world and this implies new visions and skills. The concentration phenomenon will continue, but the new commercial spaces allow for differentiation and accessibility. It is evident that if digital visibility barriers grow, the smallest will suffer even more; that's why the digital concentration we're living – in the hands of very few players – is one of the topics to discuss at a structural and legal level.

Student activities

Choose a brand and based on your choice:

- define the sustainability actions to be applied in the future;
- identify the combination product/price segment/target where to diversify;
- identify a social media and the content typology to be developed;
- define which of the following formats – brick-and-mortar mono-brand store, brick-and-mortar multi-brand store, shop-in-shop in department stores, online mono-brand shop and online multi-brand platform – need to be developed the most;
- verify the degree of synergy among the aesthetic elements of the latest collection: the fashion show, social networks, mono-brand store windows and the advertising campaign.

Notes

1 In 1983, the production of men's underwear was cancelled.
2 The brand, despite launching a men's line, is strongly perceived as a women's brand.
3 Chanel, Hermès, Louis Vuitton and Prada.
4 Giorgio Armani does not offer silk nightgowns; for this reason, we have analysed Dolce & Gabbana.
5 Zara has no nightwear line.
6 Pianoforte Holding controls several brands including Yamamay and Carpisa.

11

BRANDS SPECIALISING IN ACTIVEWEAR

Reading: the fashion influencer

The influencer is a person able to influence consumers' opinion of a brand and their product choices. They do so by leveraging on their prestige and knowledge, gained through the experience acquired in a certain field. The expertise then leads to a following on online channels, including blogs or social networks. This figure is the evolution of the opinion leader or tastemaker; the influencer and relative marketing are an integrating part of the promotion and communication strategies of many companies, as well as a support to traditional strategies. The influencer, hired with collaboration and endorsement agreements, is asked to advertise a product or brand, known to their public, applying the sharing tools supplied by the different social networks, and in line with their tone of voice. The skills of influencers are mainly based on the ability to create engaging contents (e.g. posts on social media or articles and reviews on blogs); the presence of a potential audience of users to whom they will convey the content (followers); the capability to diffuse that content, that is, the action and interaction with followers who, in turn, amplify the original message by sharing it. The influence of a user allows the client brand to amplify a message and generate trust among consumers, who consult more and more social networks before making a purchase decision. In the fashion industry, the influencer is any user of the internet with a significant following, able to impact the purchasing decisions of their audience, as well as dedicated and active in the fashion system.

11.1 Who are they?

The group comprises companies whose offer was originally focused on only sports apparel, footwear and accessories for activities like tennis, running, football and basket. To this cluster belong brands having different peculiarities: leaders like Nike and Adidas which, thanks to a very comprehensive assortment – now also including casualwear – and considerable investments in sponsorships, have achieved very high revenues; but also smaller niche brands specialised in a particular sport (e.g. Speedo in swimsuits and Reebok in CrossFit).

Since the product needs to be constantly improved to satisfy the necessities of a more and more demanding target, for all these brands, investments in research and development are one of the key factors of success. Furthermore, this sector has assisted with the emerging and consolidation of a strategy based on the launch of very successful capsule collections. In addition to the above-mentioned companies, we also consider Robe di Kappa, Fila, Dimensione Danza, Freddy and Puma.

11.2 Style, in collaboration with Daniela Guariento

In the apparel industry, the activewear niche is very important. The stylistic identity of its companies is defined according to the technical needs they satisfy and the fashion content.

On one side stand historic leaders like Adidas and Nike, which, in addition to designing collections with an adequate fashion content and an accurate material and accessories selection, often promote capsule collections signed with ready-to-wear brands (see paragraph 11.7.7).

On the other side, we find brands like Robe di Kappa, specialised in causal collections. The product range is exhaustive and includes practical and functional products characterised by an adequate fashion content.

Fila, instead, constantly keeps an eye on trends; this attitude results in an experimental research on materials, on technical, super-light and laminated fabrics that are then matched with jersey. The outcome is a very good combination of sport, fashion and functionality.

Some niche companies specialise in one typology of product and are also recognisable for satisfying a specific need; in the field of dance, for instance, we find Dimensione Danza and Freddy. The former designs basic and functional products made of jersey and stretchy fabrics; the very visible application of the logo on garments makes the collections recognisable. Freddy chooses to employ functional materials consisting mainly of bi-elastic jersey; its wearabilities and cuts enhance shapes and silhouettes.

11.3 Supply chain and sustainability, in collaboration with Celeste Corso

For these companies, one of the key factors of success, as we will see in the following paragraphs, is to be associated with athletes and/or sports teams in which they allocate most of their financial resources. For this reason, they do not invest in direct production: almost the entire manufacturing is delegated to hundreds of sub-suppliers located in many countries. On its website, Nike informs consumers that its supply chain encompasses 527 long-term partners from 41 different countries (Nike, 2019a).

The DNA of these brands is a mix of technology, technicality and design. However, in order to reach an excellent positioning, these features are not enough anymore. In the last few years, sustainability has emerged as an indispensable aspect. So, leveraging on their natural ability to embrace change, they have set ambitious goals, defining successful long-term programmes that have strengthened their credibility.

For instance, Adidas has taken care of sustainability since 1989. The brand is fully committed and embraces several aspects of the issue: speaking of ethics, it makes sure its partners guarantee the respect of workers' rights, putting an end to the past controversy about child labour; concerning the environment, since 2015, the brand has supported *Parley for the Ocean* and contributes to the cleaning of the coasts of Maldives from plastic.

Even Nike is an activist brand when referring to sustainability. For instance, the label designed *Nike Grind*, a range of regenerated materials used to produce shoes and apparel, as well as *Fly Leather*, a lighter and more-resistant-than-leather material obtained from the waste of the manufacturing process, and with reduced water consumption and CO_2 emissions (Nike, 2019b).

Niche brands like Arena and Speedo are still bound to the concept of performance and, as a consequence, they leverage more on the technical aspect of the product rather than on sustainability.

11.4 Segmentation strategies

A cluster including tens of brands necessarily encompasses different segmentation strategies; we hereby describe some examples.

On the one hand, Nike and Adidas adopt a lifestyle strategy; we now consider the former. The evolution undergone by the company shares some characteristics with many brands implementing the same strategy: at first, it pivoted on product and target; afterwards, it extended the merchandise offer to satisfy different needs (undifferentiated strategy), and, later on, the brand image became associated with values such as victory, the legendary Michael Jordan, iconic products, free time, community and innovation: factors able to convey a universal message and a lifestyle (lifestyle strategy). Despite all these values conveying a universal message and despite the corporate being strong, the main product – sneakers – are not overshadowed, but rather strengthened.

On the other hand, we find labels applying a product-driven strategy, focused on a specific macro use occasion for many targets: this is the case with Reebok, which is involved in marketing apparel, footwear and accessories for a universal idea of fitness: "We believe that fitness is for everybody – and every BODY" (Adidas Group, 2019).

Finally, others implement an even more specific strategy focusing on a micro use occasion: see, for instance, Speedo that states: "Since the launch of our first swimsuit in 1928, Speedo has continued to focus on two things: swimming and people who love to swim" (Speedo, 2019).

11.5 Brand

To analyse the branding strategies of this cluster, Adidas and Nike, leaders of the industry, were selected together with Fila, a follower, and Dimensione Danza, a niche company.

Adidas and Nike have common roots as they both debuted in shoes manufacturing: football shoes for the former, training shoes for the latter[1]; Fila, instead, debuted with an underwear collection, while Dimensione Danza with trendy dance apparel.

The evolution followed by the first three is similar: at first they extended their product assortment to other sports; subsequently, they encompassed the new athleisure segment in their offer. Furthermore, Adidas also included products that did not belong to its traditional product base such as watches and fragrances, and stood out for the launch of capsule collections. Conversely, Dimensione Danza, consistent with its niche strategy, did not detach from its core business.

These labels differ for the chosen naming strategy: Dimensione Danza and Fila have kept the same brand name, which is extended to every product category, encompassing also the values and the aesthetic codes of the brand. Adidas and Nike have adopted a similar strategy for most of their products, whereas, for some iconic categories of merchandise, they added a suffix: see, for instance, the legendary Adidas Originals or the Air Jordan by Nike.

Speaking of perceived and actual quality, we can state that for the two leaders, the former is superior to the latter. This result was obtained thanks to a strong reputation consolidated by decades of marketing and communication activities such as the sponsoring of very important events, clubs and athletes, as well as collaborations with famous artists and designers. Due to the lack of the above-mentioned factors, Dimensione Danza's perceived quality is the same as the actual one. On the contrary, thanks to the Made in Italy it boasts, Fila's perceived quality is greater than the real one.

Concerning iconic products, Nike and Adidas have plenty of them and, like the most famous designer labels, they are pillars of the brand identity. Among them, we may remember: Superstar, Gazelle and Stan Smith shoes for the former; Air Jordan 1 and Nike Air Max for the latter. For Dimensione Danza and Fila we can speak of symbol-products, which, however, lack in the legendary value that is typical of iconic ones.

Most of the sportswear items are carryovers and there are no significant differences between fall-winter and spring-summer collections. Nevertheless, the offer is not reinvigorated by regular launches of new merchandise and capsule collections. The most significant are those by Adidas and Kayne West, and with British designer Stella McCartney.

The made-in meant as place of production is not important for sportswear brands, whose production relies on hundreds of sub-suppliers located in low-labour-cost countries. On the contrary, the same concept, meant as country of origin, for some brands is definitely an added value: the association between Nike and USA, Fila and Italy, and Adidas and Germany is immediate. Their Creative Directors are not fashion stars, even if the above-mentioned collaborations have allowed some brands to be linked to the designers with whom they have partnered. This, in turn, has contributed towards building a brand identity that makes these labels be perceived as closer to the fashion world.

Even these brands have permanent stylistic codes, in particular, the logo: see, for instance, the legendary logos of Nike and Adidas. Among the analysed brands only Nike offers its customers the possibility to customise the product both on the website and in some stores.

11.6 Pricing, in collaboration with Benedetta Breschi

We hereby consider the price of women's sneakers to compare the positioning of unspecialised and specialised companies.

Concerning the highest segment, we confirm the considerations and reasons explained in Chapters 2 and 3. Dior and Hermès, for the previously mentioned reasons, are characterised by a consistently superior price positioning (+172% and +141.7%) as compared to Y3 ADIDAS.

Even the contemporary brand Giorgio Armani has a price higher than Y3 ADIDAS and Stella McCartney for Adidas. It is interesting to notice how the price of the latter is more than the double of the standard Adidas product, thanks to the partnership with the British designer. Nevertheless, it remains much lower than the price of the more renowned Milanese company, whose brand image is more consolidated.

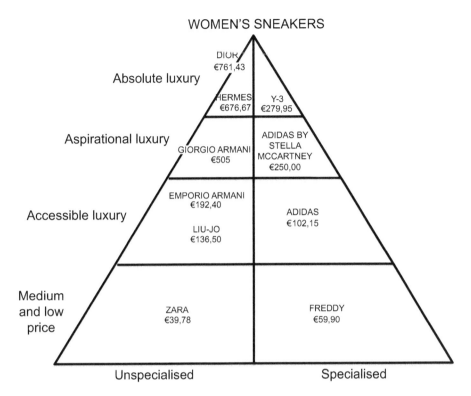

FIGURE 11.1 Golizia's pyramid of women's sneakers
Source: Prepared by Dario Golizia.

In accessible luxury, Liu Jo's positioning is arguable; in fact, its price is 33.6% higher than Stan Smith's, the iconic Adidas product.

In the medium–low segment, the specialised brand Freddy has a 50.5% higher price compared to Zara's; the latter is not very appealing in this segment.

11.7 Communication

We now proceed with the definition of the image of the cluster; afterwards, we study how the marketing and communication function is organised and managed by a company from the same group. Finally, we outline the communication mix applied by some brands.

11.7.1 Cluster image

Sneaker, innovation, technical materials, running, football, comfort and lifestyle (for leaders) are the most commonly associated words to this cluster's brands. In this group, we find brands whose identity is strongly bound to a specific sport (e.g. Speedo and swimming) or to a product (e.g. New Balance and sneakers), while others, despite being firmly connected to both (e.g. Nike and football and sneakers), are able to convey a lifestyle image to consumers.

11.7.2 Marketing function and communication, in collaboration with Michele Leoni

Kappa, brand property of Basic Net, is endowed with two different "souls": Kappa Sport and Kappa Authentic.

The former is the division dedicated to sport and technical apparel whose communication activities mostly consist of sponsorships in the fields of football and skiing, as well as with several sports federations. In this case, communication involves sponsorships, events, print media – the latter only dedicated to skiing and sometimes to football – social media and endorsee (only for skiing).

Kappa Authentic is the lifestyle-streetwear division. Its iconic product is the *222 Banda* re-interpreted from time to time according to the evolution of the collections. Kappa Authentic communication leverages on events – mainly connected to the music world such as Kappa FuturFestival; social media and digital projects; collaborations with other brands like Marcelo Burlon, Danilo Paura, Faith Connexion, or with musicians like Ultimo, Dark Polo Gang; shop windows and seeding of some items from the collections in collaboration with influencers.

Directly managed Kappa's marketing is developed according to the two macro areas and, taking into account the diversity of the two labels, it involves two different professional figures: one in charge of Kappa Authentic and another responsible for Kappa Sport. Relations with sports teams and federations, events organisation and collaborations are internally supervised. The brand employs consultants like creative and graphic design agencies, to be supported in the making of the most complex materials, a public relations and communication agency for external relations with the press (specifically for Kappa Authentic) to involve influencers and for digital and seeding projects.

11.7.3 Fashion shows and trade fairs, in collaboration with Andrea Doroldi

The brands from this cluster do not contribute to fashion weeks; in fact, their product portfolio chiefly comprises carryover items and does not contemplate the two traditional collections: spring-summer and fall-winter. The new periodically launched products are promoted on social media by influencers (see following paragraphs) through in-store presentations and often by sending sales agents or direct salespersons to clients to show the flash collections on iPad.

Also, for this cluster, the fairs considered in the previous chapters – Mipel and Pitti Immagine – cannot be a reference. In fact, for activewear business-to-consumer (BTC) fairs – addressed to final consumers – are more relevant than business-to-business (BTB) fairs – aimed at buyers. In October 2019, in Milan, the first *Plug-Mi The Sneakers Culture Experience* was held, designed by Fandango Club that saw the participation of Adidas, Puma, Nike and Reebok.

Even though they don't have interior design lines, some of these brands take part in Milan's Salone del Mobile – specifically in the *Fuori Salone* events: for instance, in 2018, Nike organised the *Brothers of the World* exhibition, which recalled the sports uniforms of the last 40 years, to celebrate the world of football.

11.7.4 Advertising, editorial, advertorial, in collaboration with Benedetta Breschi

Since this group had not been examined in the previous book (Golizia, 2016), only the 2019 advertising investments data is studied. As for the clusters specialised in menswear,

TABLE 11.1 Advertising, fashion editorial and advertorials of activewear-specialised brands

Activewear-Specialised Brands	L'Officiel			Vogue			Vanity Fair			Elle			Glamour			Total		
	A	FE	AD	A	FE	AD	A	FE	AD	A	FE	AD	A	FE	AD	A	FE	AD
Nike	0	0	0	0	0	0	0	0	0	0	0	0	0	0	0	0	0	0
Adidas	0	0	0	0	0	0	0	0	0	0	3	0	0	0	1	0	3	1
Freddy	0	0	0	0	0	0	0	0	0	0	0	0	0	0	0	0	0	0
Fila	0	0	0	0	0	0	0	0	0	0	0	0	0	0	0	0	0	0
Total	**0**	**0**	**0**	**0**	**0**	**0**	**0**	**0**	**0**	**0**	**3**	**0**	**0**	**0**	**1**	**0**	**3**	**1**

Source: Authors' data processing on the basis of fashion magazines published in Italy in September 2019. A, FE and AD stand for advertising, fashion editorial and advertorials, respectively.

streetwear and underwear, these brands didn't purchase any advertising page, thus being last in ranking. They prefer, among other things, to communicate by sponsoring teams and athletes of several sports and by using social media.

11.7.5 Influencers, gifting, endorsement, by Lavinia Biancalani

Activewear brands, before the arrival of social media, already relied on celebrities and world-famous athletes to communicate their identity and promote their products. Today, those celebrities have become influencers because they speak to millions of people.

Nike and Adidas implemented well-defined social media and influencer marketing strategies. Both brands have been innovators in the use of new technologies such as apps for running designed to motivate, inspire and share the experience of runners and conquer the heart of their communities.

In 2011, Adidas launched *MiCoach*, a voice which acted as a personal trainer for its users. Nike presented the app *Nike + Run Club* that proposed a new way of training together with the possibility to share their performances online to its users.

Both brands leveraged on emotions. Adidas, by relaunching some classics like Stan Smith and Gazelle that epitomised a nostalgic past. Nike, with its slogan *Just Do It*, touched the emotional side of its consumer and generated memorable experiences exemplified in the digital campaign *Dream Crazy* in collaboration with quarterback Kaepernick.

The influencer marketing strategy of the two giants is based on a preliminary selection of celebrities/influencers for the product launch; in the second phase, other influencers and web personalities may be employed.

In 2015, Adidas launched *Yeezy* shoes designed by rapper Kanye West, a very successful initiative thanks to the effective communication of Kayne. It's, in fact, the rapper who promotes the brand through its offline visibility during his concerts and events, and online with the endorsements of his wife Kim Kardashian and some VIP friends. It is important to stress how, among young people interested in trends, the celebrity's approval is a powerful WOM (word of mouth) marketing tool; the endorsement by celebrities boasting millions of followers directs the attention to the product and makes the hype[2] and the desire to acquire a product grows together with a sense of exclusivity. In the case of *Yeezy*, the shoes were not available in any store, and the launch date was secret and had to be found out online by potential customers.

Nike collaborates with very different personalities and transforms its online partnerships into events that actively involve the entire community. The American brand selects influencers and web personalities according to the segment of reference. On the one hand, we find athletes like James LeBron, NBA player of Los Angeles Lakers, Cristiano Ronaldo for football and Serena Williams for tennis, personalities whose enterprises are followed both offline and online thanks to their numerous followers. On the other hand, the brand organises collaborations aimed at reaching a fashionista target choosing Chiara Ferragni, who, on her blog, explains how she uses the app *Nike NTC*.

Puma, after losing a bit of appeal, has recently tried to compensate with new communication strategies on social media. In 2014, the company declared its intention to reach the new target of Millennials, introducing a new streetwear line. For this purpose, the brand worked with Rihanna's Fenty collection: a line worthy of its own Instagram profile. Most posts did not portray Rihanna; however, the account gained visibility thanks to the sharing on her profile followed by more than 87 million users. Still in the attempt to appeal to Millennials, Puma has promoted the launch of *Fierce* – a super-light shoe – with the help of Kylie Jenner, model, entrepreneur and girlfriend of rapper Tyga. Conversely, for the launch of the #IgniteXT line, to give visibility to the product and to raise awareness and engagement on social media, the brand chose to collaborate with about 60 international macro and micro influencers.

Freddy, specialised in sports and casualwear, used to rely on social networks only for product promotion. Lately, the brand has modified its strategy to stress its values. Its channels offer high-quality contents with an accurate social media storytelling; ideas are designed ad hoc and consistent to the payoff *The Art of Movement* that links art and sport. #Moveyourmind are free appointments that spread the knowledge on yoga, the discipline that embodies the payoff. Celebrities like Cecilia Rodriguez, Federica Fontana as well as numerous *influencers* like Ludovica Valli and Irene Cioni participate and promote the events thanks to medium- or long-term collaborations.

11.7.6 Social media

The cluster analysis was carried out focusing mainly on leader brands like Nike and Adidas, as other follower brands imitate their strategies. The study is mainly dedicated to Instagram, Facebook and YouTube.

Concerning Adidas, the three keywords are *attract, engage* and *activate*. The first is aimed at encouraging the user to watch the content several times to catch their attention; an example can be those posts that display products spontaneously worn by celebrities that push users to follow them in their daily life. The term *engage* describes stories with a social content for which Adidas does not choose celebrities, but ordinary people; for instance, the initiative *Find your Match* that explains to women how to choose the most suitable training bra. Finally, *activate*, whose stories tell about the love for the brand and explore the product details and its technical features, to increase desirability. An example is the description of shoes grip and waterproof material. In any case, contents are generated keeping in mind the social platform, and the target it addresses (Rodrigues, 2019).

Nike promotes the concepts of fitness and lifestyle, the core of its identity. The brand priority is quality rather than quantity. Its storytelling is aligned with the objectives, aspirations and lifestyle of consumers, and celebrates positivity and empowerment. In its social media campaigns, nothing is left to chance. On Facebook, the frequency of posts changes according to the launch of advertising campaigns or international sports events involving its ambassadors. Its narration-based – and not product-based – storytelling strategy has proven to be successful. On YouTube, the methodology is opposite: the product is the protagonist of the scene and the videos describe its production (Ravi, 2019). Nike's predominance of inspirational contents is translated into a good image–video balance where the latter are particularly effective in their storytelling. The product is present in every content, even though it is never explicitly stressed; the narration is in fact focused on protagonist athletes who are asked to promote a lifestyle and an identity in line with the brand community. The contents, exclusively conceived for Instagram, have an intense emotional component to generate engagement and contribute to the creation of an editorial offer that emulates magazines.

Adidas follows a similar path offering inspirational themes with an editorial angle. Compared to Nike, we occasionally find a major focus on the product and on sponsored events. The presence of photos and videos is balanced and emphasises the topic of training rather than the social and cultural implications of sport in the world; this topic, instead, is at the base of Nike's offer.

In both cases, the most employed social media is Instagram where Nike and Adidas, respectively, reach 122 million and 26 million users; conversely, both Facebook profiles have been less and less updated since the second semester of 2018.

Adidas aims at becoming the best sportswear brand in the world and, to do so, it invests a considerable portion of its resources in digital marketing. The company interacts with customers creating premium and customised experiences. Adidas takes care of each exchange of information with its mobile, social media and retail audience to offer a unique, consistent and multichannel experience (Erkilic, 2018). However, the final scope is revealed by Adidas Global Director, Eric Liedtke, according to whom it is important to convert social media followers into buyers (Bloomberg, 2016).

Creating a community is Nike's ultimate goal. This purpose is made explicit in a statement by the Social Media Manager Wes Warfield, according to whom it is essential to be perceived as human even when speaking on behalf of a brand like Nike. He declared that the company wants to be part of the journey of its customers, as well as of their lifestyle. The brand has started investing in people (the community) on social media, because it is the place where they meet and spend their time. Social media are a very good opportunity to build relationships (Peters, 2019).

A final and short description is dedicated to the topics of inclusivity and sustainability, which despite not being stressed on social media, are not completely overlooked. Speaking of gender equality and inclusion, Nike is committed to increasing the number of women and black people at the head of the company. Adidas, on occasion of the *Equal Pay Day*, launched the campaign *#20PercentCounts* to prove that women are paid 20% less than men for the same job (Bertoletti, 2018).

With regard to sustainability, according to a report by Global Fashion Agenda (GFA) and Boston Consulting Group (BCG), the above-mentioned brands are differently dedicated to the issue. Nike has chosen to invest in technology and collaborates with the London College of Fashion with which it developed *MAKING*, an app to facilitate designers' work by measuring the environmental impact of production. Adidas is among the founders of *Parley for the Oceans*, a network committed to protecting the oceans from plastic and pollution. This initiative has given birth to *Parley Ocean Plastic*, a range of sustainable materials resulting from the recycling of plastic waste (Biserini, 2018).

11.7.7 Sponsorships and co-branding

Sponsorships are the most applied communication tool among the companies of this cluster. In fact, by leveraging on the emotions of supporters and by exploiting its limited "aggressiveness", these brands invest many resources in this form of communication. The main reasons are the following: to create a community among the users that share the same values (fitness and health), to propose new and better-preforming products, to encourage purchases and, as a consequence, to increase sales.

In the cluster, we can identify three sub-groups: on the one hand stand the leaders – Nike and Adidas (focus of this analysis) – whose extremely high revenues allow them to sponsor every type of event, team and athlete. The second sub-group encompasses "other brands", which, for opposite reasons, support an inferior number of initiatives, generally of lower importance and linked to specific sports. Puma stands in between the two typologies.

The 2018 Football World Championship held in Russia is representative of this scenario: out of 31 teams, Adidas sponsored 12, Nike 10, Puma 4, New Balance 2 and 1, respectively, for Umbro, Hummel, Errea and Uhlsport. The first two brands sponsored the teams of the five continents, Puma three, the others one. Moreover, the teams sponsored by Nike and Adidas included first-rate clubs (including the rivals Argentina and Brazil), as well as medium/lower levels. Conversely, Puma and other companies sponsored less-popular teams.[3]

Moreover, activewear brands are bound not only to teams, but also to football players: two of the most talented, Ronaldo and Messi, have, respectively, signed a partnership with the two leaders, Nike and Adidas. Football and its clubs and athletes aren't the only focus of these companies that also take part into local initiatives. Most of Nike's initial success is owed to its grassroot marketing initiatives, such as the sponsoring of local school teams, which attracted several targets of consumers (Keller and Kotler, 2007). Adidas has followed a similar path: in 1992 it sponsored a very successful local basketball tournament in Berlin, which was then replicated in 66 different editions in Germany the following year (Aaker and Joachimsthaler, 2000). We can conclude that the omni-sponsor strategy applied by Nike and Adidas is justified by their extremely comprehensive product portfolio aimed at reaching a worldwide and transversal market.

What about other companies? We've mentioned before how they are often connected to the sports in which they are specialised. It is the case of Reebok, focused on fitness, which sponsored the sub-discipline of CrossFit (an intensive training method). This choice allowed the brand to hold a special place in CrossFitters' heart, a permanent bond, as if they were one (Zazzaro, 2018). Puma, as anticipated above, stands in between these two extremes: despite sponsoring different disciplines – including track and field, golf, basket – it specialises in football.

It is also worth commenting on Fila which, thanks to the sponsoring of some famous athletes from tennis, skiing to mountaineering, successfully diversified from the original product – underwear – to sport, shortly acquiring a very high awareness.

Concerning co-branding, and considering the clusters examined in the previous chapters, and also overturning the perspective, we can affirm that every typology of company implements, with a different frequency, co-branding partnerships with sports companies. See, for instance, brands belonging to big luxury groups (*Louis Vuitton x Air Jordan and Louis Vuitton x Nike*); contemporary brands (*Emporio Armani with Reebok*); ready-to-wear specialised brands (*Rick Owens x Adidas, Maison Margiela x Converse*); streetwear labels (*Lacoste x Supreme, Reebok x Vetements*) and casualwear brands (*Nike x Levi's, Adidas x Diesel*); and finally even fast fashion brands (*Adidas x Topshop, Kappa x Bershka*).

The reasons at the base of their strategy are different, but we can identify the prevailing three: to propose a sportier style, to increase brand visibility and to approach a more "urban" target. Considered the core role in terms of sales, it is not surprising that the majority of them involve sneakers. In some cases, the partnership is a long-lasting one (Puma x Alexander McQueen, Adidas x Stella McCartney), while in others, it is just a one-time collaboration.

In addition to activewear brands, fashion companies also frequently cooperate with musicians (Nike x Kanye West, Adidas x Beyonce), as discussed in paragraph 11.7.5, and rarely with retailers (Fila x 10 Corso Como) and environmental organisations (Adidas with Parley for the Oceans).

11.7.8 Museums, foundations and leisure time activities, in collaboration with Andrea Pittana

In this group, foundations play a key role; they are involved in social projects to help socially and economically disadvantaged people. Even though brands have a relevant historic heritage, the most significant values are not rooted in the past, but in more contemporary issues having a considerable impact on sports and sport performances. For this reason, the contents and the relation with the target leverage on symbolic values that recall the brand personality and image. We hereby analyse the initiative of one of the leader brands, Nike, and of a follower, Puma.

The former, through the Nike Foundation, is committed to several international charity projects in areas suffering from social and economic problems. On the occasion of the *International Day of the Girl Child*, for instance, the brand presented its first plan dedicated to young Indian girls called *Girl Effect* (Srivastav, 2019). Puma Energy Foundation is currently in charge of several projects in Africa, Asia, Oceania and Americas to help the population in case of catastrophic events.

11.8 Distribution in collaboration with Andrea Doroldi

In the 2020 Nike report, we clearly see the essential characteristics of the distribution structure of footwear, clothing and sport equipment companies as well as Nike's. "The athletic footwear, apparel and equipment retail markets in some countries are dominated by a few large retailers with many stores and accelerating digital commerce capabilities" (Nike, 2020).

In this sense, the American brand markets its products through *NIKE Direct operations* – including mono-brand stores, digital platforms – and a mix of independent distributors, licensees and sales agents worldwide. Moreover, the same report underlines the vital importance of certain stores that "have been designed and built to serve as high-profile venues to promote brand awareness and marketing activities and to integrate with our digital platforms".

In the same document, we also read that a growing number of consumer purchases on digital platforms use mobile applications to buy and interact with the brand. Hence, the need to improve their purchase experience.

Keeping this vision in mind, we now compare some of the figures of Nike, a leader brand, and of a niche company, Freddy, highlighting how the two adopt opposite strategies.

At the end of 2019, Nike counted on 935 mono-brand stores and direct shops-in-shop; the above-mentioned report does not specify the number of directly operated stores, but, for sure, those located in strategic cities like London and New York, belong to this category. In Milan, the brand has nine, the majority of which are in franchising, and with the biggest one located in Corso Vittorio Emanuele, adjacent to the famous fashion district.

The franchising mono-brand network is very broad, but even bigger is the multi-brand one, which encompasses different store typologies: footwear-specialised chains like Footlocker, unspecialised shops with an assortment of medium/high-level products, as well as a few selected luxury boutiques like Luisaviaroma. According to the above-mentioned Nike Report, in fiscal year 2020, the revenues of *NIKE Direct* represent about 35% of the total, compared to 32% in the previous year. Nevertheless, Nike aims at reaching a percentage of 50% in order to consolidate the relationship with its customers and increase profitability.

Freddy relies on about 50 mono-brand stores, of which three are in Milan (outlet included). The multi-brand network is chiefly based on sportswear-specialised multi-brand stores like Cisalfa, Sportspecialist and Maxi Sport: unlike Nike, the label is not distributed in luxury boutiques or in sportswear-specialised chains of stores like Footlocker and Aw-lab. For this reason, we deduce that the percentage of sales generated by direct retail is far inferior than the one made through wholesalers.

We now study the online distribution strategy of these brands. They have their e-commerce where the entire assortment is available. Nike is present on seven platforms, while Freddy only on two (Yoox and Amazon). The most offered categories for both brands are apparel and footwear (obviously sporty). If we compare the price of a product on their e-commerce with that of a platform, we see that Nike can impose the same price on Farfetch, whereas Freddy's price is different from Amazon's. Both companies allow for mobile purchases thanks to the responsive design of their websites.

11.9 Omnichannel, in collaboration with Sabrina Pomodoro and Benedetta Breschi

As in the case of casualwear brands, even those specialised in activewear do not develop an actual fashion tale and, for this reason, they belong to the category of *absence of integration*. The motivation of this peculiarity stands in the features of their product which is timeless, cross-seasonal and carryover; this factor distinguishes them from ready-to-wear brands which leverage on seasonality and emphasise it in their communication. In the study of the communication tools applied by Nike, Adidas, Fila and Freddy, two elements may be highlighted: on the one hand, sportswear, and on the other hand, the encouragement to join their fast and passionate world of training. Among these four brands, the only one that aims at keeping pace with the rhythms of ready-to-wear is Fila, which posts its fall-winter 2019/2020 collection on the Instagram stories' highlights.

Interview with Barbara Mora, Global Marketing Director at Fila

What are the peculiarities of activewear products and how will they evolve in the close future?
Functionality and style: the new concept of *active* is based on a stronger and stronger influence of trends. We will assist to union between aesthetic and more and more technical and performing fabrics with an eye on sustainability.

How has the activewear competitive scenario evolved in the last few years, and how will it change after COVID-19?
The pre-COVID-19 market was very competitive and searching for a stronger and stronger focus on activewear. After the lockdown, the scenario has remained the same, the concept of performance will still be at the core of collection development: a mix of suitable outfits for free time and to go to the gym.

Who is the typical activewear consumer and how will they change after COVID-19?
While a few years ago, the market had two very distinct consumers, the current trend is characterised by a single user. Technical products are becoming more and more requested. Consider, for instance, leggings, the most successful must-have of the recent seasons: more and more often, consumers tend to buy technical and performing leggings, rather than cotton and soft ones. Everyone wants to show a sculpted body everywhere, not just at the gym.

How is Fila approaching Millennials and Generation Z?
With customer loyalty and versatility. Fila has boasted Millennials and Generation Z among its consumers for some seasons now. Today, the brand is committed to working on market research to keep up with the trends imposed by the youngest.

Why have activewear brands always invested little in print press?
In the past, low investments were because activewear was considered a niche product. Today, we mainly fund the use of technology to create more sustainable and performing fabrics. Activewear is now a synonym for sustainability and, as a consequence, for cautious consumption and recycling. Product communication is now moving towards more and more dynamic methods such as social media, blogs and the concept of experience.

How important and peculiar are social media and influencers in activewear communication?
They are fundamental, but it is important to "dose" and use them correctly. While extending the range of consumers of activewear products, it is necessary to target the message correctly. Not everyone loves extreme sports or going to the gym, but this doesn't mean that they have to be excluded from the usage of performing items. This is the reason why it is necessary to wisely differentiate the message through social media and to choose the right influencer.

Do you think that price will change in the close future?
Unfortunately, the pandemic has negatively affected production. The great losses due to the "skipping" of an entire season have caused a crisis in the whole value chain. This condition could raise the price level.

What are the distribution peculiarities of activewear?
Even in this case, the stylistic peculiarity dictates distributive rules. The contamination of such divided worlds encourages the consumer to "dare" to approach sectors that had always been considered just for fashionistas. Consequently, the shopping experience explores the new interactions and emotions generated by the contact between brand and market, and changes accordingly.

How does activewear embrace sustainability?
It is a must. The green "touch" is permanently present in every production and is more and more visible. The stronger the bond between technology and sustainability, the more

successful the result. Nowadays, the supply chain tends – from the first steps – to search for and to use more and more natural products having a minimal environmental impact

What are the characteristics of Fila's strategy in a scenario dominated by giants like Nike and Adidas? Its Italian DNA: good taste, design and creativity dictated by its history that has all the requirements for a unique and alternative evolution.

Student activities

Choose a brand and based on your choice:

- define the sustainability actions to be applied in the future;
- identify the combination product/price segment/target where to diversify;
- identify a social media and the content typology to be developed;
- define which of the following formats – brick-and-mortar mono-brand store, brick-and-mortar multi-brand store, shop-in-shop in department stores, online mono-brand shop and online multi-brand platform – need to be developed the most;
- verify the degree of synergy among the aesthetic elements of the latest collection: the fashion show, social networks, mono-brand store windows and the advertising campaign.

Notes

1 Trainers – or tennis shoes – were given this name because they were mainly used to play sport; later on, due to the new athleisure trend, they were called sneaker.
2 The word *hype* is used to indicate a very desirable item, such as a new videogame, a TV series or the match of a popular sport; in this case the hype is about Yeezy shoes, a limited edition product, very desired among fans.
3 In the 2018 World Championship, a traditionally first-rate team, Italy, whose sponsor is Puma, did not participate. The team had not passed the previous selections.

12

BRANDS SPECIALISING IN STREETWEAR

Reading: the Sales Director

The role of Sales Director in fashion companies is strategic in order to achieve the set sales goals. Their main function is that of organising, managing and often carrying out in first person, with the main clients, the sales campaign (collection of orders) of the company's products/brands, at a global level. Each operation is made according to the agreed budget and financial resources. This activity is developed using channels (wholesale, retail, licensing, offline and online) and formats (mono-brand and multi-brand stores, online platforms, outlets, corners and shops-in-shops of department stores, etc.) that have been previously agreed with the CEO to whom they report directly. Often, in small-medium companies, the Sales Director also has the role of Retail, Merchandising and Marketing-Communication Director. The figures that generally report to the Sales Director are the following: Area Managers, the Customer Service Department (divided according to areas/markets of competency), the Inner Retail Department – buyers, visual merchandisers, store managers – and sometimes also the Marketing Director (if any). In order to achieve the set goals, the Sales Director draws three-year action plans as well as detailed annual and seasonal budgets. Their competences include the knowledge of international markets (key accounts, buyers and main retailers) and products, the ability to calculate the budget as well as problem-solving and team-work skills. Of course, they must be fluent in at least one foreign language (preferably two).

12.1 Who are they?

This group encompasses very recent companies inspired by urban cultures and alternative lifestyles: from rap, to hype fashion and sneakers lovers. The target is extremely young. Also, in this cluster several typologies of companies coexist: from those brands that in a very short time have become lifestyle labels like Off-White, to others whose fashion is inspired by a specific world such as Quicksilver and its bond with surfing. In addition to the above-mentioned brands, this chapter also considers the following: Vetements, Supreme, Kith, Etnies, Billabong, Stüssy, Undercover, Palm Angels, Acne Studios and Carhartt.

12.2 Style, in collaboration with Daniela Guariento

Supreme proposes limited-piece collections characterised by a very fast sell-out, which have become the object of desire of new generations. Products – from clothes to accessories – are well-constructed; they feature a studied functionality for training purposes and an adequate fashion content.

A rather refined product is designed by Off-White, a brand established by Virgil Abloh in 2013. The Ghanaian founder is a graduate and is a creative consultant for Kanye West and Creative Director of Louis Vuitton's menswear line. His garments are recognisable for their silhouettes and graphics; in his collections coexist casual and reinterpreted formal items, and they are all characterised by a sportswear touch. Accessories, bags in particular, are designed with unusual shapes and avant-garde details for a niche of consumers who are particularly interested in fashion.

Kith collections, instead, are more mainstream and characterised by less fashion content. The product, in fact, is conceived to satisfy practical and functional needs; its style is chiefly basic, but with and interesting activewear product assortment.

Volcom's collections are structured to supply a comprehensive product range, inclusive of coordinated accessories and clothing, designed to create a trendy total look for skaters. Unisex garments unite menswear and womenswear collections with a focus on sustainability and recycled materials.

Billabong, a California-based brand, epitomises the typical American casual product, simple, yet recognisable for its prints. The company produces both men's and women's collections for daily usage and for a young and informal target. The brand image is anchored to summer, while winter collections are designed focusing on outerwear and in particular on snowjackets. Likewise, Quicksilver, which has built its identity on surfers' culture, offers a complete collection inclusive of apparel, accessories, eyewear, watches and wetsuits.

Street subculture gives life to strictly young and casual collections, influenced by post-punk and hip-hop and characterised by classic-structure garments enriched by creative graphics and materials. Stüssy, for instance, designs original and daring total looks, also in collaboration with Clarks, Gore-Tex and Nike, which introduce new colours, fabrics and designs in sneakers and apparel lines.

12.3 Supply chain and sustainability, in collaboration with Celeste Corso

Streetwear brands do not supply much information about their production strategy. However, the small turnover and the variety of their product offer suggest that they do not possess enough resources to invest in in-house production, and that, consequently, they produce by outsourcing.

In fact, after its transfer from Kering to Authentic Brands Group (ABG), Volcom is still produced by licensing as confirmed by its spokesperson. New agreements have been signed with licensees in charge of clothing, footwear and beachwear production, as well as of skateboard, skiing and surfing accessories (Licensing International, 2019).

Even in the case of the American brand Quicksilver, it is not simple to understand the secrets of its productive organisation. The few information available is published on its homepage and identifies the parent company Boardriders Inc. as the company responsible for design, production and distribution. Nevertheless, the page does not clarify whether manufacturing is delegated to a third party or is direct (Quicksilver, 2019).

A thick silence seems to cover the productive strategy of Off-White. In 2018, Pampianconews wrote that a veil of mystery characterised this promising young holding. No figures were available, no strategies were revealed and even its image was enigmatic; on the website, only the logo and the brands name were available. Yet, New Guards Group (Ngg) was building a small empire in the field of emerging streetwear brands (Pambianco, 2018b).

Among the analysed brands, this is the least conventional, and the most original and dynamic. These labels target young consumers by speaking their language – also at a visual level – and by satisfying their needs also in the field of sustainability. Millennials and Generation Z are very sensitive to this topic and are willing to spend more to buy sustainable and conscious items. For them, sustainability is not just an option, but an ethical and environmental issue, and they consider it a cultural value. This explains why the players of this cluster are active and support this cause with their business.

Etnies, for instance, includes a vegan option in its collections and has also launched the *Buy a Shoe, Plant a Tree* campaign in collaboration with *Trees for the Future*; the goal is to plant 2 million trees by the end of 2020 (Etnies, 2019). Another active player is Volcom, whose *Eco True* sustainable manifesto has given the name to a mini-collection made with certified and recycled materials (Volcom, 2019).

12.4 Segmentation strategies

As stated in Chapter 2, and as demonstrated in the following paragraphs, streetwear brands have overturned the rules of the game in the fashion business. In particular, concerning the analysed strategies, it was believed that a lifestyle strategy could be implemented only after the long brand evolution described in paragraph 2.4; also, and mostly, that decades of history, and several segmentation strategies applied in the course of time, were necessary.

On the contrary, the experience of a few streetwear brands has proven that it is not mandatory to have a long brand history, nor to start from a specific product-market combination with a wholesale strategy to then convert it into a mainly direct retail policy.

What allowed these companies to skip these steps? Their being nonconformists, and their overturning of every dominating status quo of the fashion system: this is the message, the lifestyle that streetwear brands have consistently conveyed to Millennials, their young target. These companies have chosen radically different communication strategies: the hiring of influencers and the use of social media, instead of printed press advertising campaigns. They also follow a different timing and new modalities to launch their collections: regular [...], rather than the two classic collections per year. Even the creative approach is diverse: [...]oss-disciplinary and burns down the walls that separate the different fields and for[...] it does not rely on any pre-established hierarchy.

[...]nd

[...]ands have launched nonconformist, disruptive messages and overturned the

The original product varies according to the brand, but it is not always clearly identifiable. Off-White, since its establishment designing high-end apparel and accessories collections for all genders, is very popular worldwide among Millennials. Conversely, Undercover, founded at the beginning of the 90s by designer Jun Takahashi, debuted with punk-inspired T-shirts, and later extend the offer to a line comprising punk, street and sensual styles. Carhartt, however, debuted proposing denim work overalls, still representing the brand's inspiration. The original products of Billabong, established in the early 80s, were board shorts with the triple stitching that makes them more resistant.

Brands' development is heterogeneous. On the one hand, Off-White has been able to extend to different product categories: clothing, activewear, footwear, bags, shoes, jewels, eyewear, thus becoming a lifestyle brand for Millennials, in a few years. On the other hand, Billabong has added to its assortment several items (caps, flip-flops, sweatshirts and T-shirts) that are very bound to its origins – surfing – and, as a consequence, to the brand image.

Streetwear brands apply a naming strategy which implies the use of the same name for all product categories and lines; for instance, Undercover uses its name for the Snow line and the main womenswear, menswear and kidswear collections.

As in the case of industrial brands, the *made-in* is little important. The ratio of perceived/actual quality varies according to brand. For instance, for Off-White, the former is higher than the latter for several reasons; among them, the numerous collaborations with prestigious labels like Louis Vuitton and Moncler, the sponsoring by celebrities like Bella Hadid and the presence of a Creative Director who's also a fashion star. Speaking of Carhartt, the scenario is different: actual and perceived quality coincide. In fact, the brand, as compared to Off-White, leverages less on the intangible aspects of the product, to focus on raw materials which are pivotal for the use function associated with the brand.

Despite being extremely young, streetwear brands boast some garments that, even if they cannot be defined as iconic in a strict sense, have become part of the contemporary fashion history: for instance, Off-White's (yellow) industrial belt and the Mona Lisa Hoodie; for Billabong and Carhartt we may speak of iconic use function rather than products since their collections are dedicated, respectively, to surfing and workwear. The former is a living legend of surfing, whereas the latter stands out for its resistant fabrics applied to work jackets, coats and dungarees.

Speaking of the Creative Director, the group includes two extremes. On the one hand, brands having fashion stars as Creative Directors such as Virgin Abloh and Jun Takahash' for Off-White and Undercover; on the other hand, Carhartt and Billabong, which ´ have such a figure.

These brands do not have fixed stylistic codes because they address new gen° ask for constant innovations; consequently, their approach is destructured a' the numerous collaborations with other brands, as well as the continuous ´ design and materials, are an expression of this trend.

Among the typical product service, customisation is very dev' ing is the exclusive line of customised sweaters proposed bv the Metropolitan Museum of New York for the *Punk: Ch*

12.6 Pricing, in collaboration with Bene^

In this section, we consider the price of the hoodie ˟ ised and specialised companies.

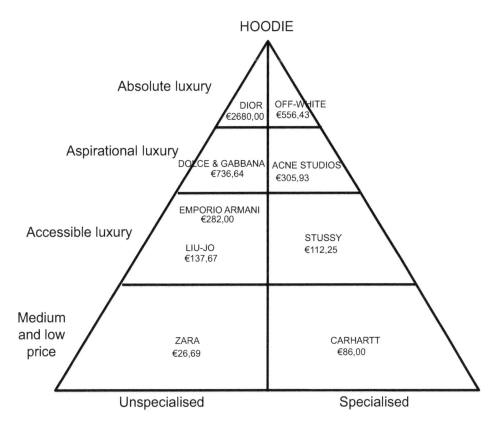

FIGURE 12.1 Golizia's pyramid of hoodies
Source: Prepared by Dario Golizia.

Concerning absolute luxury, we summarise the considerations made in Chapters 2 and 3. Dior is characterised by a definitely superior price positioning (+381.6%) compared to Off-White. To the reflections made in Chapter 2, we may add that streetwear-specialised brands are relatively young and haven't had the time (as Valextra – in the category of bags – has had) to elaborate and convey an identity that allows them to compete, in terms of price, with the most famous historic labels. Moreover, the target of the French brand is older and with a higher spending power than Off-White's.

This statement is confirmed also by the comparison with Dolce & Gabbana, which also boasts a superior price when compared to Off-White (+32.3%)

In the opposite position, for the medium-low segment, Carhartt has a 222.2% superior price than Zara's. In this segment, fast fashion brands have no "appeal" and cannot compete with specialised companies, which, conversely, have managed to create and gather a very loyal and little-price-sensitive fan base.

12.7 Communication

We now proceed with the definition of the image of the cluster; afterwards, we study how the marketing and communication function is organised and managed by a company from the same group. Finally, we outline the communication mix applied by some brands.

12.7.1 Cluster image

Street culture, urban and genderless style, T-shirt, hoodie (oversize), prints and writings, daring and fluorescent, logo, cap, co-branding, nonconformist are the words most associated with this cluster. Also, in this group, we find brands whose identity is mainly connected to an activity (e.g. Volcom and skating, Billabong and surfing) and others that, despite being strongly bound to an activity (e.g. Supreme and skating), are attempting to shape and convey a lifestyle to their consumers. For very few, the image is also linked to the founder/designer like Off-White and Virgil Abloh.

12.7.2 Marketing function and communication, in collaboration with Michele Leoni

New Guards Group's[1] headquarters for marketing and communication is located in Milan and supported by regional collaborators, agencies and press offices reporting to the central department.

The Creative Directors of the different brands are located in different areas of the world, from Asia to the USA, and their work is the result of a constant dialogue with the Milanese headquarters.

Samples are managed by external PR agencies for the different continents and relative markets.

The marketing department is in charge of strategies planning, capsule collections and the communication campaigns (together with the communication department) of all brands. The same office also takes care of events and, in collaboration with external agencies, they organise fashion shows, openings, etc., both internationally and locally.

12.7.3 Fashion shows and trade fairs, in collaboration with Andrea Doroldi

In this segment, Vetements and Off-White stand out because they present their collections with fashion shows: led by Demna Gvasial and Virgil Abloh – who are also, respectively, Creative Directors of Balenciaga and Louis Vuitton menswear – they are now considered as luxury brands. By applying the already discussed scheme for fashion shows by Vilaseca (2010), we can state that both brands belong to the theatrical typology group. Off-White's fall-winter 2020 womenswear collection was not presented on a classic catwalk but on a chess board where models moved like chess pawns.

Most streetwear brands do not participate in fashion weeks; in fact, as anticipated in the previous paragraphs, and developed in the following, brands employ social media and influencers as communication and presentation tools for collections. Consequently, on their website or social profiles, they showcase catalogues or some products worn by celebrities. These brands have a range of items including carryover merchandise and are constantly updated by periodically launched capsule collections (monthly or weekly).

The Instagram profiles of brands or of a fan club, like the very famous Highsnobiety (more than 3 million followers), show the previews of oncoming products. For instance, Supreme supplies an app with which, every Friday, it informs customers about the date of release of the weekly capsule collection; it is the brand's way to generate curiosity and encourage purchases, without imposing the typical long waiting periods associated with the fashion system.

For these brands it makes no sense to consider trade fairs like Mipel and Pitti Immagine. There are in fact many fairs organised by enthusiasts in Italy and worldwide. One of them is Sneakerness, a *reselling* platform to buy and sell sneakers and streetwear garments: it consists of a travelling fair held in many cities and that, due to the Covid-19 emergency, has not taken place in 2020.

12.7.4 Advertising, editorial, advertorial, in collaboration with Benedetta Breschi

The group of streetwear brands had not been examined in the previous book (Golizia, 2016); as for activewear, underwear and formal menswear brands, these companies didn't buy any advertising page on magazines in the period of observation. The cluster comprises a set of recently established brands that address a very young target, mainly using social media (see following paragraphs). Among the four analysed brands, two, Acne Studios and Palm Angels, are mentioned in fashion editorials. The former boasts a more consolidated brand awareness and a more heterogeneous target, which allowed it to gain the attention of three magazines: *Vogue, L'Officiel* and *Elle*. While for the latter, a lower visibility and a more focused target attracted the attention of one single magazine, *Elle*.

12.7.5 Influencer, gifting, endorsement, by Lavinia Biancalani

This cluster is rather heterogeneous if analysed in terms of digital and influencers marketing, even if all its brands are founded on the creation of a community.

Among leader brands, Off-White penetrated the industry applying promotion methodologies compliant with the rules of fashion: it participated, even if occasionally, in Paris Fashion Week. Conversely, Supreme has always had an anti-establishment marketing approach – underpinned by different digital and influencer marketing strategies – that has become stronger and stronger thanks to the success of social media.

Virgil Abloh, founder of Off-White, has worked as a style consultant for singer Kayne West; this is an essential premise to understand the digital marketing strategy of the brand, based on the fame and appeal of a set of creative personalities and celebrities of the international streetstyle scenario. The digital strategy was less transparent but more authentic; in fact, rather than structuring influencer marketing campaigns for *adv* posts, the brand organised a series of seeding and gifting initiatives with celebrities that boast a high number of

TABLE 12.1 Advertising, fashion editorial and advertorials of streetwear-specialised brands

Streetwear-Specialised Brands	L'Officiel			Vogue			Vanity Fair			Elle			Glamour			Total		
	A	FE	AD	A	FE	AD	A	FE	AD	A	FE	AD	A	FE	AD	A	FE	AD
Acne Studios	0	1	0	0	1	0	0	0	0	0	0	0	0	1	0	0	3	0
Off-White	0	0	0	0	0	0	0	0	0	0	0	0	0	0	0	0	0	0
Supreme	0	0	0	0	0	0	0	0	0	0	0	0	0	0	0	0	0	0
Palm Angels	0	0	0	0	0	0	0	0	0	0	1	0	0	0	0	0	1	0
Total	**0**	**1**	**0**	**0**	**1**	**0**	**0**	**0**	**0**	**0**	**1**	**0**	**0**	**1**	**0**	**0**	**3**	**0**

Source: Authors' data processing on the basis of fashion magazines published in Italy in September 2019. A, FE and AD stand for advertising, fashion editorial and advertorial, respectively.

online followers. The chosen personalities could autonomously post the company's products to generate buzz and hype. For instance, model Bella Hadid (35.7 million followers on Instagram) published a photo while wearing Air Jordan 1 by Virgil Abloh shoes. A look at the Instagram profile of the brand indicates the intent to create a genuine community: the brand reposts the contents generated by talents and common people on the platform and always references the source. For this reason, we can find contents conceived by micro influencers, ordinary people and celebrities that, altogether, become a community that nourishes the brand popularity.

Since the invention of social media, Instagram in particular, Supreme has based its strategy on user-generated contents freely created by the users of the platforms. Established by James Jebbia in 1994, from its debut, the brand has stood out for its unconventional approach to marketing and promotion, as well as to distribution and to the launch of collections. The hype generated by the brand is thus the mirror of its product exclusivity, presented through weekly drops – every Thursday – and in limited edition. Thanks to the approval and trust of American East Coast skaters' community, the brand has become a global phenomenon. Neither direct evidence of seeding and gifting actions nor explicit references to advertising collaborations and endorsement are found on social networks. However, two trends can be identified on social media: on the one hand, the collaboration with talents – part of the brand offline community – for editorial pictures posted on social media profiles of the company, among them Tyshawn Jones (@enwhytj (371,000 followers); on the other hand, the creation of a community of celebrities that support the brand and that are willing to post on their own profiles without an actual endorsement agreement; e.g. the case of rapper Fedez who certainly contributed to the brand popularity in Italy.

The "second-generation" brands of this cluster – Huff, Obey, Kith and Carhartt WIP (streetwear line of workwear brand Carhartt) – see Stüssy as an actual benchmark and have structured a very similar social media communication without direct endorsement and explicit seeding or gifting initiatives.

A different approach characterises performance brands. Let's consider Billabong, which despite addressing the streetwear segment, has debuted targeting surfers. The structure of its influencers marketing is traditional as it contemplates experience-based endorsement activities like the launch of capsule collections and classic paid endorsements for the promotion of new products on Instagram. In 2019, the brand supplied the equipment to some surfers of the *World Surf League*, such as Italo Ferreira and Federico Morais (784,000 and 127,000 followers, respectively, on Instagram).

12.7.6 Social media

While traditional fashion brands had to learn the new language of the internet, streetwear communities, even before the rise of social media, were already active online: forums like NikeTalk, BapeTalk, Strictly Supreme and ISS/Sole Collector were fundamental to gather information on the new drops or to buy and sell products.

Since these companies express a peculiar lifestyle, the analysis is focused on the world of streetwear, considered as one entity, rather than on single brands.

Contents, which reflect the concepts described in the previous paragraph, show two main characteristics: transparency and customisation. These brands intend to tell and share everything about themselves with their community; in particular, the behind the scenes.

Virgil Abloh confirmed the intention in an interview where he celebrated the qualities of Instagram by saying that, until the arrival of social media, it was normal, yet strange, not to reveal the steps behind the work of a designer (Schwartzberg, 2016). These brands have turned customisation into their mantra. An evidence of it is the 2016 pop-up experiment Life of Pablo by Kanye West: 21 pop-ups were located in 21 different cities, each one selling a different collection with unique colours and logos (Hope, 2017).

Contents vary according to brands; however, they all share an anti-establishment approach in their aesthetic. Despite displaying the product, the latter is included in a more comprehensive narration aimed at creating a collective imaginary to be shared and approved by all users. Hence the choice to publish raw contents without much editing, or contents "borrowed" from users of the brand community. Off-White and Supreme are exemplary cases of this approach: they match images of the campaign or of the launch of new collections with amateur contents – often videos – where the author's name is explicitly written in the credits. These posts have the purpose of creating a visual blog involving the fan base – from user to creator. No particular distinction between contents designed for Instagram and Facebook – the most used platforms – is highlighted.

While the goal of some clusters is to convey exclusivity, conceived as a top-bottom process where Creative Directors impose new trends to the market, streetwear brands have overturned this model. Their main objective is the creation of a community with a strong sense of belonging. For their fans, wearing the logo and expressing their opinion is a way to affirm that they are part of a tribe (Hope, 2017). Guram Gvasalia declared that customers buy a hoodie, wear it and take a selfie; afterwards, they post it on Instagram to feel they belong to a community (Socha, 2017).

12.7.7 Sponsorships and co-branding

Streetwear companies haven't made relevant investments in sponsorships. Their strategy, which doesn't contemplate the classic two-season annual calendar, but the regular launch of limited-availability products, is not suitable for sponsorships. According to Dahlén, Lange and Smith (2010) the aim of sponsorships is to build lasting long-term relationships, which create a mutual value.

Conversely, co-branding activities are often implemented, in particular by those companies in the segment of activewear. This choice can be justified by two reasons: on the one hand, by the ease with which these items are mixed and matched; on the other hand, by the growing trend of streetwear in the last few years. Some examples of co-branding are *Supreme x Nike*, *Vetements x Reebok*, *Off-White x Converse*, *Kith x Adidas* and *Carhartt x Converse*.

Another often-applied methodology is founded on collaborations with retailers: *Off-White x Le Bon Marché*, *Kith x Bergdorf Goodman* and *Stüssy x Dover Street Market*. This strategy satisfies several needs: first, it attracts a new target for retailers; second, it enhances product visibility and availability of young brands. These are the main reasons for its implementation. We also identified less-frequent collaborations with brands from big luxury groups (*Supreme x Louis Vuitton*), with contemporary brands (*Vetements x Tommy Hilfiger*) and with footwear-specialised brands (*Vetements x Manolo Blahnik*).

An interesting example of a collaboration with artists, whose result is not an apparel capsule collection, is the case of Off-White x Takashi Murakami. The partnership gave birth to a series of exhibitions aimed at highlighting the numerous connections between the eccentric languages of the brand and the artist.

12.7.8 Museums, foundations and leisure time activities, in collaboration with Andrea Pittana

As for activewear brands, the most meaningful values for streetwear companies are not rooted in the past, but in contemporary issues. The most important concepts are the tribe and the sharing of the same lifestyle (e.g. for surfers the concept of freedom and challenge): contents and relation must integrate in one specific language and world, which is the founding element of the "tribe".

The most dynamic brand is Quicksilver, whose foundation, operative from 2004 until 2013, donated 6 million dollars to several initiatives. Their activity had been suspended between 2013 and 2016, to later restart in the *Boardriders Foundation*.

12.8 Distribution, in collaboration with Andrea Doroldi

These brands have overturned the traditional fashion calendar and, consequently, the rules of distribution. We hereby consider two representative examples, Off-White and Supreme.

The former belongs to New Guards Group (acquired by Farfetch), a segment leader also including Palm Angels and Marcelo Burlon; its CEO, Andrea Grilli, announced that he would launch Off-White's spring 2021 collection directly in stores. He had already declared that the time frame between the collection delivery to retailers and the moment of consumers' purchase was too long. However, he reassured that the schedule of sales campaigns would not be modified and wholesalers would be able to purchase collections twice a year, in February and September. Collections would also be organised according to monthly deliveries and the comprehensive assortment would guarantee the satisfaction of any commercial need. At the same time, Virgil Abloh would have all the creative "space" he'd need (FashionMagazine, 2020).

Even Supreme applies peculiar sales strategies: its collections, as already said, are presented each Thursday, and in order to purchase an item, potential customers have to subscribe online registering their credit card number.

As a consequence, streetwear labels have a limited number of mono-brand stores – Supreme has 11, Off-White 36 (20 shop-in-shops included) – or like Vetements, they have none. Supreme opened its first store in Milan in Via Verri (besides having been available for a while at La Rinascente in a shop-in shop), while Off-White opened a shop-in-shop in 2020. These labels also rely on a selected network of multi-brand stores specialised in their product typology. In general, we can estimate that the percentage of revenues deriving from direct retail is still considerably inferior than wholesale's.

We hereby consider the online strategy of these brands. They have their own e-commerce, but only Off-White makes the whole assortment available. Supreme sells only a selection of it. The former is available on all nine platforms, Supreme on only one (Farfetch), presumably to keep its allure of exclusivity. The most offered categories are ready-to-wear, bags and shoes for Off-White, apparel for Supreme. If we compare the price on their e-commerce with that of Farfetch, we see that Off-White can impose the same price, while Supreme's prices are higher on online platforms. Both brands allow purchases with mobile devices thanks to a responsive website design.

12.9 Omnichanel, in collaboration with Sabrina Pomodoro and Benedetta Breschi

Among the examined brands – Acne Studios, Off-White,[2] Supreme and Palm Angels – only the first has a mono-brand store in Milan, while Off-White is available in Milan in a shop-in-shop located at La Rinascente department store. To summarise, except for Acne Studios, it is impossible to analyse the points of sale of sample brands.

Since it was impractical to find the advertising campaigns using the sources observed for the entire study – these four brands don't produce traditional seasonal collections – it would have been ineffective to analyse their integrated communication considering only the fashion show and the Instagram page. Moreover, from the analysis of their Instagram profiles, we can highlight how the four brands do not intend to stress the theme of a single collection, but they rather focus on a more universal concept: a contemporary, urban and streetwear style inspired by street culture and art.

Interview with Cristiano Fagnani, Chief Marketing Officer at New Guards Group

What are the peculiarities of the streetwear product and how will they evolve in the future?
Streetwear was born as an expression and extension of youth style and culture. It represents and defines the participation in a community, in a cultural movement, often rooted and originating from big – American, but not only – metropolis, and it is influenced by all the elements that revolve around it: music, sport, and art. Sneakers, hoodies, t-shirts, denim are the components of the uniforms of street culture that become (and constantly reinvent themselves) white canvas to write and draw on and tell stories about the community. In the last 10/15 years, the ability of brands and communities to communicate, connect and travel has taken streetwear out of its niche, becoming a global phenomenon, able to cross-influence mainstream culture and the fashion industry in the strict sense.

Recent brands like those specialised in streetwear have become lifestyle labels in a few years, how do you explain that?
On the one hand, the fashion system, meant as a creative and cultural one, observes, mirrors, absorbs and reinterprets the stimuli coming from the contemporary world. In this sense, it was inevitable for the industry to apply some streetwear codes and to encompass them in the most mainstream language and aesthetic. On the other hand, the accelerations and democratization (access) of digital, e-commerce and communication platforms have allowed niche brands to emancipate and gain global visibility.

How has the competitive scenario of streetwear evolved and how will it evolve in the post-COVID age
As for any brand, the ability to exist, grow, and evolve is connected to the authenticity of their story, to the originality of the product, and to the ability to reinvent themselves generation after generation (or from age to age) without losing their distinctive DNA. The acceleration witnessed in the last few years has helped brands grow their "audience" of consumers and potential market. In the post-COVID age, crucial ability for brands will be that of constantly nourishing their connection with consumers, focusing on local communities, cities, and trying to get closer and closer to their audience wherever they are. The ability to

use digital platforms, most of all social media and e-commerce, will be a decisive factor to keep the conversation active and to serve consumers in this historic moment.

What are the characteristics of the streetwear consumer and how will they change in the post COVID age?
The streetwear consumers have a personal, emotional, and cultural relationship with the brand. To these very active and influential consumers, brands will still have to offer new opportunities of interaction and engagement. Endorsement – the "validation" by these customers – is fundamental for streetwear brands. The influence of these users is the real driver of every trend. In general, we cannot deny that all consumers are moving towards digital shopping both for necessity (less international mobility, etc.) and for convenience and affinity: young customers, more than others, interact with brands and purchase products without leaving the digital platforms.

Why have streetwear brands always invested little in print press?
The strength of streetwear brands stands in their ability to connect and build a personal and organic relationship with their consumers. The direct and almost personal relationship between brand and customer (through stores, social media, and events) is the key to success. The ability of brands to be successful through consumers' word-of-mouth (physical or virtual) accelerates the visibility and sales. It is a more credible bottom-up communication that avoids the most classic forms of advertising.

How important and peculiar are social media and influencers in streetwear communication?
I don't like the word *influencer* so much; I believe it's been overused. For sure, in streetwear, opinion leaders, trusted editors, and "influencers" have had a pivotal role for their ability to discover, use, and make new brands and products known, thanks to their physical and virtual networks.

Do you think that the price of streetwear products will change in the close future?
The price of streetwear products won't undergo any change because it's already accessible and accessibility is part of its DNA, and the community would not accept any price variation. Concerning those fashion brands embracing streetwear trends, of course, other parameters, connected to product quality and manufactory, are involved.

What are the distributive peculiarities of streetwear?
Streetwear pivots on clear points of reference: the contact with the store that becomes an aggregator, being part of a project, and feeling the member of a group. Nowadays, communities are different, we have both digital and physical spaces, and the former has extended the possibility to be a group and to create connections.

How do you include the topic of sustainability in streetwear?
It is a theme that pervades the whole contemporary society. For sure, young communities are more and more sensitive to it and consider it a priority. Speaking of the product, the process is already taking place, but it requires more time.

How New Guards Group's strategy will evolve?
New Guards Group is a platform at disposal of creative personalities who, in the last few years, have been leaders and expression of an important cultural phenomenon that has helped them grow. The Group aims at balancing the "spontaneity" of creative personalities and the rules of the industry.

Student activities

Choose a brand and based on your choice:

- define the sustainability actions to be applied in the future;
- identify the combination product/price segment/target where to diversify;
- identify a social media and the content typology to be developed;
- define which of the following formats – brick-and-mortar mono-brand store, brick-and-mortar multi-brand store, shop-in-shop in department stores, online mono-brand shop and online multi-brand platform – need to be developed the most;
- verify the degree of synergy among the aesthetic elements of the latest collection: the fashion show, social networks, mono-brand store windows and the advertising campaign.

Notes

1 New Guards Group controls several brands including Palm Angles, Off-White and Marcelo Burlon.
2 Off-White, when this research had already been concluded, opened a store in Milan.

13

BRANDS SPECIALISING IN BAGS

Reading: the visual merchandiser

An effective product display considerably determines the success of a point of sale (Cavalca Altan, 2004). The visual merchandiser plays a crucial role in this sense. They are in charge of the layout of showrooms and stores and of the fitting of windows and interiors. In the past, they used to be called *window dressers*, but in the course of time, their role has evolved, turning them into actual "directors" of the store fitting; they take care of product display in order to make the merchandise appealing to potential consumers. Their work also implies the fitting of a location that, consistent with the image to be conveyed, valorises, shapes and gives life to products, emphasising their characteristics and points of strength. Even the paths designed in the store, the necessary time to visit it and the definition of thematic areas respond to the need to support the purchase process (Zinola, 2011). The visual merchandiser is thus an actual director of a play in which the store is the stage, and the product the protagonist. Creativity, besides a good knowledge of communication, is the distinctive skill of a visual merchandiser; endowed with good manual skills they have to be willing to travel to work in all the stores of important international brands. Moreover, their work should be led by curiosity and emerging trends to stimulate their aesthetic sense. They chiefly work for department stores or companies having a tight network of mono-brand shops; however, they sometimes also operate as a consultant for different points of sale.

13.1 Who are they?

This group is made of companies specialised in the production of accessories, specifically bags, to be worn with any type of apparel; they are mainly aimed at women, but men are also considered. Even the composition of this cluster is rather variegate: at the highest level we find very few specialised labels like Valextra and Zanellato. At a medium-high level, instead, some uncontested players like Coach and Furla compete, while in the low segment, numerous unbranded firms coexist with a few renowned ones. Besides the above-mentioned companies, we also analyse Coccinelle and Carpisa.

13.2 Style, in collaboration with Daniela Guariento

The style of bag-specialised brands varies according to the target to satisfy.

In Valextra, a historic Milanese brand, functionality, research and minimal, yet refined, design coexist. This mix allows the company to reach a mature target with a high spending power. Manufacturing excellence is guaranteed by very precious leathers, whereas the choice of colours makes the product fashionable. Zanellato, another excellent name in the leather industry, designs its collections with more experimental taste, materials and fashion sense (compared to Valextra) to reach a more extravagant and aggressive target.

Furla is characterised not only by simple and functional shapes, but also by trendy colours, accessories and decorations – mainly in metal – to appeal to a young target. Coccinelle, a romantic and feminine brand, designs both classic and contemporary shapes addressed to an even younger target. Carpisa offers an extended variety of collections including bags and trolleys; the product is functional, practical and made of different materials such as genuine and fake leather and fabrics, to embrace a wide market.

13.3 Supply chain and sustainability, in collaboration with Celeste Corso

Brands positioned in a high and medium-high price range partially produce in directly owned factories and sometimes collaborate with selected and controlled partners. Also, the selection and control of raw materials, integrated in the production cycle and including many hand-made procedures, are handled directly. Such a strategy is justified by the very high retail price and by the consequent importance of actual product quality, a key factor of success; hence the need for strict control. It is easy to understand how, for these players, communicating their productive skills represents an added value; their manufacturing strategy appears similar to that of formal-menswear-specialised companies. Zanellato chooses and checks the best leathers directly at the source; the brand designs and produces its collections in-house, thanks to an excellent supply chain.

Moving down to the medium-low segment, the actual quality loses importance and does not require a direct control of the production cycle. Manufacturing is, in fact, extensively delegated to external suppliers. Carpisa, for instance, mainly outsources production to Asia.

Concerning sustainability, the raw material used in this industry, leather, is the starting point of this analysis. In the common imaginary, this word recalls pollution, damage to the environment and aggressive and harmful chemicals.

However, the Italian tanning industry, the world leader of the high-end segment, has undergone a considerable green metamorphosis. Due to its polluting past and to the nature of its material processing, this sector has been strictly put under discussion for a long time. The Union of Italian Tanneries (UNIC) points out that in the last ten years, Italian tanneries have used less resources: −16% of water consumption; −8% of energy consumption; −17% of chemicals usage; −26% of waste production and −38% of emissions (La Conceria, 2019a). So, we can affirm that, at least upstream, sustainability in the supply chain is guaranteed; but, even downstream, we can identify some virtuous examples.

In the medium-price women segment, Furla participated in the *Fur Free Retailer* programme banning the use of fur and some types of wool in favour of certified and traceable ones (Tanzarella, no year).

Carpisa, operating in the low-price segment of this sector, is a virtuous example. With the *Save the Ocean* capsule collection, in collaboration with an organisation committed to safeguarding the seas, the company produced recycled-polyester bags for its spring-summer 2019 collection (Carpisa, no date a).

13.4 Segmentation strategies

In this cluster, no company has been able to implement a lifestyle strategy, with the obvious exception of those examined in Chapters 2 and 3 (Prada, Gucci, Louis Vuitton, etc.). The remaining brands leverage on product, price and target, choices that do not facilitate a life-style strategy. Consequently, brands like Valextra are specialised in classic style and expensive women's bags, whereas others like Furla and Coccinelle offer bags for a more accessible cost and aimed at women with a lower spending power.

13.5 Brand

In order to analyse this cluster, we selected four companies each competing in a different price segment: Valextra for the highest segment, Coccinelle and Coach for accessible luxury and Carpisa for the mass market. These companies all debuted, although with different products, in the leather goods sector, to then undertake a different path and development.

Valextra, which had initially based its business on women's luxury bags, later specialised in briefcases, luxury luggage and travel bags, diversifying even in footwear; Coach, which at first manufactured small leather goods, extended its merchandise range to other leather products and, later on, to footwear and ready-to-wear (Indvik, 2016); Coccinelle, which had debuted as a bag samples producer, made a downstream integration, manufacturing and selling the finished product; Carpisa, the youngest brand, made its first appearance in the market with luggage and travel bags, which are still the main business.

Despite differing in their positioning, the studied brands all share the idea that having local roots enhances the perceived value of the product (Kapferer and Bastien, 2009, 2012 reprint). In the highest price segment, Valextra leverages on its made-in to emphasise the concept of a historic brand. Its heritage is rooted in the city of Milan, one of the most important fashion capitals, a fertile ground for the most renowned fashion companies. Also, Coach, established in New York in 1941, considers the made-in a crucial characteristic of the brand "defined by a free-spirit, all American attitude"; these are the words written on its website (Tapestry, 2020). Nevertheless, the emphasis on craftsmanship is not very credible due to its price positioning. Coccinelle and Carpisa, recently established companies, stress the concept of Made in Italy, particularly for design and creativity.

Even the presence of iconic products plays a pivotal role in the perception of the market: however, only Valextra can boast iconic items, in the strict sense of the term. Its SerieS line, launched in 1961, and now iconic, was inspired by traditional trapezoid doctors' bags. Eight years later, the women's version – characterised by smoother shapes and a smaller size – was also designed.

For the other brands, it's better to speak of representative rather than iconic products. Among them, we find Coccinelle's Ambrine, Coach's Tabby and Carpisa's trolley.

The ratio actual/perceived quality is different. For Valextra, consistently with its top-level positioning, we can speak of very high actual quality, which, in turn, corresponds to the perceived one. Coach and Coccinelle offer a high perceived quality and a medium-high effective one, a typical characteristic of brands competing in accessible luxury. Concerning Carpisa, the medium perceived quality corresponds to the effective one.

All companies share the identical naming strategy, based on the usage of the same brand name, to sign the different products and transversally penetrate the brand's DNA.

Last but not least, the customisation service is effective to consolidate the target's brand loyalty, but also to embrace the concept of uniqueness, a very relevant topic for contemporary consumers. Valextra has followed this trend with its made-to-measure service that involves the customer in the unique experience of the creative process. The same service is offered, on a limited product selection, by Coccinelle, on whose website customers can select the colour of the outer shell of the bag, its lining and can even add writing (Foglia, 2016). For Coach, this service is free and aimed at conveying the concepts of craftsmanship and prestige (Loriga, 2019). Still online, Carpisa offers the possibility to add not only text to the product, but even digitally printed images, photos and patterns of specific colours, all free of charge.

13.6 Pricing, in collaboration with Benedetta Breschi

In this paragraph, we consider the price of the shopper to compare the positioning of unspecialised and specialised companies.

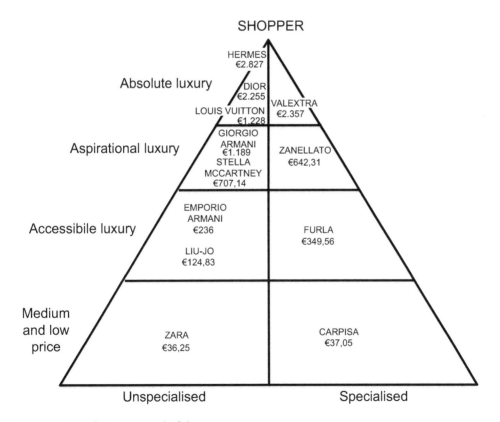

FIGURE 13.1   Golizia's pyramid of shoppers
Source: Prepared by Dario Golizia.

Speaking of absolute luxury, we summarise the considerations made in Chapters 2 and 3. Hermès boasts a superior price positioning compared to Valextra because, in the consumer's mind, it represents the most prestigious brand, in particular for leather goods. With reference to the positioning of the Italian brand, as compared to Dior, the two are similar: despite the inferior brand awareness, Valextra was able to create an image of a niche brand associated with a very high quality of raw materials and manufacturing; for this reason, it can compete with the famous French fashion house.

The price of Giorgio Armani, a contemporary brand, is definitely higher (+85.1%) when compared to Zanellato. The difference is due to the more consolidated brand awareness and image of the former.

In the opposite position, accessible luxury, Furla is characterised by a consistently superior price, as compared to Emporio Armani and Liu Jo. In this segment, the strong specialisation and a specific product and production know-how have considerable importance in terms of brand recognition and positioning.

The analysis is less interesting for the medium-low segment where the price difference between Zara and Carpisa is of 80 cents.

13.7 Communication

We now proceed with the definition of the image of the cluster; afterwards, we study how the marketing and communication function is organised and managed by a company from the same group. Finally, we outline the communication mix applied by some brands.

13.7.1 Cluster image

Bag is the keyword for all the brands of this cluster: this is because these companies are strongly specialised in this product. Also, in this case, brands differ thanks to characteristics that define their identity and positioning; for instance, extreme luxury, elegance, sobriety timeless and Made in Italy for Valextra; while Coach's DNA is based on a good price/quality rate, casual style and Made in USA.

13.7.2 Marketing function and communication, in collaboration with Michele Leoni

Orciani, an Italian brand specialised in belts, accessories and men's and women's leather clothing, was established by Claudio Orciani who, at the end of the 70s, had the intuition to design a practical buckle-free belt that was not subjected to safety checks in airports. The success of all of accessories was just a step away from the success of the *Nobuckle*; this is the name of the buckle-free belt. Orciani has its internal press office managed by the Communication Director who reports directly to the Managing Director. The marketing and communication department has its headquarters in the Italian region of Marche – where the headquarters of the company is located – as well as a second office in Milan. The corporate communication (about the brand and the company), the sending of samples for magazine shootings, events (inclusive of their graphic and creative work) are all managed internally. It is the same for the digital marketing and social media department, whereas the creation of social media contents – mainly Instagram – is entrusted to an external agency.

13.7.3 Fashion shows and trade fairs, in collaboration with Andrea Doroldi

Bags-specialised brands, generally, do not participate in ready-to-wear fashion shows. There are, instead, two very important fairs for this sector: Mipel and GDS (Global Destination for Shoes & Accessories). None of the observed brands – Valextra, Zanellato, Furla, Coach and Coccinelle – participated in the 2019 and 2020 editions; this is evidence of the decreasing interest in these trade fairs.

Nonetheless, during fashion weeks, these brands promote their collections' organising events. For instance, the #NoLogoMyLogo collection for fall-winter 2020/2021 by Valextra was presented in its mono-brand boutique of Milan. The hashtag clearly states that the company intends to strengthen its relationship with historic customers and also create a bond with new generations by providing the opportunity to customise the bag. Also, Zanellato organises events during the fashion weeks. The fall-winter 2019 collection was presented with three short films dedicated to the company's key products (Zanellato, no date). Furla, for fall-winter 2019, presented a sporty collection where several disciplines – running, tennis and fencing – inspired technical but light bags.

These brands rarely participate in the Salone del Mobile (specifically in the *Fuori Salone* events); we mention Valextra that, for the 2014 edition, had designed a limited edition glass case for a capsule collection signed by Safilo.

13.7.4 Advertising, editorial, advertorial, with Benedetta Breschi

As mentioned before, this group had not been analysed in the previous book (Golizia, 2016); in the advertising investments ranking, elaborated in September 2019, it stands in the eighth position, together with brands specialised in casualwear. Only Coccinelle purchased an advertising page on *Glamour*, with whom it shares the same target: mainly young girls and young adults. Bags-specialised brands prefer to present their collections by organising events.

13.7.5 Influencers, gifting, endorsement, by Lavinia Biancalani

The observed brands have intensively embraced social media and influencer marketing activities.

Those belonging to the luxury segment share the market with Hermès, Dior, Louis Vuitton and Prada, which, despite having diversified in other products, have built their success

TABLE 13.1 Advertising, fashion editorial and advertorials of bags-specialised brands

Bags-Specialised Brands	*L'Officiel*			*Vogue*			*Vanity Fair*			*Elle*			*Glamour*			*Total*		
	A	*FE*	*AD*	*A*	*FE*	*AD*	*A*	*FE*	*AD*	*A*	*FE*	*AD*	*A*	*FE*	*AD*	*A*	*FE*	*AD*
Carpisa	0	0	0	0	0	0	0	1	0	0	0	0	0	0	0	0	1	0
Coccinelle	0	0	0	0	0	0	0	0	0	0	0	0	1	1	0	1	1	0
Zanellato	0	0	0	0	0	0	0	0	0	0	0	1	0	1	0	0	1	1
Valextra	0	0	0	0	0	0	0	0	0	0	0	0	0	0	0	0	0	0
Total	**0**	**0**	**0**	**0**	**0**	**0**	**0**	**1**	**0**	**0**	**0**	**1**	**1**	**2**	**0**	**1**	**3**	**1**

Source: Authors' data processing on the basis of fashion magazines published in Italy in September 2019. A, FE and AD stand for advertising, fashion editorial and advertorial, respectively.

on bags. Specialised brands are thus in a position of competitive disadvantage, deriving from the single-product offer and from the limited capability to create a brand storytelling.

It is the case of Valextra established in 1937 and characterised by an intense product gifting and seeding – most of all before international fashion weeks – resulting from well-structured projects currently part of an editorial plan. For instance, in 2018, for Milan Fashion Week, the #NoLogoMyLogo campaign – dedicated to a bespoke service for the design of a unique pattern/logo for nine handbag models – was launched. The initiative was supported by a digital marketing campaign organised with seven high-profile fashion influencers like Linda Tol and Tamu McPherson.

In the medium segment, Furla represents an inspiring and "precocious" example of social networks usage aimed at building a new and younger brand identity, more aligned with global trends. In 2012, for the launch of the *Furla and I* project and for the promotion of the *Candy Bag*, the brand had already involved some influencers like Bryan Grey Yambao, known as Bryanboy. On the occasion of its 90th anniversary, the company engaged eight influencers selected from different markets and asked that a bag from the collection be interpreted for 15 days with 32 Instagram posts and stories about Furla's birthday, history and new collection. All contents were tagged with the hashtag #FurlaFeeling and #Furla90Anniversary; the first would still be used for future collaborations. Since 2018, it has been accompanied by the hashtag #TheFurlaSociety to "unite" social media talents that have represented the brand. Actually, the first edition of the *Society* project was promoted in November 2017 but it didn't include the hiring of influencers. Moreover, Furla frequently applies social media traditional endorsement strategies, by re-posting the contents of partner influencers. For instance, Chiara Ferragni has published numerous explicitly *adv* contents, in agreement with a medium-term endorsement plan for the promotion of the collection.

Carpisa concludes this analysis. In 2014, the brand promoted an initiative to support the charity event *Fashion 4 Development*, by launching a shopper during Rome Vogue Fashion Night. The bag bore the writing *No blogger, no influencer, just me*. Although the initiative didn't represent a declaration of intent about the social media and influencer marketing strategy, which in 2013 had relied on the collaboration with Chiara Ferragni to support the Carpisa Tattoo project, it definitely looked like a nonconformist statement. A final adjustment of the strategy would be made in 2015 when Penelope and Monica Cruz, the former already a brand endorser, promoted the launch of a capsule collection. A similar initiative was organised in 2018 when Kendall and Kylie Jenner, celebrities with more than 140 million followers, were chosen to design a capsule collection for bags. The strategy highlighted the brand's intention to apply endorsement strategies which have grown exponentially since the launch of the collection. The positioning of the chosen influencers is generally medium with a preference for micro influencers – having fewer than 10,000 followers – who can well interpret the brand values. Carpisa reposts on its profile the contents generated by its content creators, together with a standard caption that redirects to the advice given by influencers in their posts. Sonja Kovac and Marta Sierra are among the influencers who worked on the digital push of the fall-winter 2019/2020 collection. Finally, in 2019, for the inspirational campaign #BeAlwaysYourself, the brand involved micro influencers like models, singers, musicians and three athletes from Napoli women's football team to promote the concept of individuality and self-confidence.

13.7.6 Social media

In general, the most used social media are Instagram and Facebook, with a particular focus on the former. The brands of this cluster occasionally activate other platforms, mainly You-Tube, with the aim to support specific digital activities.

Valextra uses its social media to inform users about the brand and to keep its customers updated on the latest news. The brand has also been able to create its own community. The preferred platforms are Instagram and Facebook, which simultaneously post the same contents. The latter are product-focused and presented by means of glossy images – often sophisticated – and characterised by a high degree of photographic skills. Most of the time, images are not conceived specifically for social media, but they are taken from advertising campaigns, look-books, etc. With the purpose of creating a community and promoting aspirational values, the brand frequently posts lifestyle contents or images of celebrities and important personalities posing with the product.

Furla, among the middle-level brands of this cluster, implemented an aggressive social media strategy for the above-described reasons. The company publishes streetstyle photos or pictures where the subject is posing; the images are often taken from collaborations and influencer marketing campaigns that are activated in key moments of the year. Even this brand is product-focused and leverages on the use of personalities to construct an engaging storytelling. Posts that portray only the product are used in a limited number of occasions and mainly for the launch of new items. The majority of contents are photos; videos are only occasionally used to tell about the backstage of advertising campaigns and collaborations with talents. The latter are also published on YouTube where the brand boasts 3,000 users. Even in the case of Furla, the most employed social media are Instagram and Facebook where the same contents are posted. Twitter, less frequently used, is conceived as a means to generate traffic on the website and on the online store.

Carpisa shows a considerably different approach. The brand mainly concentrates on In-stagram where it boasts about 385,000 users and transfers the same posts to Facebook; the usage of other social networks is not significant. The company communicates its image with consistency but without users' involvement, applying a vertical brand-user communication. To do so, the brand publishes highly engaging product images. However, it is important to highlight how Carpisa, unlike other brands, employs the platform for customer service purposes, punctually answering the questions and the comments of its users. In August 2017, Carpisa was criticised for a Facebook campaign resulting from this policy of vertical communication. The campaign offered users the possibility to do an internship in the mar-keting offices of the brand. The requirements included a formal application submitted with a communication plan for the launch of a new product, but also the purchase of a bag from the new fall-winter 2017/2018 collection. The negative comments highlighted how difficult it was for the brand to horizontally dialogue with its audience and to understand how users are willing to express their opinion without being censured. The company has increased collaborations with influencers and digital talents and occasionally reposts on its profiles their contents with a standard caption recalling the styling advice given by influencers to followers.

Brands employ social media for diverse purposes.

In 2019, during a speech held for the annual event *Next Design Perspective* organised by Altagamma, Sara Ferrero, CEO of Valextra, underlined the importance of building a community. The CEO declared that the luxury company aimed at creating a timeless product as well as an engaging relationship with every generation. To do so, creativity is essential (Altagamma, 2019).

In 2012, Furla had already invested in the creation of projects specifically conceived for social media and had restructured its final-user communication. Since most of the sales are related to the CRM (customer relationship management) activities implemented, at Furla social networks have always represented a crucial leverage in this sense.

Carpisa's goal, in the usage of social networks, is to generate both traffic in the online store and conversions. For this reason, the Instagram shopping function is implemented in most posts and the company is very proactive in supplying information and directions to its users in the comments. This activity proves the intention to convert the highest possible number of posts into sales.

13.7.7 Sponsorships and co-branding

Bags-specialised brands do not contemplate conspicuous investments in sponsorships. Those competing in the very high price segment could apply this strategy supporting ultra-exclusive events consistent with their image; however, they do not possess the financial resources to make such an investment.

Moreover, even the examples of co-branding are rare. The experience of Valextra with designer Michael Anastassiades, which was born from a mutual passion for beauty, is worth mentioning. For both the brand and the artist, beauty is the result of the dialogue between aesthetic and functionality (Maggiore, 2019).

Brands competing in the medium-price segment stand out neither in the field of sponsorships nor in that of co-branding. We may remember some collaborations with artists (*Coccinelle x Karen Wall, Furla x Maho Tonouch*) and retailers (*Furla x Saks Fifth Avenue*).

13.7.8 Museums, foundations and leisure time activities, in collaboration with Andrea Pittana

These brands did not invest significantly in the implementation of heritage and lifestyle.

Those positioned in the luxury segment reach a very niche target and communicate by means of very exclusive events. The eventual development of the heritage, even if potentially interesting, would need very high investments for their scarce economic resources.

In the medium-low price segment, however, financial resources are mainly allocated to branding strategies, traditional communication and retail (off and online); an eventual investment in brand heritage wouldn't be justified as the value proposition is based on accessible price.

13.8 Distribution, in collaboration with Andrea Doroldi

The distribution structure varies according to the brand positioning. Those belonging to the high and medium-high segment, Valextra and Zanellato, respectively, have a rather small distributive network. The great competition because of lifestyle brands like Hermès, Louis Vuitton, Gucci, Chanel and Prada – studied in Chapters 2 and 3 – doesn't allow them to reach high turnovers, and, as a consequence, an extensive distribution structure is not necessary. In fact, Valextra's merchandise is available in only two mono-brand stores in Italy – one in Milan – few shop-in-shops located in the most famous international department stores, and in very few prestigious multi-brand boutiques like Antonia in Milan. Zanellato has a similar structure: its products are available in three mono-brand stores – one of which in Milan – few shop-in-shops in worldwide famous department stores and few luxury multi-brand boutiques. For both brands, the estimated percentage of the direct retail channel is allegedly inferior than the wholesale one.

Conversely, at a medium and medium-low level, brands like Coach, Furla and Carpisa rely on an extensive distribution network for the opposite reasons. Unspecialised brands in these segments, due to their very low appeal (as explained in paragraph 13.6), and inferior revenues generated by leather goods, do not need a broad distribution network, thus leaving more "space" for specialised firms.

In the 2020 Tapestry Report,[1] we clearly see the essential characteristics of Coach's distribution structure. Coach sells through its own network inclusive of directly operated and online stores, shop-in-shops in concession, as well as wholesalers. However, the latter only represents 9% of the total turnover[2]; the remaining percentage is made by means of 958 directly operated stores including flagship stores, shop-in-shops in concession and independent outlets. The first are bigger and represent the highest expression of the world of Coach; the second offer a product assortment chosen according to the size and position of the shop (Tapestry, 2020).

This is a structure similar to Furla's, which relies on a retail network of 490 mono-brand stores, of which 285 are directly operated, 163 are in franchising and 42 are in travel retail, and on more than 1,000 multi-brand shops. In Milan, the brand can count on three mono-brand stores, one in the very central Piazza Duomo, and the remaining two in high streets. The turnover percentage represented by retail in 2018 was about 70%.

Also, Carpisa is equipped with an extensive distribution network that includes more than 650 mono-brand stores, mainly in franchising (Carpisa, no date b); of these, six are in Milan and all are located in central streets, but none of them in the fashion district.

We now consider the online distribution strategy of the same brands.

They all own their e-commerce where the whole assortment is available. Valextra is sold on seven platforms, Zanellato on three (Farfetch, Luisaviaroma, Yoox), Furla on four (the previous three and Amazon), Coach on six and Carpisa on only Amazon. The most representative category is bags. If we compare the price on their e-commerce and on Farfetch, we see that Valextra's, Coach's and Carpisa's prices are identical, while the price on the websites of Zanellato and Furla are higher. The five brands all allow purchases with mobile devices thanks to a responsive web design.

13.9 Omnichannel, in collaboration with Sabrina Pomodoro and Benedetta Breschi

Concerning bags-specialised brands, one of them stands out for a high degree of integrated communication and belongs to the *creative-idea-led integration* category: Carpisa. The brand focuses its communication for fall-winter 2019/2020 on the ideas of diversity and inclusion. The company aims at emphasising the beauty and uniqueness of diversity: *#BeAlwaysYourself* is the hashtag of the campaign, also found on its Instagram posts with different images and statements such as *Be confident, Be strong, Be different, Be Authentic, Be Happy* and *Be Unique.*

Moreover, the images of the campaign, accompanied by some iconic statements of the collection, become the fitting of the shop window.

Zanellato belongs to the *collection-led integration* category thanks to the idea of colour – the driving element of the collection – applied to the entire fashion tale. The classic Postina bag, the core product of the brand, is proposed in a new version with many colourful decorations that are, in turn, used to embellish the walls of the store.

Coccinelle, because it only applies the same image on the different means of communication without conveying a specific concept, belongs to the lower level of *visual and iconic integration*. Even though the brand aims to underline the importance of friendship – portraying in its campaign girls from different ethnic groups hugging each other and carrying a bag on their shoulders – it simply publishes the same campaign on magazines, billboards, on the Instagram page as well as on the walls of the boutique.

Speaking of Valextra, no synergy among the advertising campaign, the store and Instagram is found (*absence of integration*). The shop is minimal and the windows only display the product without any particular fitting. On the Instagram page, the collection is visible only in a "sneak peek" of the stylist and Creative Director walking and holding a bag, which is not even the same as the one shown in the shop window.

Interview with Claudia Orciani, president of Orciani

How is the scenario of the bag industry evolving?
Nowadays, more and more "disposable" icons are being born, next to real classics and big brands like Hermès. We see the birth of falling stars that disappear in a couple of seasons, we see fashion houses that chase this quick success and then fade away. After all, our company guarantees style, functionality, as well as a service and a very good price-quality ratio. These are the values at the base of *Sveva*, our it-bag.

What type of consumer do you target?
Federica, my sister and Creative Director, and I love saying that there is no Orciani woman, but there are Orciani women: the versatility of our bags is not just represented by their function, but also by their style. A wide range of women, multi-tasking, of course.

How are you facing the challenge of new consumers: Millennials and Generation Z?
We are a niche brand and "new" consumers represent a desirable target with whom we started a "virtual" dialogue two years ago. For instance, keeping (also) them in mind, we have designed some more ironic "mini-bags" that preserve our brand DNA.

Is the control of production still a key factor of success?
I reply with a question: is the control of breathing still indispensable in a polluted world? Yes, a correct understanding of the needs, producing without having unsold merchandise, and guarantying customer service are still at the base of success and longevity.

How are you tackling the sustainability challenge?
I can say that we had already accepted this challenge in 2013 with the making of solar power and geothermic plant for renewable energy production. In the last few years, we have committed to becoming a plastic-free company and in June we launched *Planet*, a fully sustainable backpack.

How have the brand communication levers changed?
The levers are the same, while the channels, the rhythms and the speed with which the message reaches the consumer are changing. Today, more than ever, brands need a heritage to resist in such a superficial and not-always-positively-evolving market.

Have investments in print media less importance than in the past?
We can't deny that print press investments have a different importance and are addressed to a more mature target with a higher spending power.

Consequently, they're still effective to push sales. Our customer still considers fashion magazines as a good source of shopping advice; the trust in traditional media hasn't decreased and, as a consequence, these media – provided they understand readers' needs – will coexist with digital ones. Today, print press cannot and shouldn't be the only medium of communication … digital is "trendy".

Will the price of the premium segment change in the close future?
It has already changed because in 2008 we lived a real social and economic transformation that became even more significant in 2011, when we all realised that it didn't make sense to talk about the middle class. Today, the gap between the "poor" and the "rich" is even more evident; by "poor" I don't just mean needy people, but also all that part of the middle class that cannot afford those little luxuries they used to enjoy before.

What was the impact of e-commerce and shopping experience on distribution strategies?
For a brand like ours, e-commerce, shopping experience and omnichannel are three concepts that identify a very clear strategy aimed at developing and strengthening and traditional channels (boutiques) and online shops (direct and indirect).

Student activities

Choose a brand and based on your choice:

* define the sustainability actions to be applied in the future;
* identify the combination product/price segment/target where to diversify;
* identify a social media and the content typology to be developed;
* define which of the following formats – brick-and-mortar mono-brand store, brick-and-mortar multi-brand store, shop-in-shop in department stores, online mono-brand shop and online multi-brand platform – need to be developed the most;
* verify the degree of synergy among the aesthetic elements of the latest collection: the fashion show, social networks, mono-brand store windows and the advertising campaign.

Notes

1 Tapestry controls the following brands: Coach, Kate Spade and Stuart Weitzman.
2 This data refers to Tapestry and not just to Coach.

14

BRANDS SPECIALISING IN FOOTWEAR

Reading: the H&R director

We felt it was appropriate to conclude the section dedicated to company profiles with an interview with Mr. Vaghi, Global H&R and Organization Director at Dolce & Gabbana.

How has the role of management changed in the last few years in fashion companies?
It is necessary to make a distinction. On the one hand, there are few giant companies such as Kering and LVMH, where the great importance given to managerial skills has allowed for the achievement of excellent results. On the other hand, there are many small/medium companies to which no sufficient or equal importance has been given.

How difficult is it to make such different souls – respectively creative genius and rational management – coexist?
Their coexistence is possible and necessary, but each soul must be able to "listen" to the other. If the creative soul can grasp and understand the needs of the managerial one (and vice versa), a virtuous process is generated; if there is no dialogue and coexistence between the two, it is impossible to reach very good medium/long-term performances.

What are the most requested professions by fashion companies?
On the one hand, they require classic fashion professionals like patternmakers, dressmakers and employees for quality check. Recently, and this is something new, industrial engineers are very requested, in fact, their skills are fundamental to have a structured approach. On the other hand, fashion companies search for employees in the retail sector, in particular, store managers. Lately, also merchandisers have been very sought for, as well as all the roles that deal with digital communication and e-commerce.

What do you think about digital marketing?
Communication and marketing online are substituting traditional ones. It is a huge phenomenon: a process of transition between "old" and new generations, between "old" and new values and, consequently, between a traditional and innovative way of organising and managing human resources.

You talked about new values, what do you mean?
New generations, millennials, have different values from the less young. For the latter, the most important, and sometimes the only, value was work. On the contrary, new generations are very careful in keeping a good balance between work and private life.

How important is passion in the fashion system?
Passion is an essential factor at any level, from warehouse workers to CEOs. Passion makes you overcome obstacles; without it, it's impossible to work in a fashion company. Obviously, the company contributes to nourishing this passion.

What advice would you give for a job interview?
It sounds banal but having clear ideas is the first piece of advice. When I ask a young candidate: "what would you like to do?" and they reply: "anything", they don't stand a chance. Vice versa, if they answer that they would like to work (for instance) in the product department because they have seen the website and visited the store, they show they have passion.

14.1 Who are they?

In this chapter, we consider those companies that market only (or chiefly) footwear. This sector is dominated by specialised companies, with the exception of sneakers whose leader are activewear-specialised brands. A business where multiple typologies of firms coexist. From historic, exclusive and prestigious brands like Santoni, offering a classic artisanal product for a mainly masculine elite, to trendsetter labels like Manolo Blahnik, Jimmy Choo and Louboutin, characterised by an equally luxurious product, yet addressed (almost) exclusively to women. In the same cluster, we also find brands like Geox, competing at a medium-low level and addressing a more extended and transversal market. In addition to the above-mentioned companies, in the same chapter, we also examine Giuseppe Zanotti, Sergio Rossi, Tod's, Pollini, John Lobb, L'Autre Chose, Hogan and Nero Giardini.

14.2 Style, in collaboration with Daniela Guariento

A characteristic shared by high-end footwear brands is the usage of excellent materials, skilled craftsmen labour and an outstanding product quality. However, style changes from label to label and becomes the distinctive element of their brand identity. Giuseppe Zanotti stands out for its contemporary design and luxury materials. Geometrical lines are the distinguishing feature of Sergio Rossi, offering chiefly a classic, elegant and refined product. Concerning men's footwear, Santoni epitomises perfection and classic timeless design; its products are rigorously hand-made.

Collections of medium-low level are characterised by a lower quality of finishing and materials. Moreover, they do not possess a stylistic code and, for this reason, they mainly include basic and carryover items, while trendy products are just a small portion of the offer. Geox, instead, shows a different approach: this company has leveraged on the combination of technology, design and functionality.

14.3 Supply chain and sustainability, in collaboration with Celeste Corso

Productive strategies in the footwear industry show many analogies with bag manufacturing. Even in this case, high-end brands boast an in-house production for most of their items, the remaining part is assigned to external suppliers.

The main reason is the same, that is, to control the excellent quality of the entire productive cycle. Consequently, it is pivotal to communicate the history of artisanal production, at the expense of ultra-mechanised techniques that speed up the process and allow for the manufacturing of very high quantities. As further proof of this strategy, Sergio Rossi's CEO, Riccardo Sciutto, affirms that technology is necessary to improve logistics and traceability, but not production speed, which is not an added value for a high-end brand (La Conceria, 2019b). Also, Tod's group mainly produces directly; on the website the company writes that production takes place in the group's factories and in a small number of specialised workshops, with whom the brand has established consolidated and long-term relationships. For every item, the parent company is in charge of monitoring the purchase of raw materials, all the productive phases and their final outcome, even when external suppliers are employed (Golizia, 2016).

In the medium-low price segment, the productive strategy is the opposite, due to the reasons already explained such as the minor importance of actual quality and the inferior need to control the productive cycle. Geox, for instance, one of the co-leaders in terms of turnover, relies on external partners for both production and supply of raw materials (Geox, no date).

The concepts expressed for bags companies (see previous chapter) can be similarly applied to this cluster. The raw material is the same: leather, which, as explained in Chapter 13, is the antithesis of sustainability. However, something is changing.

Manolo Blahnik has been one of the pioneers in this sense; in 2011 the brand launched a footwear line in collaboration with the eco-designer Marcia Patmos, whose objective was to reach zero impact in the luxury industry.

In the medium-high segment of the market, Pollini takes care of the environment using only green leather and installing solar power systems (Merli, 2019). In the medium-low segment, Geox tackles the issue of carbon footprints by launching the programme *La scarpa che fa respirare il mondo* (the shoe that makes the world breathe).

14.4 Segmentation strategies

Also, in this cluster, we cannot identify any company able to implement a lifestyle strategy. This is due to a very strong bond with a specific product – footwear – and sometimes its style, as well as with the target and the price segment. The bond is so tight that it prevents successful diversification in other categories of merchandise or targets. Consequently, brands such as Louboutin and Jimmy Choo adopt a segmentation strategy focused on the product (shoes) and target (women) with a very high price; as well as Santoni and John Lobb whose target, however, is men; whereas others, such as Geox, implement a strategy focused only on the product, as they reach a wider market.

14.5 Brand

To understand the characteristics of the cluster, we have identified the following companies: Giuseppe Zanotti and John Lobb, competing in the high-price segment; the former addresses a feminine target, and the second a masculine one; Tod's and Geox, addressing both genders and operating, respectively, in the medium-high and medium-low segments. Despite following different strategies, all these companies debuted in footwear.

Concerning diversification, John Lobb, the brand with the superior heritage, only "slightly" extends its range to accessories, to mainly focus on footwear. Zanotti and Geox have embarked on a selective diversification with small women's "leather-to-wear" collections (Eytan, 2015).

Tod's, instead, has implemented the most comprehensive diversification policy. From the launch of its renowned *Gommino* moccasins (Sylvers, 2019), it has extended its production to leather accessories and bags, which were fairly successful. Later on, the company also expanded to ready-to-wear and eyewear: through this thorough extension, the company attempted to build a brand lifestyle. However, the operation was not very successful since the perception of the market is still strongly associated with footwear and in particular with *Gommino* moccasins.

The origin of the brand is a crucial element also for these companies in order to increase the perceived brand value (Kapferer and Bastien, 2009, reprint 2012).

In the upper price segment, Zanotti, Lobb and Tod's leverage on the made-in to emphasise the concepts of heritage and craftsmanship and augment the perceived quality. The heritage of the former is based on the story of the founder and on his place of birth in Emilia Romagna, an Italian region famous for its footwear tradition (Sabino, 2016). Consequently, the Made in Italy is strongly anchored to the artisanal productive techniques and to the extravagant design of the brand.

The same considerations are applicable to Tod's, a brand strictly bound to the town of origin of its owners and to local production. The former is located in Italy in the province of Fermo, a footwear district (Sylvers, 2019) which still hosts the production plants of the brand. Conversely, John Lobb summarises the identity of different countries and of their respective specialisations. It unites Paris – production location and inspiration in terms of elegance and design – and the UK, recognised for its tradition of luxury footwear. Unlike the above-mentioned brands, Geox stresses the concept of Made in Italy only for its design, whereas it outsources production to directly owned companies or to suppliers located in low-labour-cost countries like Serbia (Chamberlain, 2016). In each of these cases, the crucial role of the country of origin "drives" the consumer's choice and adds authenticity to both brands and products.

Also, the presence of iconic elements plays a pivotal role in the consumer's perception and each company is characterised by their own. For instance, for Giuseppe Zanotti we may speak of iconic styles rather than products. Some of them have become such, thanks to the endorsement of celebrities: Adele wedge sandals, designed for Lady Gaga in 2012, are a clear example. Even Geox doesn't really boast an "iconic" product but rather an "iconic" technology allowing for breathable and comfortable soles.

For John Lobb, we can speak of iconic products in the classic sense of the term; its monk-strap moccasins and the *Chukka* boots are constantly reinterpreted must-haves. Tod's, among the four analysed brands, is the one with the most iconic product, the moccasin, regularly re-proposed in its collections.

Concerning the naming strategy, some differences were observed. On the one hand, Giuseppi Zanotti and John Lobb, leveraging on the strong personality of their founders, "sign" the entire product portfolio with their own names. The former relies on the celebration of the homonymous founder and Creative Director, recognised as an undisputed star designer (Sabino, 2016). The latter, established in 1866, bears the name of its founder whose legend has endured thanks to the celebrated craftsmanship and productive excellence of its merchandise.

On the contrary, Tod's has not embraced a patronymic naming strategy; however, even though the name cannot be traced back directly to the founder, the current majority share-holder, Diego Della Valle, is strongly rooted in the brand and associated to it by public opinion.

Speaking of Geox, the brand has not employed a patronymic naming strategy, consistent with its low price positioning.

Symbol of men's bespoke shoes production, John Lobb offers in-store customisation and bespoke services for a selection of "historic" models. Obviating the problem of the cost of these services, Giuseppe Zanotti can ingeniously create a distinctive product service, offering the opportunity to check the authenticity of the shoes purchased from third-party retailers. The above-described incentives are based on a direct exchange with the client; Tod's, in order to engage the consumer, chooses a more anonymous and digital strategy based on the online customisation of its Gommino moccasin.

14.6 Pricing, in collaboration with Benedetta Breschi

We hereby consider the price of women's pumps to compare the positioning of specialised and unspecialised companies.

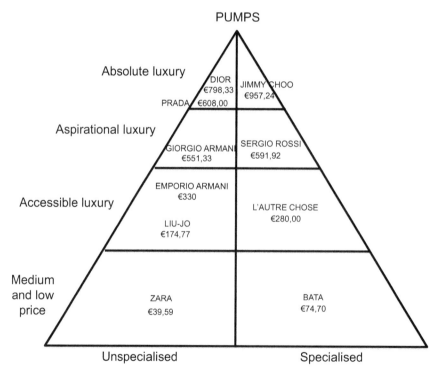

FIGURE 14.1 Golizia's pyramid of pumps
Source: Prepared by Dario Golizia.

Concerning the highest segment, we reiterate the considerations made in Chapters 2 and 3. The specialised brand Jimmy Choo, which has a higher price than Dior and Prada's, has been able to conceive and convey an image of a trendsetter brand worn by celebrities; this has guaranteed it a superior positioning.

The price of Giorgio Armani, a contemporary brand, is slightly inferior (−7.3%) as compared to Sergio Rossi's: the former's pluses in terms of image, already described in Chapter 4, are compensated by the latter with its superior product and production know-how (see interview at the end of the chapter).

As in the bags sector, and for the same reasons – specific product and production know-how – in accessible luxury, L'Autre Chose has a much higher price (+60.2%) than Liu Jo's. Likewise, in the medium-low segment, Bata's price is almost double (+88.6%) that of Zara's, due to its higher brand awareness in this category of merchandise.

14.7 Communication

We now proceed with the definition of the image of the cluster; afterwards, we study how the marketing and communication function is organised and managed by a company from the same group. Finally, we outline the communication mix applied by some brands.

14.7.1 Cluster image

For this cluster, the shoe is the variable associated with every brand. Even in this group, the positioning and identity of brands are defined by other characteristics: scarlet red sole, very high heels, chic and sexy Parisian glamour for Louboutin; breathable, essential design, family-friendly for Geox.

14.7.2 Marketing function and communication, in collaboration with Michele Leoni

Jimmy Choo's marketing and communication headquarters is based in London. The brand has a press office for each country in which the brand is distributed. For those nations in which sales are conspicuous, the press office is internal and reports directly to the headquarters in London, whereas for emerging markets or for those in which distribution is not sufficiently expanded, the brand employs external communication consultants and agencies, still managed by the Marketing and Communication Director. The latter reports to the CEO of the brand. All internal and external press offices take care of corporate communication and of the management of collection samples for fashion editorials. The VIP office, the pivot of brand communication, is based in Los Angeles where the digital marketing office is also located. Events organisation is internal and also includes the setup design, while its actual realisation is supplied by an external producer, mainly for the presentation of collections during Milan Fashion Week.

14.7.3 Fashion shows and trade fairs, in collaboration with Andrea Doroldi

Also, brands specialised in footwear do not organise fashion shows. Nonetheless, a specific trade fair, Micam, is held in Milan. Among the observed brands – Louboutin, Cahovilla, Manolo Blanik, Raparo, Nero Giardini and Geox – only the last two, positioned in the medium-low segment, participated in the event in 2019. Luxury brands do not take part in it since they prefer organising presentations and special events, often in their showrooms or in other specific locations.

For instance, during the spring summer 2020 haute couture week in Paris, Christian Louboutin presented a collection inspired by Bhutan. Guests got on the *Loubhoutan Express*, a railway carriage styled like the Orient Express and painted in red to recall the brand identity, which took them to a Bhutanese temple. In the temple participants were shown the collection consisting of 13 shoes reflecting the 13 forms of art recognised in the Kingdom (Hirshmiller, 2019). Manolo Blanik and Zintala, instead, present the pre-collections on their social media with a link to the e-commerce of the brands where the whole collection is available.

14.7.4 Advertising, editorial, advertorial, in collaboration with Benedetta Breschi

As mentioned in Chapter 2, this group had not been considered in the previous book (Golizia, 2016) and research; referring to the analysis outlined in Chapter 2, brands specialised in footwear are fifth in ranking for the number of purchased advertising pages. Nevertheless, it is worth observing how Jimmy Choo, Geox and Hogan choose to advertise, consistent with their positioning, on two different magazines. Jimmy Choo, which is a luxury brand, purchased two advertising pages from the equally prestigious fashion magazine, *Vogue*. Conversely, Hogan and Geox, whose targets, although different, are more inclusive, chose *Glamour*, a more mainstream publication.

14.7.5 Influencers, gifting, endorsement, by Lavinia Biancalani

In the course of time, shoes, traditionally a functional item, have turned into an object of desire and have become increasingly important in men's and women's outfits. Instagram, the most used social media, together with Facebook, represents the ideal channel to speak about the brand, to involve followers, to generate buzz and curiosity and to give users the opportunity to consult a sort of online catalogue. Communication pivots on the product and most posts are inspired by the editorial style of fashion magazines. Many seeding and gifting activities as well as celebrity endorsements and influencer marketing campaigns are carried out. Some brands have planned strategies that imply the creation of ad hoc contents

TABLE 14.1 Advertising, fashion editorial and advertorial of footwear-specialised brands

Footwear-Specialised Brands	L'Officiel			Vogue			Vanity Fair			Elle			Glamour			Total		
	A	FE	AD	A	FE	AD	A	FE	AD	A	FE	AD	A	FE	AD	A	FE	AD
Hogan	0	0	0	0	0	0	0	1	0	0	0	0	1	1	0	1	2	0
Geox	0	0	0	0	0	0	1	1	0	0	0	0	1	1	1	2	2	1
Jimmy Choo	0	0	0	2	0	0	0	0	0	0	1	1	0	0	2	2	1	3
Louboutin	0	0	0	0	0	0	0	0	0	0	0	0	0	0	0	0	0	0
Total	**0**	**0**	**0**	**2**	**0**	**0**	**1**	**2**	**0**	**0**	**1**	**1**	**2**	**2**	**3**	**5**	**5**	**4**

Source: Authors' data processing on the basis of fashion magazines published in Italy in September 2019. A, FE and AD stand for advertising, fashion editorial and advertorial, respectively.

for social media; sometimes they differentiate according to channel, but pictures prevail over videos and animations.

Louboutin, whose red heel is a distinctive trait, is extremely appreciated by celebrities who promote it through word of mouth, and by influencers that proudly show off the latest model, a forbidden dream for many women. Evidence of how appreciated the brand is, is the song dedicated by Jennifer Lopez in 2009. The company boasts many successful collaborations like the one with Disney: in 2012 Louboutin designed the shoes of the modern Cinderella for the launch of the new cartoon. In the same year, the brand implemented the first noteworthy digital initiatives such as the launch of the Louboutinize app that allows users to create wish lists, to learn about the product story and to access unpublished contents. The brand is endowed with well-structured social media channels (almost 14 million followers on Instagram) and with an editorial plan that includes product and lifestyle images. The company also likes experimenting with new tools such as apps, but, above all, it has understood the importance of communicating the brand world and of building a community on social media. Hence, the creation, in 2015, of the #LouboutinWorld campaign: a hashtag conceived to encourage users to share their brand experience and to become part of an online story. This campaign made the brand win the *Marketer of the Year* award during the *29th FN Achievement Awards*. No evidence of particularly structured influencer marketing campaign is available, even though activities of gifting and seeding, as well as public relations, are carried out in Italy and abroad.

In 2016, Geox, which organised some seeding and gifting initiatives with influencers, began a repositioning process aimed at communicating a more modern brand image. With its #startbreathing campaign, the scope of the brand was to involve users by combining fashion and experience. In the same year, the #walkforaweek Instagram campaign was presented: ten international artists showed the usage of the new Nebula line. *GeoxDragon* (racing car team) is a noteworthy initiative, having its own Instagram page, and organised for the 2019 Formula E championship with the involvement of racers Brendon Hartley and Nico Muller, both counting on a considerable community on social media.

Nero Giardini celebrates Italian style with a collection specialised in shoes and with a medium-low positioning. The brand is active on the main social networks: on Instagram it keeps a rather institutional tone of voice and presents product images – mainly still life – and campaign photos. In 2016, the company began its repositioning – also online – launching a new website and restyling its social networks. The work implied a new selection of more balanced contents including products, atmospheres, occasions of use and style. The brand is evidently applying an editorial plan based on advertising and contents sponsoring campaigns on both Instagram and Facebook. No evidence of influencer marketing activities was found.

14.7.6 Social media

The resilience of this sector has allowed its brands to adopt diversified social media communication strategies. The latter are often addressed to the main platforms and focused on both the product and the company philosophy and culture. Instagram is the preferred social media of the fashion industry; it is an image aggregator and an information supplier (in captions) that creates a sort of blog to communicate the brand values. Specific attention is paid to the product, often associated to the description of initiatives, and cultural and social responsibilities (economic, environmental, etc.) programmes. Unlike other clusters, which have embraced several social networks without distinction, this one designs specific editorial plans for each platform, being aware of their different targets. Moreover, this group shows the ability to build a community – through social media – aimed at generating customer loyalty and at increasing brand awareness and retention.

Louboutin is one of the main players of the luxury segment. The brand is particularly loved by celebrities and boasts 13.7 million followers on Instagram, 3.3 million on Facebook and 3.9 million on Twitter. The first noticeable characteristic is the conspicuous presence of videos specifically conceived and made for social networks: about 30% on Instagram, well-balanced with photographic contents. The company publishes contents of its campaigns for the launch of new products, as well as formats written and designed to promote events and special occasions such as *the exhibition(nist)*, an exhibition that celebrated the 30th anniversary of the brand. The production of videos – often enriched with special effects and illustrations – differentiates the brand from competitors. The editorial plan is almost the same for all social media, with a careful adaptation of the tone of voice in captions. The engagement rate is average considering the high number of followers of each channel and the average number of video visualisations.

Concerning Geox, in 2016, the brand started a repositioning process with the purpose of communicating a more modern image. The brand is active on main social media, YouTube and LinkedIn included, but not on Twitter. On Instagram, the company privileges a standard visual communication, mainly based on photos, and video contents that chiefly describe the product. Contents are made ad hoc for social media, but sometimes they are an adaptation of advertising campaigns; in the photos shoes are worn, pictures normally portray a setting, even though still lives are also used. The brand implements few collaborations with talents and brand ambassadors, but it has signed an interesting partnership with Lisa Casali, an environmental scientist, to support the causes of sustainability and technological innovation. Instagram counts on about 290,000 followers, and Facebook on more than 1.5 million with a constant growth. Interaction is very high for product information requests (in particular for kids' collections); a good conversion is noticed for sustainability contents.

Nero Giardini, active on the main social networks (240,000 followers on Instagram), opts for photographic contents rather than videos. Posts mainly concentrate on both worn and still life product images, many of them made in the studio. On Facebook (676,000 followers), the brand publishes videos of its campaigns but also ad hoc formats that aim to describe the product and the company through the narration of craftsmen's work and the concept of *Made in Italy*. The acquisition of followers on social media grows regularly and boasts a good engagement rate. The fan base is in fact very participative, interested in the product (particularly on Instagram) and in the topic of *Made in Italy* (chiefly on Facebook). No specific influencer marketing initiative is observed.

Brands employ social media for diverse purposes.

Louboutin uses social networks to work on its identity. This historic brand doesn't just describe the product, but narrates a world, a creative concept conveyed through the designer's words and with the help of his or her muses (from Monica Bellucci to Dita Von Teese). This approach generates a sense of belonging.

Geox acts bearing in mind specific objectives: to increase traffic in both online and offline stores and to generate conversations about sustainability and product innovation in order to change its positioning.

Likewise, Nero Giardini, particularly on Facebook, promotes the concept of Made in Italy in the attempt to develop a sense of belonging for its community. The final objective is to increase sales and brand awareness.

14.7.7 Sponsorships and co-branding

Footwear-specialised brands invest little resources in sponsorships and collaborations.

Concerning the former, an example is the experience of Louboutin, which supported the refurbishing of Palais de la Porté Dorée in Paris, located in the district where the artist spent his childhood, and where an aquarium, which had inspired one of the designer's first styles, is based. The reasons for this choice can be found in the bond with the local territory and with a symbolic product. Another interesting case is the partnership between Geox and the American Dragon Racing team competing in Formula E. The latter is a championship dedicated to electric cars: the partnerships is thus aimed at stressing the connection between the brand and sustainability.

Speaking about co-brandings, the most popular are those signed with other fashion companies (Christian Louboutin x Louis Vuitton, Manolo Blahnik x Vetements and John Lobb x Paul Smith), or with brands from other industries but with which they share an absolute luxury lifestyle (John Lobb x Aston Martin).

14.7.8 Museums, foundations and leisure time activities, in collaboration with Andrea Pittana

For the luxury brands of this cluster, the development of their heritage in order to strengthen their positioning would be a convenient move. However, their economic resources are mainly allocated to distribution strategies and alternative communication policies. The only initiative is the creation of foundations aimed at promoting projects, aligned with the brand values, and at fostering the growth of the territory where the company is located. For instance, in 2019, Tod's supported a project by FAI, *The National Trust for Italy*, for the restoration of Recanati, home town of poet Giacomo Leopardi, located in the Marche region, where Tod's headquarters is located. Two years before, in Arquata del Tronto, in the same region, the brand had opened a shoe production plant to help the area, which had been harshly damaged by an earthquake.

Concerning medium-low-segment brands, the same considerations made in Chapter 13 are applicable.

14.8 Distribution, in collaboration with Andrea Doroldi

The distribution structure of the studied footwear-specialised brands varies slightly according to their positioning. In fact, they are leaders of their segments and need a broad distributive structure to reach their targets.

Unlike bags-specialised companies, the firms positioned at a high and medium/high level, Jimmy Choo and Tod's, respectively, are characterised by a very extended distributive structure. This is because the lifestyle brands described in Chapters 2 and 3, in the footwear segment, do not have the same competitive strength they have in that of bags.

Jimmy Choo sells through 226 direct mono-brand stores (of which 47 outlets) – one of which is in the fashion district of Milan – and 554 wholesale stores; the brand is also distributed in prestigious multi-brand boutiques such as Giò Moretti in Milan, a luxury multi-brand located in the fashion district.

Tod's is characterised by a similar structure: its products are available in 215 mono-brand stores, of which 137 are directly operated, 2 of which are in Milan – one in Via Montenapoleone, and the other in the luxury spot Galleria Vittorio Emanuele II. The brand also sells its products through a selected multi-brand network including Biffi in Milan, a historic luxury apparel and footwear shop. For both the estimated percentage of direct retail is allegedly inferior to the wholesale one.

Also, and even more so, in the medium-low segment, one of the co-leader brands relies on an extensive distribution network.

In fact, Geox counted on 974 mono-brand stores, of which 454 are directly managed, and more than 10,000 multi-brand shops that equally represent almost the respective halves of the firm's turnover.

We now consider the online distribution strategy of the same brands. They all have their own e-commerce where the entire merchandise offer is available. While Jimmy Choo and Tod's are present on seven and six platforms, respectively, Geox is on only three (Farfetch, Yoox and Amazon) due to its lower positioning. For Jimmy Choo and Geox only shoes are available, while for Tod's we also find accessories and bags. If we consider the price of their product on Farfetch and on their e-commerce, all brands manage to impose the same price. For all three brands, it is possible to make purchases with mobile devices thanks to a responsive website design.

14.9 Omnichannel, in collaboration with Benedetta Breschi and Sabrina Pomodoro

Among the brands specialised in footwear, Geox communication reaches a high degree of integration (*creative-led integration*). For fall-winter 2019/2020, the brand hired exceptional endorsers of different ages, professions, culture, experience and aspirations, such as actor Corrado Tedeschi, freestyle wrestling champion Frank Chamizo and the travelling and photography enthusiasts Marco and Natalia Morello. The theme of the campaign, set in Rome and called "Love is love", is self-love. In the caption of an Instagram post, the brand wrote "#Love comes in many forms. Its power has transcended age, wealth, culture, gender and social background, throughout history. The Geox Fall-winter 2019 Collection encapsulates love in all senses of the word".[1] Geox also promotes its advertising campaign on social networks, encouraging its followers to "discover" its photos.

Even Hogan adopts a *creative-led integration* approach between point of sale, advertising and social media. The protagonist of the shop windows is a white fur framing one of the garments of the collection; the same item is worn by the model for the advertising campaign. Also, on the feed of the Instagram page, the brand posts images of the shop window and of the store, as well as pictures of the advertising campaign. Moreover, in the campaign photo, besides a close-up of the shoes, the user can catch a glimpse of the white fur, the same displayed in the shop windows.

Moving on to the analysis of John Lobb and Jimmy Choo, we can identify in both a weak integration classifiable as *visual and iconic integration*. A video posted on John Lobb's

Instagram page recalls the fall–winter 2019/2020 collection, even though the only element that stands out is the shoe which is also the protagonist of the advertising campaign. Several clips of the advertising campaign video are posted on Instagram stories highlights. Conversely, Jimmy Choo doesn't promote its collection on Instagram; nonetheless, the advertising campaign and the shop windows are consistent: in the former, the model Kaia Gerber is "leaning" on the logo of the brand, the blow-up of the two steel initials, which are also displayed in the shop window.

Interview with Riccardo Sciutto CEO at Sergio Rossi

How has the fashion system evolved in the last few years?
The fashion system has become more complex; the paradigm that used to work five years ago is not effective anymore; in the past, advertising on *Vogue* and having a store in through Montenapoleone were enough to be successful. In the last few years, we have assisted to a Copernican revolution that has overturned the rules of the game. The brand is not the core anymore, as in the 80s and 90s, it's been replaced by the consumer whose needs must be understood to guarantee the most desirable experience.

How important is it to have a defined business model?
It is paramount and it pivots on the control of the whole value chain: if the customer is at the centre of the system, production and distribution must be in-house. This allows for flexibility and effective management of time-to-market.

What are the productive strategies applied by women's footwear-specialised companies like Sergio Rossi?
Production in this industry is outsourced to numerous micro-producers. To make a pair of shoes, a company on average delocalises to 20 different suppliers. Sergio Rossi produces directly 86% of its merchandise (other brands only 10–15%, other none). This allows the company to have the utmost control on quality as well as to flexibly respond to the needs of clients to whom we deliver the ordered products every month. We are going towards the future, nevertheless, we respect the heritage and the tradition of a historic brand like Sergio Rossi. My motto is: think heritage, play digital.

How do you include sustainability in fashion?
We must give Millennials credit for breaking the past schemes; they want to be more participative, to influence change, to understand what's behind the product and where and how it was made. And Sergio Rossi has taken huge steps in this direction. All the waste of leather deriving from production is regenerated by a German firm that re-sells it to other brands making more accessible products. Moreover, since 1 January 2020, we use 100% certified green energy, whose 20% is produced by our solar panels, and 80% from power suppliers.

How does Sergio Rossi – a brand strongly specialised in women's shoes – tackle the challenge of competing with mega-brands?
By telling a unique story; the brand boasts a very high awareness worldwide and a know-how in high-end shoes which has become exemplary. One of my first initiatives was the recreation of the history of the company: I have rebuilt the historic production archive by personally buying the shoes; I have done it to understand what direction to take for an innovative valorisation of the past, and to reset production time to make it more effective.

Footwear industry, new generations and digital world, how is the scenario changing?
The challenge started five years ago when I stopped offline investments to focus on digital communication and, on Instagram, with the support of an internal team shooting 700 pieces of contents per season. However, most of fashion companies delegate the management of digital communication to external agencies; I believe it is a mistake, they should internalise this new culture.

Omnichannel and the evolution of the distributive structure.
Omnichannel is not the future anymore: by now it is widespread; if the customer is our focus and stands at the core of the system, companies have to be well-structured to reach them through all the possible channels. I still believe in shops, provided they are dynamic and offer a superlative customer experience and customization.

Do you think that prices will change in this sector?
I reckon that price will tend to increase because, as previously said, complexity has augmented. The business model encompassing omnichannel and in-house production is very expensive compared to the past and the average profitability has decreased due to smaller margins.

How has the scenario evolved after Covid-19?
Besides the serious health emergency, Covid can be an opportunity for daring. What I mean is that it has simply accelerated an inevitable process that had just begun and had to evolve. We have to realise that consumers have radically changed habits and that companies need to react to this new scenario. How? By humanising technology. In the past, we proposed two opposite worlds: the cold technology and the in-store physical experience; today, we need to offer a balance between innovation and feelings, between technology and quality, taking the store to customers' homes. Sergio Rossi's flagship store in through Montenapoleone generates a very high amount of sales thanks to "human technology": the customer can connect online with the store manager who describes the collection and shows the product live, thus making them live an incomparable experience.

Student activities

Choose a brand and based on your choice:

- define the sustainability actions to be applied in the future;
- identify the combination product/price segment/target where to diversify;
- identify a social media and the content typology to be developed;
- define which of the following formats – brick-and-mortar mono-brand store, brick-and-mortar multi-brand store, shop-in-shop in department stores, online mono-brand shop and online multi-brand platform – need to be developed the most;
- verify the degree of synergy among the aesthetic elements of the latest collection: the fashion show, social networks, mono-brand store windows and the advertising campaign.

Note

1 Geox Instagram page posted on 10 September 2019.

15

CONCLUSIONS

Shared critical factors of success and future scenarios of the fashion industry in collaboration with Sennaith Ghebreab

Now that we have reached the conclusion, we do not intend to proceed with a tedious comparison of the 13 clusters, but to point out the most relevant characteristics of this study by identifying the future trends that are, and will be, affecting the fashion industry, also in consideration of the Covid-19 emergency.

What has emerged from the analysis carried out in the previous chapters, from the interviews reported at the end of each of them and from those made specifically to draw these conclusions?

Summarising, we can say that we agree with David Pambianco when, in the interview, he maintains that in luxury – except for some cases – the most successful business model is the *buy* one applied by big groups, whereas in the medium-low segment, the most effective is the *make* strategy implemented by fast fashion brands. Speaking of accessible luxury, instead, which is endowed with great potential, a reference model has not emerged yet. We have also come to the understanding that relying on a well-defined business model is now more important than ever. Speaking of which, an alternative interpretation was proposed by Massimo Piombini, who in an unpublished interview from 2019 had stated that:

> In the recent past, I noticed that the classification and nomenclature were rather stiff and brands followed a clear scheme. Nowadays, due to the evolution of the industry, and as a consequence of the market, business models are much more overlapped.

An interesting position is also that of Sama who stated that it "is important ... to renew the business model by adapting it to the commercial and technological evolutions".

Nonetheless, they all share the vision that a successful business model should always be rooted in the original brand values and its authenticity, rather than running after market trends. For this reason, possessing and telling a unique story is crucial, in particular for those specialised brands that have to compete with mega companies. Fagnani stated: "as for any brand, the ability to exist, grow, and evolve is connected to the authenticity of their story ... the ability to reinvent themselves generation after generation (or from age to age) without losing their distinctive DNA".

And here comes another key factor of success, lifestyle: whether it is specialised or unspecialised brands, a common characteristic of prosperous companies is the ability to convey a lifestyle to their consumers.

But the latter are the new protagonists of the current competitive scenario, Sciutto has even spoken about a "Copernican revolution that has overturned the rules of the game. The brand is not the core anymore; it's been replaced by the consumer whose needs must be understood in order to guarantee the most desirable experience". Freschi adds that when relating to consumers it is necessary "to create an empathic, and more democratic relationship." Yet, it is not simple. In fact, according to Sallorenzo: "among new generations it is difficult to identify targets and consumption models."

Nevertheless, to conquer the consumer's heart, successful companies apply the best practice of customisation, which has moved from being an opportunity to being a necessity. It is not simple to implement, since businesses, in order to supply this service, have to reorganise both logistics and production, inevitably increasing the complexity of their management.

Even sustainability and diversity are now integrating factors of successful business models; these are topics of interest chiefly for new generations, as confirmed by Sciutto: "We must give Millennials credit for breaking the past schemes; they want to be more participative, to influence change, to understand what's behind the product and where and how it was made". And since in the next few years, a considerable part of the business will pivot on this target, fashion companies are investing many resources in the safeguard of the environment. However, the analysis we carried out shows that only few of them have really included sustainability in their system of beliefs; we should not forget what Pambianco affirmed: "sustainability is simply connected to brand reputation; in the short term, almost all the players have had to adopt sustainable conducts; so, being sustainable won't represent an added value for the brand anymore, but a prerequisite of the product".

We mentioned the issue of diversity, which is another important asset companies are leveraging on. Piombini supplies us with an interesting interpretation when affirming that

> diversity means equal opportunities: a chance is given to everyone; however, diversity becomes a mistake when it is used as a protection for the lack of talent: a company should find a balance between offering opportunities and recognising someone's talent.

However, all the interviewed professionals agree that presumably the most important factor shared by the most successful companies is omnichannel; if the customer is like the sun on which the whole system pivots, firms need the necessary structure to reach them with all the possible channels, including distributive and promotional, and always applying the same storytelling. Actually, the specific research carried out for the purposes of this book has proven that only few virtuous companies can accomplish a high degree of communication integration.

Nonetheless, the omnichannel wouldn't exist without the boom of digitalisation. Evidence was given on how offline advertising investments underwent a slump and how they were integrated/substituted with online ones, in particular the usage of social media and influencers, more effective and efficient in terms of cost per contact, visibility and usability. Sciutto stated: "The challenge started 5 years ago when I stopped offline investments to focus on digital communication and, on Instagram". Yet also in this field, the challenge is complex: it is not enough to create a profile and post videos. The research has proven how successful companies create contents in line with the brand positioning in structured – and not improvised – digital marketing campaigns. According to Freschi: "Digital platforms have allowed brands to reach a more and more extended audience and have given a voice to everyone". The real difficulty for every business is language: "The most important concept that emerges from social media is that of community; youth speaks a different language, and this must be understood; managers still communicate 'vertically', while what is needed is a horizontal dialogue", maintains Sallorenzo.

Digitalisation has changed not only communication methods, but the distributive ones as well. Although Pambianco affirmed that it is more and more "difficult and useless to separate online and offline sales since the latter influence the former", it is necessary to state that the most profitable companies are giving more importance to direct retail, at the expense of wholesale; the main purpose is always the same: having a direct contact with the consumer and making them live a superlative experience. How? By offering a "human technology". In the past, the cold technology and the in-store physical experience were two opposite poles: nowadays, and more and more in the future, virtuous brands are reorganising so to "take" the store to the homes of their consumers, thus creating a balance between innovation and feelings. As maintained by Sciutto: "the customer can connect online with the store manager who describes the collection and shows the product live; thus making them live an incomparable experience". According to Cavalli, "sales campaigns will employ more and more digital tools to compensate for the impossibility to travel, and the same methodology will be applied to the presentation of collections that will have to comply with social distancing regulations". Of course, artificial intelligence – magic mirrors, virtual shop assistants, etc. – is extremely helpful in this sense, and, despite being less "visible", it represents another asset fashion companies are investing in.

Concerning price there are different opinions; Freschi stated: "the market evolution will not necessarily affect prices"; Sama affirmed: "we're living in a period of deflation rather than inflation"; and finally Sciutto who said: "that price will tend to increase because complexity has augmented".

In 2020, the Covid-19 pandemic broke out. The above-described trends are still applicable; nonetheless, the author thought it was appropriate to integrate them with some ad hoc interviews.

The new reality will lead to systemic changes in the fashion industry in a post-Covid world: changes in consumer behaviour and a reset of the distribution footprint (as mentioned above) are reflected by the current situation. Felix Krueger, Partner & Associate Director, Fashion & Luxury, at BCG, argues: "Accelerated behavioural changes include a further shift in category mix towards casualwear, polarization of price points, increasing importance of sustainability, health and sport and a new trend in luxury, which is harder hit in Europe due to repatriation of (Chinese) luxury consumption.

The distribution reset includes further DTC (direct to consumer) push, less wholesale and online being more and more at the core".

Structural shifts include a new model of profit & loss, industry polarisation, increased company digitalisation as well as new leaders. According to Krueger:

> New Profit & Loss shape is characterized by store revenues which are dampened for a longer time, therefore requiring strict cost management across COGS (cost of goods

sold), rent, personnel and company costs. In addition, required to free up funds in order to invest in increased demands from consumers regarding digital distribution and sustainability.

Looking at polarisation, an essential aspect is sales volumes: smaller and mid-sized players would be threatened without a clear value proposition. "Likely seeing a next wave of vertical & horizontal integration through M&A. This time we'll see digitization of businesses for real, as all brands now acknowledge the importance of E2E (End to End) digitization and personalization of consumer pathways".

But a new era needs new leaders to be able to invest in all relevant forward-looking goals; leaders should de-clutter with the aim to invest in the next company milestones. "Building the artificial intelligence (AI) and tech backbone to digitise core processes, including product development and e-commerce, into elevated consumer needs around brand purpose, product offering and sustainability". Furthermore, digitising the entire process to shift from a mass media to a customised communication requires the hiring of specialised personnel. Krueger concludes affirming that "leaders of the future need to move away from a single product/store focus to owning the direct consumer relationship in a personalised manner with a clear brand purpose and a digital-first mindset".

A complementary and interesting vision is supplied by Andrea De Santis, Engagement Manager at McKinsey, Milano. He affirmed that "the crisis has certainly shaken some industry's foundations".

First, wholesale: independent wholesalers and family-owned boutiques in Europe look particularly vulnerable; also at risk are some of the big existing luxury department stores, and wholesale remains a very important channel across all key markets especially for non-vertically integrated distribution brands, as well as for upstream brands. De Santis stated: "Covid-19 has further reduced the wholesale vital space (already shrinking due to growth of e-commerce and brand's increasing vertical integration) and worsened already fragile economics". Wholesale is taking dramatic steps to escape the crisis, some of which will have adverse consequences on brands: "diversion of business to online flash sales, adapt terms for merchandise swap (e.g., refund one item from past season for every new collection items purchased); increase flexibility on payment days; ally with marketplace".

The second aspect is the shift "from global to local shoppers". Luxury is a multinational market that speaks to customers around the world. The purchases that consumers make outside their home country constitute about 30% of business sales; Chinese customers play a central role within the "world shopper". According to De Santis, "brands should understand how to re-activate their international Asian clients in their home countries. This will require brands to focus on creating more-tailored local experiences, to refine their digital offerings, and to engage more deeply with consumers".

The third aspect is related to "shows without an audience". Fashion weeks and trade shows are an important part of how brands sustain a lively relationship with their consumers and business partners; while we foresee a return to normality on this front,

> the luxury industry should explore what could be an alternative way to preserve their experience and magic; brands will be called also to simplify and streamline their presentation calendars; this should happen in coordinated manner, rethinking the calendar of fashion.

Finally, a general overview of the value chain that has to be redesigned. Still De Santis maintains that

> As the Covid-19 crisis lingers, technology can help luxury companies to maintain productivity – from remote working to virtual show rooms – and perhaps even improve it for good. There is a great opportunity to digitize the E2E supply chain, to increase efficiency and effectiveness at product level, both in terms of offer productivity and speed. This will require investments in innovation that will help companies moving toward intense application of digital prototyping and sampling. Also the commercial elements, such as virtual show room, would be a plus to keep an alive relationship with buyers in time of restricted travelling policies.

Although the book analysed the business model of existing companies, we should not forget the relevant role of start-ups, as confirmed by Stefano Galassi, Managing Director at Startupbootcamp:

> For the sake of the fashion industry's future, we need more start-ups which bring innovative and disruptive solutions to the industry; a rising number of companies are collaborating with start-ups because they believe that the technology takes their business one step ahead.

Of course, as Freschi stated: "we need to ask about the role of fashion today. The crisis that has hit the world is an opportunity to think, to re-align everything, to define a more authentic and true framework".

We conclude with a consideration of the great Giorgio Armani who in the middle of the Covid-19 crisis declared that "this crisis is a perfect opportunity to slow down and re-align everything, to define a more authentic reality" (Pollo, 2020).

Further reading

Anouti, C., Graham, B. (2018) *Promoting Fashion*. London: Laurence King Publishing.
Chevalier, M., Mazzalovo, G. (2012) *Luxury Brand Management: A World of Privilege*. New York: Wiley.
Corbellini, E., Saviolo S. (2009) *Managing Fashion and Luxury Companies*. Milano: ETAS.
Kapferer, J.N., Bastien, V. (2009, 2012 reprint) *The Luxury Strategy. Break the Rules of Marketing to Build Luxury Brands*. London: Kogan Page.

BIBLIOGRAPHY

Aaker, D.A. (1991) *Managing Brand Equity: Capitalizing on the Value of a Brand Name*. New York: The Free Press.

Aaker, D.A., Joachimsthaler, E. (2000) *Brand Leadership*. 7th edition. Milano: FrancoAngeli.

Abell Dereck, F. (1980) *The Starting Point of Strategic Planning*. London: Prentice-Hall Englewood Cliffs.

Adidas Group. (2019) [Online] Available from: https://www.adidas-group.com/en/brands/reebok/ [Accessed: 16 March 2021].

Allérès, D. (2003) *Luxe... Stratégies Marketing*, 3rd edition. Paris: Economica.

Altagamma. (2019) *Lo sguardo di Altagamma sul futuro: Next Design Perspectives 2019* [Online] Available from: https://altagamma.it/news/info/137/ [Accessed: 16 March 2021].

Amarca, N. (2017) *How Alexander Wang Used Social Media to Win in Fashion* Highsnobiety.com [Online] Available from: https://www.highsnobiety.com/2017/09/27/alexander-wang-interview/ [Accessed: 16 March 2021].

Anouti, C., Graham, B. (2018) *Promoting Fashion*. London: Laurence King Publishing.

Armani. (2020) [Online] Available from: https://www.armani.com/experience/it/corporate/social-responsibility/ [Accessed: 16 March 2021].

Aull, A. (2019) *How Timberland Is Embracing the Future of Content Marketing* Percolate [Online] Available from: https://blog.percolate.com/2017/10/timberland-content-marketing-strategy/ [Accessed: 16 March 2021].

Badia, E. (2011) *Zara*. Milano: Egea.

Benetton. (2019a) Fondazione benetton [Online] Available from: http://www.benettongroup.com/it/gruppo/profilo/fondazione-benetton/ [Accessed: 16 March 2021].

Benetton. (2019b) Fondazione unhate [Online] Available from: http://www.benettongroup.com/it/gruppo/profilo/fondazione-unhate/ [Accessed: 16 March 2021].

Benetton. (2020) [Online] Available from: http://www.benettongroup.com/it/sostenibilita/ [Accessed: 16 March 2021].

Bertoletti, C. (2018) *Nike, Adidas, Reebok: lo sportswear per la parità di genere* MarkUp [Online] Available from: https://www.mark-up.it/nike-adidas-reebook-lo-sportswear-per-la-parita-di-genere/ [Accessed: 16 March 2021].

Bhasin, K. (2019) *Ralph Lauren's Plan to Lure Younger Shoppers: Hype* BoF [Online] Available from: https://www.businessoffashion.com/articles/news-analysis/ralph-laurens-plan-to-lure-younger-shoppers-hype [Accessed: 16 March 2021].

Bini, V. (2011) *La supply chain della moda*. Milano: FrancoAngeli.

Biondi, A. (2019) *Is Streetwear Finally Ready for Women?* Vogue.com [Online] Available from: https://www.voguebusiness.com/fashion/streetwear women opportunity designers market aries danielle-cathari-aleali-may [Accessed: 16 March 2021]

Biron, B. (2017) *Social Media Is Driving Growth in the Luxury Menswear Market* Glossy.com [Online] Available from: https://www.glossy.co/evolution-of-luxury/social-media-is-driving-growth-in-the-luxury-menswear-market?utm_source=digiday.com&utm_medium=referral&utm_campaign=digidaydis&utm_content=biron-social-media-driving-growth-luxury-brands# [Accessed: 16 March 2021].

Biserini, F. (2018) *Moda sostenibile: il primo passo è la progettazione* D.Repubblica [Online] Available from: https://d.repubblica.it/moda/2018/07/31/news/moda_e_sostenibilita_design_sviluppo_impatto_ambientale-4031761/ [Accessed: 16 March 2021].

Bloomberg. (2016) *Adidas Looks to Harness Instagram Fans to Maintain Its Momentum* BusinessofFashion [Online] Available from: https://www.businessoffashion.com/articles/news-analysis/adidas-looks-to-harness-instagram-fans-to-maintain-its-momentum [Accessed: 16 March 2021].

Bloomberg. (2019) *Adidas's New Price Target Leaves Nike in Its Wake* BusinessofFashion [Online] Available from: https://www.businessoffashion.com/articles/news-analysis/adidass-new-price-target-leaves-nike-in-its-wake [Accessed: 16 March 2021].

BoF. (2019) Gucci and Saint Laurent Face Uphill Battle to Get Green [Online]. Available from: https://www.businessoffashion.com/articles/news-analysis/gucci-and-saint-laurent-face-an-uphill-battle-to-get-green. [Accessed: 16 March 2021].

Bolelli, G. (2019) *Woolrich vuole diventare un marchio globale* FashionNetwork [Online] Available from: https://it.fashionnetwork.com/news/Woolrich-vuole-diventare-un-marchio-globale,1054306.html [Accessed: 16 March 2021].

Business People. (2018) [Online] Available from: http://www.businesspeople.it/People/Protagonisti/Chi-e-Sandro-Veronesi-mr-Calzedonia-103862 [Accessed: 16 March 2021].

Calzedoniagroup. (2019a) [Online] Available from: https://www.calzedoniagroup.com/world-in-progress/il-nostro-modello-e-contributo/gestione-responsabile-della-catena [Accessed: 16 March 2021].

Calzedoniagroup. (2019b) Fondazionesanzeno [Online] Available from: https://www.fondazione-sanzeno.org/chi-siamo [Accessed: 16 March 2021].

Camera Moda. (2019) *Max Mara presenta Camelux* [Online] Available from: https://www.camera-moda.it/it/associazione/news/1566/ [Accessed: 16 March 2021].

Camuffo, A., Cappellari, R. (1997) *Forall Pal Zileri*. Torino: ISEDI.

Camuffo, A., Romani, P. Vinelli A. (2002) *Economia & Management*. gennaio-febbraio, p. 94.

Canali. (2019) [Online] Available from: https://www.canali.com/it_it/black-edition.html [Accessed: 16 March 2021].

Carpisa. (No date a) [Online] Available from: (https://www.carpisa.it/it_it/save-the-ocean// [Accessed: 16 March 2021].

Carpisa. (No date b) [Online] Available from: https://www.carpisa.it/it_it/about-us/ [Accessed: 16 March 2021].

Cavalca Altan, E. (2004) *La moda allo specchio*. Milano: FrancoAngeli.

Chamberlain, G. (2016) *The Expensive 'Italian' Shoes Made for a Pittance in East European Sweatshops*. The Guardian [Online] Available from: https://www.theguardian.com/fashion/2016/aug/20/shoes-uk-high-street-made-for-a-pittance-eastern-europe-sweatshop [Accessed: 16 March 2021].

Chevalier, M., Gutstatz, M. (2012) *Luxury Retail Management*. New York: Wiley.

Chevalier, M., Mazzalovo, G. (2012) *Luxury Brand Management: A World of Privilege*. New York: Wiley.

Chodha, D. (2019) *Ermenegildo Zegna Asks: What Makes a Man?* Wallpaper.com [Online] Available from: https://www.wallpaper.com/fashion/ermenegildo-zegna-asks-what-makes-a-man [Accessed: 16 March 2021].

Cochrane, L. (2018) *Virgil Abloh Named Artistic Director of Louis Vuitton's Menswear*. The Guardian [Online] Available from: https://www.theguardian.com/fashion/2018/mar/26/virgil-abloh-named-artistic-director-of-louis-vuitton-menswear [Accessed: 16 March 2021].

Corbellini, E., Saviolo S. (2009) *Managing Fashion and Luxury Companies*. Milano: ETAS.

Corneliani. (2019) [Online] Available from: https://www.corneliani.com/it/it/corneliani/ [Accessed: 16 March 2021].

Crivelli, G. (2019) *Sostenibilità: le strade scelte da Massimo Alba, Triump, Uriage* [Online] Available from: https://www.ilsole24ore.com/art/sostenibilita-strade-scelte-massimo-alba-triumph-e-uriage-ACkZwxY?refresh_ce=1 [Accessed: 16 March 2021].

Curci, M. (2019) *Sfilata Dior Cruise 2020: il viaggio tra Mediterraneo, Europa e Africa di Maria Grazia Chiuri*. Grazia [Online] Available from: https://www.grazia.it/moda/tendenze-moda/sfilata-dior-cruise-2020-abbigliamento-borse-accessori [Accessed: 16 March 2021].

Dahlén, M., Lange, F., Smith, T. (2010) *Marketing Communications: A Brand Narrative Approach*. Ney York: Wiley.

Danziger, P.N. (2018) *Why Zara Succeeds: It Focuses on Pulling People in, Not Pushing Product Out* Forbes [Online] Available from: https://www.forbes.com/sites/pamdanziger/2018/04/23/zaras-difference-pull-people-in-not-push-product-out/#45adcb4123cb [Accessed: 16 March 2021].

DeKlerk, A. (2016) *Gucci Launches a Personalisation Service*. Harpers Bazaar [Online] Available from: https://www.harpersbazaar.com/uk/fashion/fashion-news/news/a37236/gucci-launches-a-personalisation-service/ [Accessed: 16 March 2021].

Diciotto. (2018) [Online] Available from: https://diciotto.net/2018/10/18/martin-margiela-svela-il-motivo-per-cui-ha-lasciato-la-moda/ [Accessed: 16 March 2021].

DolceGabbana. (2020) [Online] Available from: https://www.dolcegabbana.com/it/dgyourself/ [Accessed on: 16 March 2021].

Elevent. (2020) *Top Sponsorship – H&M We Love Horses* [Online] Available from: https://elevent.co/blogs/sponsorship/top-sponsorships-h-m-we-love-horses [Accessed: 16 March 2021].

Erkilic, G. (2018) *6 Things You Should Know About Adidas' Digital Marketing Strategy* DigitalAgencyNetwork [Online] Available from: https://digitalagencynetwork.com/digital-marketing-strategy-of-adidas/ [Accessed: 16 March 2021].

Etnies. (2019) [Online] Available from: https://www.etnies.com/eu/buy-a-shoe-plant-a-tree/ [Accessed: 16 March 2021].

Eytan, D. (2015) *Shoe Master Giuseppe Zanotti on His 20-Year Career and Working with Beyoncé*. Forbes Magazine [Online] Available from: https://www.forbes.com/sites/declaneytan/2015/03/19/giuseppe-zanotti-announces-beyonce-collaboration-and-reflects-on-his-20-years-in-business/#7d2fc67e4527 [Accessed: 16 March 2021].

Fabris, G. (2009) *Societing*. Milano: FrancoAngeli.

Fabris, G., Minestroni, L. (2004) *Valore e Valori della marca*. Milano: FrancoAngeli.

FashionMagazine. (2020) *Off-White salta lo show di Settembre e lancia la Spring 2021 in store a Febbraio* [Online] Available from: www.fashionmagazine.it https://www.fashionmagazine.it/trend/new-guards-group-rivoluziona-le-consegne-off-white-salta-lo-show-di-settembre-e-lancia-la-spring-2021-in-store-a-febbraio-105360 [Accessed: 16 March 2021].

FashionNetwork. (2017a) *Levis e l'importanza dell'esperienza reale nel mondo digitale* [Online] Available from: https://it.fashionnetwork.com/news/levi-s-e-l-importanza-dell-esperienza-reale-nel-mondo-digitale,891794.html [Accessed: 16 March 2021].

FashionNetwork. (2017b) *Ferragni costumista per show Intimissimi* [Online] Available from: https://it.fashionnetwork.com/news/Ferragni-costumista-per-show-intimissimi,839384.html [Accessed: 16 March 2021].

FashionUnited. (2018) *Ermenegildo Zegna: i clienti indicano la strada da seguire* FashionUnited.it [Online] Available from: https://fashionunited.it/news/business/ermenegildo-zegna-i-clienti-indicano-la-strada-da-seguire/2018120618859 [Accessed: 16 March 2021].

Foglia, A. (2016) *My Coccinelle, il nuovo servizio di personalizzazione* [Online] Available from: https://www.alessiafoglia.com/fashion/my-coccinelle-il-nuovo-servizio-di-personalizzazione-online/ [Accessed: 16 March 2021].

Forbes. (2019) [Online] Available from: https://forbes.it/2019/02/28/kiton-alta-moda-italiana-maschile-lusso/ [Accessed: 16 March 2021].

Forrester. (2019) *Victoria Secret's Cautionary Brand Tale: When Intimates Fail to be Intimate.* Forbes [Online] Available from: https://www.forbes.com/sites/forrester/2019/11/25/victoria-secrets-cautionary-brand-tale-when-intimates-fail-to-be-intimate/#1a68422d5aee [Accessed: 16 March 2021].

Freed, J. (2019) *Hunting for Hype: How Social Media Influences Streetwear Fashion.* TheGlobeandMail [Online] Available from: https://www.theglobeandmail.com/life/style/article-hunting-for-hype-how-social-media-influences-streetwear-fashion/ [Accessed: 16 March 2021].

Fuorisalone. (2019) *RoBOTl: il supereroe della sostenibilità.* Fuorisalone [Online] Available from: https://fuorisalone.it/2019/it/magazine/focus/article/182/robotl-il-supereroe-della-sostenibilita [Accessed: 16 March 2021].

Gap. (2020) [Online] Available from: https://www.gapinc.com/en-us/values/sustainability [Accessed: 16 March 2021].

Geox. (no date) [Online] Available from: https://www.geox.biz/it/sostenibilita/supply-chain.html [Accessed: 16 March 2021].

Giannelli, B., Saviolo, S. (2001) *Il licensing nel sistema moda.* Milano: RCS libri.

Golizia D. (2016) *Fashion Business Model.* Milano: FrancoAngeli.

Guardian Fashion. (2013) *New Models: How Rick Owens's Dancers Conquered Paris Fashion Week* The Guardian [Online] Available from: https://www.theguardian.com/fashion/fashion-blog/2013/sep/27/rick-owens-models-dancers-paris-fashion-week [Accessed: 16 March 2021].

Gucci. (no year) *Gucci-Dapper Dan: The Collection* [Online] Available from: https://www.gucci.com/us/en/st/stories/advertising-campaign/article/pre-fall-2018-dapper-dan-collection-shoppable [Accessed: 16 March 2021].

Guess. (2020) [Online] Available from: https://sustainability.guess.com/ [Accessed: 16 March 2021].

Hirshmiller, S. (2019) *Christian Louboutin's Presentation Involved a Replica Train Carriage Dubbed the 'Loubhoutan Express'.* Footwearnews [Online] Available from: https://footwearnews.com/2019/fashion/designers/christian-louboutin-spring-2020-paris-haute-couture-1202800302/ [Accessed: 16 March 2021].

H&M. (2019) Hm Foundation [Online] Available from: https://hmfoundation.com/hm-foundation/ [Accessed: 16 March 2021].

H&M. (2020) [Online] Available from: https://hmgroup.com/sustainability.html [Accessed: 16 March 2021].

Hope, A. (2017) *How Are Streetwear Brands Targeting Today's Youth?* Dalziel&Pow [Online] Available from: https://www.dalziel-pow.com/news/brands-targeting-youth [Accessed: 16 March 2021].

Hubstyle. (no date) *Coco Capitan per Gucci* [Online] Available from: https://hubstyle.sport-press.it/2017/07/27/coco-capitan-x-gucci/ [Accessed: 16 March 2021].

Il Post. (2013) *La storia di Victoria's Secret* [Online] Available from: https://www.ilpost.it/2013/10/31/victorias-secret/ [Accessed 16 March 2021].

Inditex. (2020) [Online] Available from:https://www.inditex.com/en/our-commitment-to-the-environment/closing-the-loop/collect-reuse-recycle/ [Accessed: 16 March 2021].

Indvik, L. (2016) *Why Coach Is Now Focusing on Ready-to-Wear.* Fashionista [Online] Available from: https://fashionista.com/2015/09/coach-1941-stuart-vevers-interview [Accessed: 16 March 2021].

Ironico, S. (2014) *Fashion Management.* Milano: FrancoAngeli.

Jarnow, J., Dickerson, K. (1997) *Inside the Fashion Business.* Upper Saddle River: Prentice-Hall.

Kapferer, J.N., Bastien, V. (2009, 2012 reprint) *The Luxury Strategy. Break the Rules of Marketing to Build Luxury Brands.* London: Kogan Page.

Keller, K.L., Kotler, P. (2007) *Il Marketing del nuovo millennio*, 3rd edition. Milano: Pearson Prentice Hall.

Kent, S., Guilbault, L. (2019) *LVMH Gets Competitive about Sustainability.* BoF [Online] Available from: https://www.businessoffashion.com/articles/professional/lvmh-gets-competitive-about-sustainability [Accessed: 16 March 2021].

Keshni, U. (2015) *Our Guide to Louis Vuitton Leather and Canvas. What Makes the Strongest Bags in the World so Strong?* Tradesy [Online] Available from: https://www.tradesy.com/blog/our-guide-to-authentic-louis-vuitton-leather-and-canvas/ [Accessed: 16 March 2021].

Kiton. (2018) [Online] Available from: https://kiton.com/en/2018/04/29/the-elegant-man-milan-april-2018 [Accessed: 16 March 2021].

Kors. (2019) Final Annual Report [Online] Available from: http://s22.q4cdn.com/557169922/files/doc_financials/annual_report/Final-Annual-Report-on-Form-10-K-with-Wrap.pdf [Accessed: 16 March 2021].

Kotler, P. et al. (2008) *Principles of Marketing.* 5th European Edition. London: Prentice Hall.

Krishan, H.S. (1996) Characteristics of Memory Associations: A Consumer-based Brand Equity Perspective, *International Journal of Research in Marketing,* 13.

La Conceria. (2019a) [Online] Available from: https://www.laconceria.it/conceria/la-pelle-italiana-dati-e-primati-lx-factor-e-la-sostenibilita/ [Accessed: 16 March 2021].

La Conceria. (2019b) [Online] Available from: https://www.laconceria.it/calzatura/per-sergio-rossi-linnovazione-e-utile-in-tutto-ma-non-in-produzione-sbagliato-correre-la-manovia-di-lusso-vuole-il-suo-tempo/ [Accessed: 16 March 2021].

Lea-Greenwood, G. (2016) *Fashion Marketing Communications.* New York: Wiley.

Lettly. (2016) *Social Media Tricks among Lingerie Brands* Medium.com [Online] Available from: https://medium.com/@Lettly/social-media-tricks-among-lingerie-brands-45efbbd71ec2 [Accessed: 16 March 2021].

Levi's. (2019) Levistrauss [Online] Available from: https://www.levistrauss.com/values-in-action/levi-strauss-foundation/ [Accessed: 16 March 2021].

Licensing International. (2019) [Online] Available from: https://licensinginternational.org/news/liberated-brands-buys-volcom-brand-from-kering/ [Accessed: 16 March 2021].

Lonati, V. (2019) *Fuorisalone 2019: gli eventi di oggi mercoledì 10 aprile.* Amica [Online] Available from: https://www.amica.it/2019/04/10/fuorisalone-2019-eventi-mercoledi-10-aprile/ [Accessed: 16 March 2021].

Long, C. (2018) *Virgil Abloh Named as Artistic Director of Louis Vuitton Menswear.* Financial Times [Online] Available from: https://www.ft.com/content/48fbc39c-30e1-11e8-ac48-10c6fdc22f03 [Accessed: 16 March 2021].

Loriga, M. (2019) *Coach Create: Giacche e Sneakers Personalizzate.* Fashion-times [Online] Available from: https://www.fashiontimes.it/2019/05/coach-create-giacche-sneakers-personalizzate/ [Accessed: 16 March 2021].

Lvmh. (2020) *Life. Social & Environmental Responsibility* [Online] Available from: https://www.lvmh.com/group/lvmh-commitments/social-environmental-responsibility/life-initiative-lvmh/ [Accessed: 16 March 2021].

Maggiore, F. (2019) *Argilla e rabdomanti, dietro le quinte delle ceramiche di Antonio Marras e Kiasmo.* Elle Decor [Online] Available from: https://www.elledecor.com/it/people/a27014573/fuorisalone-2019-antonio-marras-kiasmo-ceramiche/ [Accessed: 16 March 2021].

Maloy, S. (2018) *An Inside Look at Alexander Wang's Playful, Inclusive Social Strategy.* Adaptly.com [Online] Available from: https://adaptly.com/inside-alexander-wang-social-media-strategy-retail-fashion-design/ [16 March 2021].

Merli, A. (2019) *Il focus di Pollini è su heritage e Middle East.* MFFashion [Online] Available from: https://www.mffashion.com/news/livestage/il-focus-di-pollini-e-su-heritage-e-middle-east-201906111950444592 [Accessed: 16 March 2021].

Mffashion. (2020) [Online] Available from: https://www.mffashion.com/news/livestage/hermes-strizza-l-occhio-ai-giovani-201811141624146279 [Accessed: 16 March 2021].

Misani, N., Varacca Capello, P. (2017) *Fashion Collections.* Milano, EGEA.

Moncler. (2020) [Online] Available from: https://www.moncler.com/it/monclernow/moncler-one-house-different-voices/ [Accessed: 16 March 2021].

Mooney, M. (2017) *Gap Foundation: 40 Years of Good* [Online] Available from: https://corporate.gap-inc.com/en-us/articles/2017/09/gap-foundation-40-years-of-good [Accessed: 16 March 2021].

Morgan, C. (2019) *Paul & Shark 'goes green' in Spring/Summer 2020 Collection.* MoodieDavittReport [Online] Available from: https://www.moodiedavittreport.com/paul-shark-goes-green-in-spring-summer-2020-collection/ Accessed: 16 March 2021].

Mosca, F. (2010) *Marketing dei beni di lusso.* Milano – Torino: Pearson Italia.

Nazir, S. (2019) *How Does Zara Survive Despite Minimal Advertising?* Retail Gazette [Online] Available from: https://www.retailgazette.co.uk/blog/2019/01/how-does-zara-survive-despite-minimal-advertising/ [Accessed: 16 March 2021].

Nike. (2019a) [Online] Available from: http://manufacturingmap.nikeinc.com/# [Accessed: 16 March 2021].

Nike. (2019b) [Online] Available from: https://www.nike.com/it/it_it/c/sustainability [Accessed: 16 March 2021].

Nike. (2020) [Online] Available from: https://s1.q4cdn.com/806093406/files/doc_financials/2020/ar/NKE-FY20-10K.pdf [Accessed: 16 March 2021].

Okonkwo, U. (2007) *Luxury Fashion Branding.* New York: Palgrave Macmillan.

Otb. (2019) [Online] Available from: https://www.otb.net/en/staff-international/production/ [Accessed: 16 March 2021].

Pambianco, C. (2008) *I signori dello stile.* Milano: Sperling & Kupfer.

Pambianco. (2017) *Prada firma conferenza su sostenibilità e innovazione.* Pambianco [Online] Available from: https://www.pambianconews.com/2017/03/21/prada-firma-conferenza-sostenibilita-innovazione-211218/ [Accessed: 16 March 2021].

Pambianco. (2018a) *Giorgio Armani racconta e si racconta* [Online] Available from: https://www.pambianconews.com/2018/11/15/giorgio-armani-racconta-e-si-racconta-247973 [Accessed: 16 March 2021].

Pambianco. (2018b) [Online] Available from: https://www.pambianconews.com/2018/02/19/ngg-il-nuovo-polo-italiano-che-cresce-nel-segreto-di-off-white-230693/ [Accessed: 16 March 2021].

Pambianco. (2019) *Dolce & Gabbana dà più peso alla moda curvy.* Pambianco [Online] Available from: https://www.pambianconews.com/2019/06/18/dolce-gabbana-da-piu-peso-alla-moda-curvy-264573/ [Accessed: 16 March 2021].

Parah. (2019) [Online] Available https://www.parah.com/eu-it/azienda-parah.aspx [Accessed: 16 March 2021].

Patagonia. (2020) [Online] Available from: https://eu.patagonia.com/it/it/activism/ [Accessed: 16 March 2021].

Pellicelli, G. (2005) *Strategia.* Milano: Egea.

Peters, B. (2019) *Nike's Secret to Success on Instagram: Building an Engaged Community* Buffer [Online] Available from: https://buffer.com/resources/instagram-community-nike [Accessed: 16 March 2021].

Pollo, P. (2020) "Sfilare non più di due volte l'anno", *Corriere della Sera*, 30 May 2020, p. 25.

Pomodoro, S. (2017) "Integrated Communication Strategies in Spring Summer 2015 Ready to Wear Fashion Tales" in "Fashion through History, Costumes, Symbols, Communication" (vol. II), Edited by Giovanna Motta and Antonello Biagini. Newcastle: Cambridge Scholars Publishing, 394–406.

Porter, M. (1980) *Competitive strategy. Techniques for Analysing Industries and Competitors.* New York: The Free Press.

Porter, M. (1985) *Competitive Advantage Creating and Sustaining Superior Performance.* New York: The Free Press.

Posner, H. (2011) *Marketing Fashion. Strategy Branding and Promotion.* London: Laurence King Publishing Ltd.

PVH. (2019) [Online] Available from: https://www.pvh.com/-/media/Files/pvh/investor-relations/PVH-Annual-Report-2019.pdf [Accessed: 1 April 2021].

Quicksilver. (2019) [Online] Available from: https://www.quiksilver.com.au/about-us [Accessed: 16 March 2021].

Ramakrishnan, V. (2019) *The Key to Victoria's Secret Social Media Success.* Unmetric [Online] Available from: https://blog.unmetric.com/victorias-secret-to-success-on-social-media [Accessed: 16 March 2021]

Ravi, K. (2019) *6 Ways Nike Built a Strong Brand on Social Media.* Unmetric [online] Available from: https://blog.unmetric.com/nike-social-media [Accessed: 16 March 2021].

Ricca, M., Robins, R. (2012) *Meta-luxury.* New York: Palgrave Macmillan.

Rinaldi, F.R., Testa, S. (2013) *L'impresa moda responsabile.* Milano: Egea.

Rocca, F. (2011) *Hermès.* Torino: Lindau.

Rodrigues, L. (2019) *Do It Like Adidas — How to Convert with Killer Digital Content.* Medium [online] Available from: https://medium.com/@lilianarodrigues.pr/do-it-like-adidas-128078ef18fe [Accessed: 16 March 2021].

Sabbadin, E. (1997) *Marketing della distribuzione e marketing integrato.* Milano: Egea.

Sabino, C. (2016) *High-Art Footwear Rocks the Fashion World from Giuseppe Zanotti.* Haute Living [Online] Available from: https://hauteliving.com/2016/09/high-end-footwear-rocks-the-fashion-world-from-giuseppe-zanotti/620166/ [Accessed: 16 March 2021].

Sacchi, M.S. (2017) Kering. Rivoluzione Gucci. *Corriere della Sera,* 25 April 2017, p. 10.

Sacchi, M.S. (2020) Così la filiera della moda sostiene già la ripartenza. *Corriere della Sera,* 27 April 2020, p. 7.

Sahli, E. (2019) *Le borse di Anastassiades per Valextra sono le architetture da indossare quest'inverno.* Elle DÉCOR [Online] Available from: https://www.elledecor.com/it/lifestyle/a29191794/borse-valextra-michael-anastassiades-flute/ [Accessed: 16 March 2021].

Scafati, L. (2019) *H&M, la nuova capsule collection tutta green.* Vanity Fair [Online] Available from: https://www.vanityfair.it/fashion/red-carpet/2019/04/05/hm-capsule-collection-conscious-exclusive-2019 [Accessed: 16 March 2021].

Schwartzberg, L. (2016) *How Off-White's Virgil Abloh Uses Social Media to Teach and Inspire.* FastCompany [Online] Available from: https://www.fastcompany.com/90460346/philips-hue-security-risk [Accessed: 16 March 2021.

Sherman, L. (2017) *Decoding Chanel's Gen-Z Strategy.* BOF [Online] Available from: https://www.businessoffashion.com/articles/professional/decoding-chanels-gen-z-strategy [Accessed: 16 March 2021].

Socha, M. (2017) *CEO Talks: Guram Gvasalia of Vetements.* WWD [Online] Available from: https://wwd.com/business-news/business-features/ceo-talks-guram-gvasalia-vetements-10829782/ [Accessed: 16 March 2021].

Speedo. (2019) [Online] Available from: https://www.speedo.com/on/demandware.store/Sites-spdgbgbp-Site/en_JE/GeoShow-Content?cid=careers [Accessed: 16 March 2021].

Srivastav, T. (2019) *Girl Effect Uses Social Content to Empower Adolescent Girls in India* [Online] Available from: https://www.thedrum.com/news/2019/10/11/girl-effect-uses-social-content-empower-adolescent-girls-india [Accessed: 16 March 2021].

Stansfield, T. (2015) *Fancy Owning a Pair of McQueen's Armadillo Boots?* Dazed Digital [Online] Available from: https://www.dazeddigital.com/fashion/article/25474/1/fancy-owning-a-pair-of-mcqueens-armadillo-boots [Accessed: 16 March 2021].

Stella McCartney. (no date) *About Stella* [Online] Available from: https://www.stellamccartney.com/experience/us/about-stella/ [Accessed: 8 February 2020].

Stoneisland. (2020) [Online] Available from: https://www.stoneisland.com/experience/it/zdhc-roadmap [Accessed: 16 March 2021].

Sylvers, E. (2019) *Tod's Loafers Have Won Over Royals and Hollywood—But Not Many Millennials.* The Wall Street Journal [Online] Available from: https://www.wsj.com/articles/tods-loafers-have-won-over-royals-and-hollywoodbut-not-many-millennials-11550336401 [Accessed: 16 March 2021].

Tanzarella, C. (no year) *Furla ancora in prima linea per l'environment.* MFFashionr [Online] Available from: https://www.mffashion.com/news/livestage/furla-ancora-in-prima-linea-per-l-environment-201907151117275298 [Accessed: 16 March 2021].

Tapestry. (2020) [Online] Available from: https://tapestry.gcs-web.com/static-files/211db552-8b97-460b-b24b-e4ba34780d31 [Accessed: 16 March 2021].

Tecchiato, A. (2019) *H&M. Fast Fashion o Fast Sustainable?* Thismarketerslife [Online] Available from: https://www.thismarketerslife.it/marketing/branding/hm-fast-fashion-o-fast-sustainable/ [Accessed: 16 March 2021].

Timberland. (2020) [Online] Available from https://www.timberland.it/responsibility.html [Accessed: 16 March 2021].

Tortora, L. (2019) S*alone del Mobile 2019: Fendi Casa presenta 'Back Home' di Cristina Celestino e la sua nuova strategia*. Vogue [Online] Available from: https://www.vogue.it/moda/article/salone-del-mobile-2019-fendi-casa-presenta-back-home-di-cristina-celestino-e-la-sua-nuova-strategia [Accessed: 16 March 2021].

Triumph. (2019) [Online] Available from: http://www.triumph.com/it/it/13517.html#.XaczKeg-zbDc [Accessed: 16 March 2021].

Tungate, M. (2005) *Fashion Brands*. London: Kogan Page.

Valdani, E. (1995) *Marketing Strategico. Un'impresa proattiva per sviluppare capacità, market driving e valore*. Milano: Etas.

Various authors. (2010) *Ermenegildo Zegna*. Ginevra-Milano: Skira.

Vergani, G. (2010) *Dizionario della moda*. Milano: Baldini Castoldi Dalai.

Vilaseca, E. (2010) *Fashion Show: Come organizzare una sfilata di moda*. Modena: Logos.

Volcom. (2019) [Online] Available from: https://www.volcom.com/blogs/campaigns/eco-true [Accessed: 16 March 2021].

Zanellato. (2019) [Online] Available from: https://www.zanellato.com/it/storia [Accessed: 16 March 2021].

Zanellato. (no date) [Online] Available from: https://www.zanellato.com/it/storia [Accessed: 16 March 2021].

Zanzi, C. (2019) *Veronesi: "Per il gruppo Calzedonia, green, giovani e retail"*. PambiancoNews [Online] Available from: https://www.pambianconews.com/2019/10/08/veronesi-per-il-gruppo-calzedonia-green-giovani-e-retail-273843/ [Accessed: 16 March 2021].

Zazzaro R. (2018) *CrossFit, Reebok vs. Nik: 2010–2020, storia di una grade sfida*. Gqitalia [Online] Available from: https://www.gqitalia.it/gq-inc/economia/2018/06/27/crossfit-reebok-vs-nike-2010-2020-storia-di-una-grande-sfida/ [Accessed: 16 March 2021].

Zegna. (2019) Fondazionezegna [Online] Available from: http://www.fondazionezegna.org/archivio-storico/ [Accessed: 16 March 2021].

Zinola, A. (2011) *Dietro le quinte della moda*. Milano: GRUPPO 24 ORE.

INDEX

Milton Keynes UK
Ingram Content Group UK Ltd.
UKHW010038200924
448541UK00008B/87